The Invisible Caring Hand

The Invention of Brownstone...

The Invisible Caring Hand

American Congregations and the
Provision of Welfare

Ram A. Cnaan

with
Stephanie C. Boddie, Femida Handy,
Gaynor Yancey, and Richard Schneider

Foreword by John J. DiIulio

NEW YORK UNIVERSITY PRESS
New York and London

NEW YORK UNIVERSITY PRESS
New York and London

© 2002 by New York University
All rights reserved.

Library of Congress Cataloging-in-Publication Data
Cnaan, Ram A.
The invisible caring hand : American congregations and the provision
of welfare / Ram A. Cnaan ; with Stephanie C. Boddie.
p. cm.
Includes bibliographical references and index.
ISBN 0-8147-1617-2 (cloth : alk. paper) ISBN 0-8147-1618-0 (pbk. : alk. paper)
1. Church charities—United States.   I. Boddie, Stephanie C. II. Title.
HV530 .C617 2002
361.7'5'0973—dc21   2002003565

New York University Press books are printed on acid-free paper,
and their binding materials are chosen for strength and durability.

Manufactured in the United States of America
10 9 8 7 6 5 4 3 2 1

Dedicated with appreciation and admiration to the tens of thousands of clergy who serve the spiritual, religious, personal, social, and political needs of their communities. May this book bring you the support and the recognition you deserve.

Contents

viii | *Contents*

Foreword

JOHN J. DiIULIO, JR.

In this path-breaking book, Ram Cnaan admirably achieves two things that are very rarely achieved at all, let alone together. The first achievement is timeless, world-class scholarship. This book contributes mightily to our objective understanding of critically important social phenomena and institutions. It will inform interested academic researchers and their students for decades to come. The second achievement is timely, policy-relevant scholarship. This book promises to influence greatly key real-world decision makers, both public and private. It will discipline their present debates and leaven their future deliberations. Let me commence with the latter achievement as it pertains to certain ongoing public policy debates about religion in the public square.

The 2000 U.S. presidential election contest between Republican Governor George W. Bush, of Texas, and Democratic Vice President Al Gore, of Tennessee, began as one of the most contentious, and ended as one of the closest, presidential elections in American history. But, on at least one aspect of national social welfare policy, the two candidates agreed far more than they disagreed. During the first months of the battle, both Bush and Gore gave major campaign speeches calling for greater partnerships between government and religious organizations to combat poverty, cut crime, and ameliorate other social ills. Right up to election day, despite their deep ideological and partisan differences on other domestic issues, both candidates continued to proclaim that so-called faith-based organizations, including local congregations (churches, synagogues, mosques, and others), played a vital, if largely unheralded, role in delivering social services to needy children, youth, and families in this country and to propose that the national government do more to assist sacred places that serve civic purposes in our poorest neighborhoods.

Specifically, both Bush and Gore called for expanding "charitable choice," a wide-ranging provision of the 1996 federal welfare reform law that, among other features, permits religious organizations to compete to administer certain federal social welfare programs on the same legal basis as any other non-governmental or nonprofit organization, and to accept public funds for these purposes without thereby automatically having to divest themselves of their religious iconography or losing the so-called ministerial exemption, granted under Title VII of the 1964 Civil Rights Act, that allows them to take religion into account in making employment decisions. Gore called for expanding charitable choice to certain federal housing, juvenile justice, and drug treatment programs. Bush called for expanding it primarily to these same areas but also to several others.

Far more significant, however, than their specific points of policy agreement were their kindred basic assumptions about the strengths and limits of community-serving religious organizations as means of delivering social welfare services. Three continue to stand out. First, both Bush and Gore argued that greater support for so-called faith-based organizations could supplement, but not substitute for, conventional public social welfare programs; second, both insisted that these organizations needed not just more public support but also far greater private (individual, corporate, philanthropic) support; and, third, both emphasized that not just fewer bureaucratic barriers or more money but also more capacity-building and technical assistance, would be needed to forge effective community-serving public/private and religious/secular partnerships. Bush's rendering of these assumptions was particularly striking, coming as it did from the standard-bearer of a party whose leaders, from Ronald Reagan in the 1980s through Newt Gingrich in the 1990s, had consistently promoted the wholesale devolution of federal social welfare programs onto state and local governments, private companies, and charitable organizations.

The Invisible Caring Hand suggests that these assumptions are essentially correct. While making a compelling case that America's estimated 350,000 or so congregations do provide an eclectic range of social welfare services (my favorite is chapter 8's tale of small congregations in Council Grove, Kansas), Cnaan is candid in stating that "we know almost nothing about the scope, nature, and dynamics of congregations engaged in social service provision" and equally forthright in stressing that, given what we do know thus far, the idea that government can be replaced by religious charities in serving the needy is fanciful at best. Of the many important and policy-relevant lessons this book teaches, none is more critical than the following: "Congregations cannot assume the role that government plays in social services provision and caring for needy people. They can, however, be the quiet partner that constitutes the first line of help."

The Invisible Caring Hand reaches its policy-relevant conclusions by means of a multifaceted methodological approach that encompasses archival research, hundreds of in-depth interviews, and an ethnographically sophisticated rendering of how independent congregations in different cities (including one non-U.S. city, Ontario, Canada) network, form community-serving coalitions, provide services, and affect not just individual beneficiaries but entire neighborhoods. Together, the cases empirically unearth intellectually fascinating patterns in how religiously motivated volunteers and other citizens achieve civic purposes through congregational, and intercongregational, life.

The patterns, however, are not emphasized to the exclusion of the people behind them. Throughout *The Invisible Caring Hand*, Cnaan's writing and use of key terms is precise enough to satisfy scholars but lively and accessible enough to satisfy readers without Ph.Ds. Thus, the superb account in chapter 9 of "mediating structures" and a New Orleans church federation is followed, in chapter 10, by two examples in Pennsylvania, one of which is St. Gabriel's Episcopal Church in Pennsylvania, led by Mother Mary Laney, "a trim woman in her mid-fifties with gray hair, a strong voice, and stronger convictions. . . . She asks the question, 'if I were on trial for being a Christian, what evidence would be presented and would I be convicted?' She wants the answer to be 'Yes.'"

Cnaan concludes the book by stating that local congregations are major threads in "the nation's social safety net for those most in need of food, shelter, counseling, and emotional support. Congregational involvement in social services provision is as American as apple pie, though far less recognized and celebrated." Thanks to this remarkable book, however, *The Invisible Caring Hand* will not remain so invisible or so little understood by policymakers and others, for much longer.

Preface

RAM A. CNANN

I was born in Israel and trained as a social worker in the European framework that took for granted the presence of a benevolent and wise government that assumed the responsibility for addressing all social ills. When I began working and studying in the United States, I was amazed by the limited role the U.S. government plays in civic life and the distrust most citizens feel toward their government. I noticed that, in the absence of a benevolent government welfare system, thousands of volunteers and voluntary organizations arose to meet citizens' social needs and constitute an active civic life in the United States. The right to form such groups is guaranteed in the U.S. Constitution, and the current tax structure favors their growth and development. This emphasis on—and the preponderance of—nonprofit organizations captured my attention, along with that of many other scholars. Throughout the past few years, I found numerous newspaper articles on the role of the American congregation in restoring civic life in our communities, political speeches on the importance of congregations, and legislation that encourages the participation of congregations in the public life of our society. I spent several years studying nonprofit organizations and volunteerism and their impact on the quality of life in urban America. As time passed, I was struck by the significant role religious congregations play in maintaining social care networks and community life in America. Thus, I set out to learn as much as possible about how American congregations fill this role. A major product of my studies was my first book, *The Newer Deal: Social Work and Religion in Partnership* (1999).

As I began to study faith-based organizations, I realized that most social scientists shy away from faith-based organizations in general, and congregations in particular. In fact, I could not even find a good working definition of a "congregation" in the social science literature. After studying congregations for the past five years, I am still amazed by the paucity

of literature on congregational involvement in social and community services provision. Thus, I offer this book as the culmination of years of
studying congregations and as a step toward increasing our understanding
of local religious congregations and their contributions to society.

As the author, I have opted to use the editorial "we" in grateful acknowledgment of the important contributions of many colleagues and
friends. Four wonderful individuals significantly contributed to this book,
and I happily acknowledge them as cocontributors. Stephanie C. Boddie
was, at the time of this writing, a doctoral student at the University of
Pennsylvania School of Social Work and the research director at the Program for the Study of Organized Religion and Social Work. She conducted
many of the interviews, contributed to many chapters, and is responsible
for bringing many chapters together into a cohesive whole. Femida Handy
coauthored the chapters that deal with Ontario, Canada, and Council
Grove, Kansas. We traveled often to these places and shared not only new
knowledge but, eventually, also our lives. Femida is a member of the Faculty of Environmental Studies, York University. Richard Schneider, a retired lawyer, was also a student at the University of Pennsylvania, as well as
a board member of Urban Bridges. He contributed and wrote most of the
material in the chapter on St. Gabriel's Church. Last but certainly not least,
Gaynor Yancey actually awakened my intellectual interest in this field. If
she had not been next to me in the beginning stages of this research, I
would not have ventured into this area. Her support and knowledge have
guided me for a long time. She contributed to the chapter on volunteerism,
and her ideas and insights can be found throughout the book. Gaynor conducted many of the original interviews, and together we pretested and fi-
nalized the research instruments used in this book. After receiving her doctoral degree from the University of Pennsylvania, she joined the faculty at
Baylor University.

As in my previous book, the responsibility for the theses presented in
this book rests solely with me. My arguments represent a synthesis of many
years of research on the role of faith-based organizations in the provision
of social services. Clearly, I was influenced by discussions with the people
who helped me write the book and by many knowledgeable colleagues. Although I am indebted to them, they are not responsible for any of the
statements made in this book.

The concept for this book began with research grants from the Lilly Endowment to study the role of the religious community in the welfare system toward the end of the twentieth century and to disseminate the find-

ings. I am in debt to Craig Dykstra, Jeanne Knoerle, and Fred Hofheintz, who listened to my embryonic ideas about the role of congregations in society and gave me generous support. They saw the potential in my work even before I was aware of it, and if not for their support I might have studied something altogether different. I received considerable emotional and intellectual support from Fred Hofheintz, my program officer. When I first met Fred, I had come to ask for the Endowment's support but was so captivated by our intellectual discussion that, hours later, I forgot to ask for support. Fortunately, Fred remembered.

In order to carry out additional field work, I was assisted by grants from other sources. Each arrived just in time for me to complete the task at hand. I wish to thank the Kellogg Foundation, the Manhattan Institute, the Kahanhoff Foundation, the University of Pennsylvania Research Fund, and the University of Pennsylvania School of Social Work. Together, grants from these institutions enabled me to extend the scope of the study to a degree that would otherwise have been impossible. My dean, Ira M. Schwartz, was most supportive and helpful. I cannot thank him enough for his encouragement and for his willingness to allow me to do things my way. I learned the true meaning of leadership by observing him letting me try my best and thus guiding me in his way. He also supported me in hard times, and I am grateful. Similarly, Peter Vaughan was always there with a word of encouragement when I needed him. I was lucky to have these people around when I most needed them.

I am particularly indebted to Diane Cohen and Robert (Bob) Jaeger, codirectors of Partners for Sacred Places, a national, nonprofit, nonsectarian organization founded in 1989 to help Americans embrace, care for, and make good use of older and historic religious properties that continue to play a critical role in the lives of their communities. In appreciation of their support, which enabled me to carry out my pilot study on this topic, as I did with those from my previous book, I am donating all royalties from this book to Partners for Sacred Places so that they may continue to support the social and structural needs of America's congregations.

Special thanks are in order to the people who assisted in data collection. While a third of the interviews were carried out by the authors, many others were carried out by committed and insightful groups of interviewers. They are Susan Alborell, Chicago; Jill Borden, San Francisco; Henry Brown, Mobile; Ayala Cnaan, Houston and Mobile; Michelle Kaiser, New York City; Wendy Carver Landes, Indianapolis; Carol Okun, Philadelphia; and Benjamin Plotinsky, Indianapolis.

Other individuals supported this endeavor in many ways. I cannot begin to list them all, but I want to mention a few. Peter Dobkin Hall, now at the Kennedy School at Harvard University and formerly of the Yale Program on Nonprofit Organizations, enabled me to present some of my initial findings at Yale University. He also introduced me to many scholars and practitioners in the nonprofit field who provided me with new perspectives on the topic. I am grateful to David Mason, of Mason Enterprises, of Corpus Christi, Texas, who read a previous manuscript of mine (one that had been rejected for publication) and wrote to me that he was so fascinated that he shared my work with fellow travelers on a flight from Alaska. It was a morale boost I needed at the time, and I am grateful for it, for David's consistent encouragement, and for his provision of relevant material for this book. My friend Robert Wineburg matched me with Partners for Sacred Places, and we spent many hours of discussing and disagreeing on many issues. Through him, my interest in the area grew, and I am fortunate to have known him for the past two decades.

Colleagues who critiqued earlier versions made many cogent comments and suggestions that helped me to improve the quality of this book. The errors are still mine, but they are fewer in number thanks to their detailed and constructive critiques. They are John DiIulio, of the University of Pennsylvania; Edward Newman, of the Temple University School of Social Administration; and Heidi Unruh, of the Eastern Baptist Theological Seminary. David Hammack, of Case Western Reserve University, provided me with helpful comments on the chapter on the historical development of congregations in America. Jill Sinha and Vanmala Hirarandani read earlier drafts of the manuscript, and their comments and careful criticism helped avoid numerous errors and helped focus the book. Mona Basta helped in library work. Hauquing Zhao managed the database for this study and was instrumental in making sure we had a working database to analyze. Ami Dalal and Ayala Cnaan entered most of the data for this project. Finally, I wish to acknowledge Eileen Lynch, who has provided superb editorial assistance. Eileen has been my editor for the past fifteen years, and, thanks to her careful and most intelligent review of my work, people think I am smart. The credit should go to her. Thank you, Eileen. At a later stage, additional editing was provided by David Estrin, and he gave the book its final form.

To all of those I have named, I am grateful. But, most of all, I am thankful to the many clergy and congregational leaders who took the time to talk with us and who provided us with insight into and some understanding of the important role congregations play in urban America. There is no way we could have done this work were it not for those individuals who generously gave us their time and attention and who answered our endless questions. If this book is of value, it is because of their input and careful responses. I hope that they will find some reward for their lost hours by the knowledge gained and by the possible recognition of their important work. I came out of this project impressed with their work, the immense level of uncertainty, and the number of areas in which clergy are expected to be versed and competent. Few people in America can be called at any hour of the day or night to counsel a distressed family, week in and week out carry out a religious service that is meaningful and uplifting, efficiently manage an organization, and also actively care for those in need. I take my hat off to them, and I dedicate this book to their individual and collective sacrifices.

PART I

An Overview of Congregations

1

Congregations in Society

The intermingling of church and state is as old as the history of civilization. For the people, religion offered a means of understanding the power of nature and acted as a source of confidence that their intent and behavior might bring about prosperity and prevent natural calamities. For the state, religion was a tool to keep people in order and to give them some form of hope in the face of hunger, wars, and inequality. For religious organizations, a group of believers was a form of power vis-à-vis the state. At times, the two collaborated and supported each other, while at other times they fought bitterly. As we show in chapter 2, the United States began as a communal place populated by people who disliked one form of religion and traveled across the Atlantic to practice another religion. They created and governed communities while preserving their own form of religion.

In colonial times, converting the unchurched to organized religion was a charitable cause. At that time, there was little distinction between the church and state. The theory was that unchurched people lack moral guidance, tend to drink alcohol, engage in crime, and threaten the public order. On the other hand, the theory posited that religious people who belong to a congregation tend to be less engaged in antisocial activities and make it easier for public authorities to keep order (Berger, 1969). Today, in the United States, the propagation of religion is no longer considered a charitable activity—and, as we document in this book, congregations have found other ways to develop human capital.

At the dawn of the twenty-first century, we are living in the era of what we can call the "Newer Deal." Those of us who remember the 1960s cannot but be amazed at the dramatic changes in our society in the past forty years. The government that once considered itself the protector of the weak and indigent and that championed the "War on Poverty" has now shed its social responsibilities (Ferejohn & Weingast, 1997; Hovey, 1999; Salamon, 1995; Smith & Lipsky, 1993). There is no doubt that the federal government is by far the major actor in ensuring certain entitlements. Medical support for people in financial hardship, for example, is provided through the Social Security Administration. However, as a society we have lost our compassion for poor people. Between the war on poverty and the civil rights movement of the 1960s and the newer-deal era of the 1980s the country turned its back to those in need and a spirit of profit-making at all cost prevailed. Elected officials throughout the country followed the Reagan cues and cut on welfare as part of a populist quest to win middle-class electoral votes. Whereas until the late 1970s almost every state had a full program of cash assistance (public welfare) for poor people regardless of their marital status and age, in the early years of the twenty-first century such programs have ceased to exist or are time limited. Aid for Families with Dependent Children (now Temporary Assistance for Needy Families), which guaranteed minimum income to single parents, is now limited to sixty months lifetime and twenty-four consecutive months. Public housing for the poor was also halted, and help is now limited for the most part to vouchers that reach fewer people than at any other time in the program's existence. The growth of homelessness in our midst is yet another indication of government's (and society's) lack of will to care for the poor unless the poor show willingness to care for themselves.

The Reagan administration began a "devolution" of the social welfare system by downsizing the government and by introducing the philosophy of "New Federalism." With the desire for a smaller government and the move to place responsibility at the local levels of government and to provide funding through block grants, the federal government has become merely a contractor and a funder of services. Thus, nonprofit organizations have come to the forefront as social service providers, with services ranging from housing to mental healthcare (Smith & Lipsky, 1993). In fact, the size of the federal government has not grown since the early 1960s; given government's increased involvement and U.S. population growth, this amounts to a shrinking public sector. However, it is estimated that for each federal employee in any public agency in any part of the world, there are six other nongovernment employees whose salaries are fully paid through a grant or contract from the government. (Due to increased complexity, government everywhere is involved in more fields, such as AIDS, drug abuse, border control, and some wars.) Moreover, in recent years, for-profit providers have become increasingly important in social welfare service provision (Salamon, 1995).

Nevertheless, these structural changes do not hide the growing public recognition that our welfare system has failed to meet public expectations. The assumption, dating from the Progressive Era, was that poverty would be eradicated through the application of an effective and scientific public welfare system. The much-publicized failure to eradicate poverty not only disappointed public officials but became a significant issue in public and political discourse. The poor people on welfare became the demons who caused economic stagnation and reduced our competitiveness in the world market. However, criticism without alternatives was insufficient. Faith-based organizations and local religious congregations received the "call."

There has been a plethora of calls to eliminate the existing welfare system and to replace it with effective and inexpensive faith-based providers. The retreat from public responsibility was first demonstrated by Lawrence Mead's attack on welfare, *Beyond Entitlement: The Social Obligations of Citizenship*, published in 1986. Mead shifted the discourse away from moral responsibility and toward a view of welfare as a program that bred dependency among its beneficiaries while draining the public coffers. The second trendsetting book was Marvin Olasky's 1992 book, *The Tragedy of American Compassion*. Olasky claimed that in the past only those people willing to undergo religious transformation received assistance. Moreover, he felt that they were the only ones "worthy" of any welfare assistance. Olasky was a pioneer in the advocacy of congregational social service provision from an evangelistic perspective. Olasky's ideas were embraced by Newt Gingrich, Speaker of the House of Representatives from 1995–1998, and were integrated into the "Contract with America" promulgated by conservative Republicans. In the early 1990s, Congress showed a strong inclination to finance social services through religious groups. This approach was adopted by many Republican governors, notably Governor George W. Bush, of Texas, Kirk Fordice, of Mississippi, Tommy Thompson, of Wisconsin, and John Engler, of Michigan.

The argument, accepted by many policymakers and much of the public, is that congregations and their members can offer multifaceted care that professional caregivers cannot equal. The alleged superiority of faith-based service provision rests on the idea that professional caregivers focus on "the problem," while faith-based providers view the person as a whole. Implicit in this idea is that faith-based providers seek a transformational change, while professional providers are interested primarily in "solving the problem." Thus, the parable of the Good Samaritan is the most common metaphor for the quality of faith-based care. The parable depicts a good-hearted, everyday person who gives the best care, while the trained (and higher status) helper ignores the person who is needy. This tale is often used to contrast careless professional helpers who lack compassion with the religious people who will go the "extra mile" to help someone in need. Finally, the common public perception is that exposure to moral and religious people will cause the needy to "see the light" and be transformed into productive members of society. It should be emphasized that this newly found expectation that the solutions for society's woes rest with the religious community is not based on empirical research or an in-depth understanding of how congregations and other faith-based organizations function.

The result of this positive public sentiment and of the political "rediscovery" of America's religious community was the Personal Responsibility and Work Opportunity Reconciliation Act of 1996. This law limits the duration of welfare support available to single mothers and allows congregations to be potential social services providers. The key section, as far as congregational service provision is concerned, is Section 104, known as "charitable choice." Charitable choice allows congregations that are not incorporated as regular nonprofit organizations [501(c)(3) in the IRS tax code] and other sectarian organizations to apply for public funds to provide publicly funded services while maintaining their religious character. In January 2001, President Bush made faith-based help for the poor his key domestic policy. By establishing the White House Office of Faith Based and Community Initiatives (OFBCI), the president demonstrated that care for the neediest members of our society will be encouraged to come from the local faith-based organizations and mainly from congregations.

Nevertheless, we lack sufficient knowledge about congregational life and its ability to play a key role in social service provision. The role of congregations in social services provision is often discussed by politicians, policy analysts, and the media. They praise the personal attention and moral care congregations give to the people they help. Omitted from such discussions, however, is the question of capacity. Despite the assumption that congregations can help many needy people in our society, it is still unclear whether many wish to do so, or whether they have the tools necessary to become significant providers in the social service arena. We lack knowledge of congregational experience in providing services and of congregation's inclination to partner with the world around them. Specifically, we lack systemic knowledge about congregational involvement in social service provision; we know little about religious groups' inclination to expand the scope of their current involvement in helping others.

The new policies and the establishment of OFBCI raise a plethora of policy issues. Too few data exist that can shed light on them. Yet, these issues should guide our public debate and policymaking in the years to come. The first issue, already mentioned, is congregational capacity. Can congregations manage to deliver the services expected of them? Do they have the technical skills and the qualified personnel required for social services provision? Second are issues surrounding the First Amendment. Is giving money to a religious group for the purpose of providing social services compatible with constitutional boundaries? At the time of this writing, the first legal challenge to charitable choice was beginning to make its way through the courts, as the first legal challenge to a faith-based organization and the state was filed in Texas (Cnaan & Boddie, 2002). Third, we do not know what impact these policies will have on existing nonprofit organizations. The lack of additional money for social programs coupled with increased competition from faith-based groups means that some traditional providers will find themselves out of public contracts and hence defunct. Once these organizations cease to exist, it will be difficult to resurrect them if the faith-based organizations prove ineffective or incapable. Fourth, when congregations and other faith-based organizations provide social services, there is the risk that they will serve only members. That is, they are more likely to apply exclusionary practices, as they are accustomed to doing in their spiritual spheres. Fifth, it is not clear whether the voluntary and compassionate spirit that is now assumed to dominate faith-based services will survive and exist, let alone grow, when professionalism and contract regulations step in as part of government contractual routines. Can people who are required to log and report contact hours in order to be reimbursed be compassionate and extend themselves as congregational volunteers can? Sixth, people in the congregational camp are worried about the impact that such collaboration with the government may have on the congregation as a place of worship. It is possible that congregations will be forced to apply practices that are not well accepted by members and that will impinge on their religious freedom and sense of being. The experience of transforming volunteer programs into professional and paid ones is often accompanied by increased bureaucratization (known also as "Michels's law of oligarchy") and stagnation. Seventh, the spirit of volunteerism and enthusiasm in congregations may subside when some members or people are paid for work that other formerly provided voluntarily. When a program that has relied on a group of volunteers finds itself in the position of employing workers, tension may build between the paid staff and the traditional volunteers, and the volunteers may withdraw. Eighth, overreliance on faith-based organizations carries with it the implication of reduced government involvement and responsibility for people's welfare and well-being. It enables government on all levels to wash its hands of caring for and helping the needy and uses the heroic efforts of faith-based organizations funded by the public sector as the fig leaf to cover its own diminished role in this sector. Finally, a great variability in eligibility and in methods of service delivery will emerge. Every contract between a certain county and a faith-based provider is expected to form a new mode of service delivery that is different from others. This will be a nightmare for evaluation researchers, as well as for policymakers who will wish to replicate local success elsewhere. All these worries are legitimate because we know too little about congregational involvement in social services delivery or its resilience in the face of these worries.

This book attempts to fill that void. We investigated what congregations are doing to care for people who need help. In the process, we learned a lot about a special American norm: "Once in a congregation, you are expected to assist the group in caring for people in need." This norm is so pervasive that congregations from all religions and denominations accept it and adhere to it.

We titled this book *The Invisible Caring Hand: American Congregations and the Provision of Welfare*, in part because the phrase "the invisible hand" was used by Adam Smith, who laid the foundations for modern economics in his book *The Wealth of Nations*. Smith argued that the market would manage itself if it was "free"—if it was left alone. Smith believed that free and unrestricted competition would bring optimal prices and general prosperity. Using Smith's idea of the invisible hand in a country that espouses the strongest belief in free-market principles, we were amazed to discover that welfare and social care are also provided by an invisible hand: a caring hand driven by religious gatherings and theologies. No government can force congregations and religious groups to help the needy. Only an invisible caring motivation that is partly normative, partly religious, and uniquely American can describe the work of religious congregations in ameliorating the pain, suffering, and poverty of millions. This hand has been invisible not only to the government but also to the media and to most of the public. In fact, most people we interviewed in the congregations did not appreciate or comprehend the scope of social care provided by local religious congregations. The impressive achievements of congregations in social services provision have gone unnoticed. They are invisible in an era of mass media and advanced marketing. We attempt to highlight and celebrate this work. Yet, the reader should not, for even one moment, assume that this invisible caring hand can or should replace the most invisible hand of the government. Congregations cannot assume the role that government plays in social services provision and in caring for needy people. They can, however, be the quiet partner that constitutes part of the first line of help.

Our Limited Knowledge about Congregations

It is important to distinguish the two types of organizations in the religious community that can help people in need: local religious congregations and faith-based organizations. In the United States, congregations are considered tax-exempt entities by virtue of being religious organizations and the assumption that they are charitable organizations. All other faith-based organizations are required to register with the Internal Revenue Service and get a formal certificate of incorporation. Incorporated nonprofit organizations such as Catholic Charities, Jewish Family and Children Services, Episcopal Youth Services, and other smaller, less well-known organizations, were eligible to apply for public funds for service delivery even before charitable choice legislation. Some organizations, those with a fundamentalist orientation, have declined to apply for public funds, however, fearing that a relationship with the public sector would compromise their religious integrity. Congregations that had been barred from applying for public funds are the hope of the "Newer Deal" era. Congregations, made up of compassionate individuals, are now called upon to save the welfare system and to instill values and pride in the hearts of needy Americans, as well as to provide them with both skills and work opportunities.

It is estimated that there are more than 350,000 local religious congregations in the United States. They are thus the most common and widespread institution in our society. It is also estimated that more than half the population holds active membership in a local religious congregation (Finke & Stark, 1986). The Republican and the Democratic presidential candidates in 2000 announced that, if they were elected, congregations and faith-based organizations would play a key role in their social policy agenda. And President Bush fulfilled this promise in his second week in office. Yet, we know almost nothing about the scope, nature, and dynamics of the congregations engaged in social service provision.

It is amazing that this important local institution has rarely been studied by social scientists (Miller, 1999; Wuthnow, 1994b). In fact, for many years it was almost a taboo topic in most social sciences, so much so that even the term "congregation" had not been systematically defined. The term was used broadly to denote places of worship for people from all religions and denominations but it never received a specific definition by social scientists. For example, the figure given earlier for the number of U.S. congregations is an estimate based on telephone directories, which clearly omit many congregations. The problem is that there is no complete and reliable listing of congregations; other estimates range from a low of 200,000 to a high of 500,000.

The current discourse on the role of religious congregations in social services provision often occurs without reliable data and outside the historic context. As we demonstrate, congregational involvement in social service delivery is a phenomenon unique to the United States that began only 150 years ago. While religious organizations—the Church with a capital C—has sponsored many social programs throughout the world, congregations have historically been reluctant to become involved in social programs. After all, the primary mission of a congregation is to provide a religious framework and a communal site for worshiping. Its second mission is to sustain the congregation and to guarantee resources sufficient to carry out its primary mission. Social services delivery can come only after these two missions are achieved.

It was only when church and state separated (official disestablishment) that congregations sought to become a more meaningful part of the lives of their members. The result was innovation and public involvement. This change coincided with massive immigration and urbanization, and a dramatic increase in social problems, as well as a threat to the Protestant hegemony. Congregations committed themselves to helping the newcomers, hoping to transform them and thus to attract new members to the denomination, if not the congregation. Non-Protestant groups, especially Jews and Catholics, were afraid of losing members and developed parallel services. However, these groups developed regional services that were removed from the congregations; it was only in the twentieth century that they encouraged congregational-based and para-church activities.

Our view is that congregations in the United States are made up of people with common interests and attributes, rather than simply neighbors.

Congregations in the United States are unique social institutions that serve as major social service providers. They provide services that are publicly delivered in many other advanced democracies. This book documents the impact of congregations as vitalizing community units. As such, they are already engaged in helping people in need, and it is doubtful that they have the capacity to take on additional responsibility in the American welfare system.

The impressive role that congregations play in providing social care has gone, to a large extent, unnoticed. This book explores what some had guessed but no one had systematically studied. This is the first study of the scope, nature, dynamics, and variability of congregational social services provision. We discovered that belonging to a congregation is a powerful prosocial experience, one that overshadows even religious beliefs. Indeed, we found that the group dynamics of belonging to a "moral community" brings people to care for others much more than "individual religious beliefs." This conclusion, along with the impressive social load congregations already undertake, should be incorporated into public and political discourse and considered when planning the incorporation of congregations in social services provision.

The Methods of Study

In order to provide a broad and comprehensive picture of congregational social services provision in the United States, we employ a set of complementary research methods. No single approach can provide a comprehensive answer in any social investigation, especially one as complex and understudied as this one. Thus, the following methods were used in this study: in-depth interviews with clergy and lay leaders, case studies, reviews and document analysis, and historical overview.

The interviews are discussed in the Methodological Notes (Appendix); the reader may wish to refer to this appendix throughout our discussion in chapters 4 through 8. We spent many hours in each of the 251 congregations we studied; the questions we used were prepared and piloted in Philadelphia. Many of the questions were close-ended, but others were open-ended, and we carefully read the results and analyzed the answers. In chapters 8, 9, and 10, we provide three complementary case studies. In one case, we spent time in a small town (Council Grove, Kansas) and studied the arrangement of congregational social service provision. Here we studied the networking of independent congregations and how they plan their services vis-à-vis other congregations and the local needs. In another case, in New Orleans, we studied a coalition of congregations and its impact on the city and the quality of life of its residents. In the final case study, in Philadelphia we studied one congregation that was on the brink of closure but was saved through brave leadership and the provision of relevant social services. Finally, we reviewed many historical accounts, documents, and secondary material to provide a historical review of congregations in the United States (chapter 2) and to guide our analysis in the concluding chapters.

Terminology

This book deals with religious communities of many religions and denominations. Thus, the term *congregation* is used as a comprehensive and inclusive term. We chose not to use religious-specific terms such as synagogue, mosque, ashram, or church. On a few occasions, we used the word *church* as a broad term to denote a specific organization or in quoting from other sources.

We chose not to use the term *parish* because it focuses on the geographical unit and assumes, in its purest form, that all residents in the same geographical unit worship together regardless of their interests or preferences. Warner (1994) uses the following metaphor to highlight the distinction between a congregation and a parish:

> The congregation may be made up entirely of people who subscribe to the same selection of highbrow magazines, whereas the parish has to deal with the "whole magazine rack." The congregation is an exclusive "private club," where as the parish is a "human zoo," made available as a "public utility for everyone." (pp. 68–69)

Our preference for the term *congregation* is also based on our focus on the "people," as opposed to the "place" where people meet to exchange goods and information (congregate) while expressing their faith. We use the congregation as the fundamental unit of religious communities.

Finally, we selected the term *social programs* or *social services* over *social ministries*. Although these three terms have similar meanings, the latter is more Christian in nature, and we use it where we discuss only or mostly

Christian churches, such as the chapter on the Greater New Orleans Federation of Churches. Our definition of social services captures a broad range of activities that congregations engage in for their members or for the community. These services may be familiar to most, such as counseling for families and visitation of the sick, or they may be highly professional, such as housing development and vocational training. We assumed that each congregation was involved in at least one activity that was not solely religious and that provided some social benefit to the individuals and/or the community.

The Book's Structure

The book is divided into four parts. Part I introduces the study of congregations and presents the background of our subject. In addition to this introduction, in chapter 2 we provide an understanding of the historical development of congregations in America, with a special reference to their role as social services providers.

In part II, we focus on our study of 251 congregations in the United States and forty-six congregations in Canada. As we discussed in chapter 2, we contend that American congregations are unique in their massive social services involvement. To that end, we carried out a cross-national comparison. In chapter 3, we present the characteristics of the congregations in our study. In chapter 4, we report level of congregational involvement in various areas of social and community care. We highlight the many areas in which congregations improve the quality of life for others. In chapter 5, we discuss in greater detail congregational programs and their fiscal value, as well as who is being served. In chapter 6, we try to answer the question "Which congregations are more inclined to get involved in the provision of social and community services?" The findings suggest that there is no specific profile of such a congregation: in fact, almost all congregations are active in social services provision. In chapter 7, we compare the social services provided by local congregations in Ontario, Canada, with those provided in the United States and compare the distinct abilities of congregations in the two countries to cope with emerging local needs. While Ontario congregations are also active in social services provision, their contribution is somewhat weaker, and their impact on the larger society is only marginal, as their per capita number, in comparison to the United States, is quite small.

In part III, we report the results of three additional studies that illuminate other aspects of congregational social services provision. In chapter 8,
we report how congregations in the small midwestern town of Council
Grove, Kansas, are networking and collaborating to meet a wide range of
human needs. Focusing on such a place sheds light on the work of congregations in rural America, as well as on how congregations informally
negotiate and collaborate in serving their needy neighbors. In chapter 9,
we describe the development and achievements of a coalition of congregations in New Orleans. This case highlights how congregations join forces
to solve a variety of social problems while enhancing the voice and presence of organized religion in the region. In chapter 10, we present a case
study of St. Gabriel's Episcopal Church, in Philadelphia, a congregation
that was on the brink of closing its doors but was revived and invigorated
by the social service vision of a new clergy and the cooperation of the
community.

Part IV consists of four chapters of observations and comments that,
combined, present our conclusions and their implications. In chapter 11,
we discuss volunteerism in religious contexts and how congregational
membership enhances volunteerism. It is our view that congregational affiliation, and not only religious beliefs, enhances volunteerism. In chapter
12, we discuss the reasons that congregations in the United States are so
involved in the field of social services provision. This chapter is based on
our study in part II and discusses the motives reported by clergy and congregational members as well as some that are hidden. In chapter 13, we
present congregational community involvement as a cultural norm and
discuss why this congregational activity has become so powerful. We argue
that there is a societal expectation that organized religion in the United
States will help those in need. Moreover, civil society is significantly
strengthened because of the generosity of congregations and their members. Finally, in chapter 14, we discuss the implications of our findings.
What does it mean to live in a society in which local congregations serve
as de facto social service providers?

It is our hope that our book will give people a sense of appreciation of
the civic contribution of congregations and the important role they play
as our social safety net. We also hope that our findings and ideas will open
a debate on the role of congregations as community advocates and social
services providers.

2

The Historical Development of American Congregations

> In theological language, I am convinced that there will inevitably be a wide range of responses to change, a range that will move toward a new religious ecology that serves a new community.
> —Nancy T. Ammerman, *Congregation and Community* (1997)

The roots of the current American congregation go back to the seventeenth century, when the first congregations were established by people who fled Europe to seek religious freedom or, more accurately, to escape religious persecution. This distinction is quite important in that these early settlers were themselves intolerant of other religions, and those who deviated from the accepted religious norm in a given colony or town were often persecuted and prosecuted. As a result, institutional crises related to church authority arose early in the seventeenth century. In the Antinomian controversy of 1636, several of the most prosperous and outspoken members of the Massachusetts Bay Colony challenged the authority of the ministry to dictate doctrine to congregations. These members, known as the Antinomians, were prosecuted and exiled. One of their leaders, Roger Williams, fled to Rhode Island, where he established a colony founded on liberty of conscience and whose government eschewed the power of the state to interfere in religious matters. Yet, even here, a state church was soon established.

To understand the evolution from the authoritarian colonial congregation to today's modern, social-minded congregation, it is important to understand the key trends that have characterized the more than 350-year history of this unique local institution. Holifield (1994) identified four major phases in the historical development of American congregations. These phases—the comprehensive congregation, the devotional congregation, the social congregation, and the participatory congregation —are discussed in the following sections.

The Comprehensive Congregation

The *comprehensive congregation* phase (1607–1789) is proposed as the first period in congregational life in America. While Holifield uses 1789 as the critical year for separating the periods, others view the American Revolution as a more relevant event to denote changes in the historical development of religion in America. The revolution saw the flight of many Anglican pastors from America to England, it ended the dependence of churches on the English laws and ruling, and it marked the beginning of religious disestablishment.

One established (state-supported) congregation per geographical unit (parish) characterized the comprehensive congregation phase. As Holifield noted:

> Early colonial congregations usually depended on state financing. Only among Congregationalists in Boston and a few dissenters elsewhere did voluntary contributions maintain the churches. Several other Congregationalist churches tried voluntary maintenance of ministers, but they abandoned it. By the 1650s, most New England towns outside Rhode Island had discarded the voluntary system. In New York, a trading company initially paid ministerial salary, but after 1664 the governor empowered the church to tax the inhabitants. Virginia set aside glebes (farmland) for ministers in 1619 and imposed church rates in 1623; churchwardens and sheriffs gathered the parish dues along with other taxes. (p. 30)

In the seventeenth century, most congregations were not really independent as we use the word today, but were established by a larger religious entity (the Church of England in most cases and other bodies such as central Congregationalist authorities in Massachusetts and Connecticut). It is important to remember that most settlers at that time came from England and were influenced by British tradition and social norms. Warburton (1741), as was typical of most English people of his time, asserted that an established church, in which all citizens are members and that is supported by the state, was necessary for the proper functioning of any society. The logic behind this view, as Warburton made sure to remind us, is that in order to ensure civil (that is, correct outward) behavior, the state must stress correct inward behavior, as is imposed and taught by the church. Religious freedom and tolerance of multiple religions result in secularization and the lack of correct inward orientation and doctrine, which in turn results in a lawless society of crime, deviance, and chaos. Thus, when the first settlers came from England, they came from a society in which church and state were intimately interwoven. The state supported the church and had considerable control over church affairs. For example, the King or Queen was the head of the Church of England and appointed the bishops, who, by the virtue of this appointment, were allowed to serve in the House of Lords. Little (1984) noted that those who did not accept the Church of England were called dissenters and were banned from holding public office. In 1689, dissenters were given the freedom to practice other religions, although they were still subject to the state tax used to finance and support the Church of England.

In the United States, before the Revolution and independence, religious affiliation declined to a very low rate (Finke & Stark, 1992). Even in colonies where church attendance was considered a requirement for citizenship, religious apathy and lack of church attendance were the norms. In fact, to be a clergyman in the colonial period was quite difficult. The waves of immigrants that followed the Puritan arrivals were more secular in nature; immigrants often brought with them a variety of religious heritages and were motivated by economic rather than religious concerns. As one German visitor in 1750 noted in a letter: "Pennsylvania is heaven for farmers, paradise for artisans, and hell for officials and preachers" (Gottlieb Mittelberger, quoted in Handlin, 1949).

These early comprehensive congregations had minimal involvement in the nonreligious aspects of life. They focused primarily on religious issues and viewed themselves as moral authorities. The local religious congregation (one denomination supported and financed by the colony) had public responsibilities and faced secular restrictions, similar to those that the Church of England accepts to this day (Hall, 1972). For example, in Virginia, vestries kept the records of births and burials and handled relief to the poor and homeless. Church wardens oversaw the care of orphans, corrected wayward parents, and investigated cases of child abuse. The involvement of churches in this kind of work is the basis for the claim made by some social workers that the profession originated in religion.

Anglican churches in Virginia provided these secular services in exchange for tax money (money collected directly for the church) and state financial support (money raised by the state for unspecified purposes and given to the church when it had a monetary need and applied for special assistance). Moreover, as Holifield noted:

> Almost all agreed also that worship was the responsibility of the entire community. Because they believed that worship was a public, even civic, responsibility, colonial congregations not only sought governmental assistance but also subjected themselves to civic authority. In seventeenth-century New York, governors had to approve the ministries; in Connecticut, town meetings shared in decisions about ministerial salary and tenure; in Massachusetts, between 1636 and 1692, magistrates approved or disapproved the formation of new churches. In New England, moreover, the governors also invested public authority in the churches; Massachusetts until 1664 and New Haven until 1665 admitted only full church members to the status of freemen. (p. 30)

It is important to distinguish between the role of the congregation and that of the established religion in the various colonies. While actual participation in religious services waned after 1650, the organized church in many colonies maintained its power. For example, in New England, the Puritans insisted on church membership as a qualification for voting until the British forced them to end the practice, and Puritan religious leaders intervened aggressively in family affairs (Morgan, 1966). Other important religious groups that made intensive use of church institutions to manage family and social life included Quakers, Presbyterians, and members of the Dutch Reformed Church. Even the Church of England had extensive social and family supervision responsibility, though as a broad, inclusive church, and the state church of an imperial power, it took a less severe line than did the various dissenting Calvinist groups and the Quakers. It also had to deal with resistance from people who resented its pretensions and its demands for funds (Hammack, 1998).

While various colonies had different established churches (e.g., the Congregationalists in Connecticut and Massachusetts, and the Quakers in Pennsylvania), many dissenting groups appeared, not the least of which were the Church of England and (later) the Baptists. Consequently, bitter battles over public support of churches erupted long before the American Revolution, as other Christian groups considered themselves deprived and persecuted by the established church. For example, in New York in the 1720s, dissenters attempted to take over the Church of England parsonage in Hempstead, arguing that their pastor should get the public support provided by the taxes they paid. The Church of England established its dominance in New York when it gained control over the newly created King's College (later Columbia University) in 1750. In Virginia, which publicly supported the Church of England, dissenters became vocal critics of the colony's established church. The Baptists in particular decried the Anglican hegemony; this tension no doubt contributed to Virginia's later disestablishment efforts (Miller, 1978). On the other hand, Pennsylvania was chartered as a Quaker colony, yet it did not support any religion in a formal way and thus managed to avoid many of the tensions and religious battles of the preindependence era. Even so, non-Quaker religious groups wanted to topple the Quaker social and political power structure and establish themselves as the colony's formal, state-supported church.

The formation of Christ Church, in Philadelphia, in 1695, by thirty-nine Anglican colonists illustrates some of the features of this period. Establishing an Anglican (now Episcopalian) church in a city whose political, social, and economic leadership were all Quakers was quite difficult, yet these Anglicans faced less official opposition in Pennsylvania than in any other colony (Gough, 1995). Pennsylvania had declared itself an experiment in religious freedom, and all people who believed in God were protected from persecution, even if they did not adhere to the Quaker tradition. The founders of the new Anglican Church included some prominent members of the colony, and, for a short while, members had to underwrite the cost of maintaining the congregation. The Anglicans purchased land and built their own structure with their own means. However, this independence was short lived.

In William Penn's charter for Pennsylvania, it was decreed that if twenty or more residents asked for an Anglican preacher, such a preacher had to be sent to them. Henry Compton, Bishop of London at that time, accepted this provision in order to guarantee the influence of the Church of England. The governor of Maryland, Francis Nicholson, supported and influenced the Philadelphia Anglicans' request for a preacher; as a result, in 1697 the Privy Council agreed to provide Christ Church with an annual subsidy of fifty pounds for a minister and thirty pounds for a school teacher (Gough, 1995). This case illustrates both the difficulty of forming congregations of denominations in opposition to the prominent religious group in power and the tendency of congregations to become state related.

Christ Church also provides an interesting example of how churches operated at that time. Services were held on Sunday mornings and on

Wednesday and Friday evenings. Within ten years of the church's founding, 190 families were members and supported it financially. The pastor made many trips to nearby communities to preach and to convert Quakers back to the "mother church." Education was another significant church function. The church schoolmaster was in charge of the church school; a special schoolhouse had been built as early as 1709. The schoolmaster taught children to read and write for religious, practical, and commercial purposes. Other subjects included arithmetic, prayers, grace, manners, and morals. Christ Church created the first library outside private homes and enabled members to read books that they could not afford to purchase. This social program is now handled by The Free Library throughout America.[1]

It is important to note that, even in this early period, American congregations began to diverge from their European counterparts. One reason is that they lacked the hierarchical structure common to European churches. This meant that they invariably had to make decisions on their own, without consulting an authoritarian central church. Thus, local churches, and later synagogues, were increasingly governed and influenced by the laity. "Lay vestries in Virginia; town meetings and local selectmen in New England; and congregational leaders in the Middle colonies hired their own ministers and set their own policies" (Holifield, p. 31).

At the same time, the Church of England in Virginia and in Maryland actually functioned quite well, with the College of William and Mary, in Williamsburg, Virginia, serving as an important religious and educational center. The college educated a significant portion of colonial Church of England ministers and maintained a spirit of service among them. The Church of England never established an American bishop, instead managing the colonies through the Bishop of London.[2]

Another example of the unique spirit of American congregations of the time is the Great Awakening of the mid-eighteenth century. The spreading religious fervor changed the nature of religion from a scholarly and dogmatic institution to a more charismatic and emotional one. The revival meetings, held by charismatic preachers, offered the promise of a warm, friendly, and accessible God and sent a clear threat of eternal damnation to sinners. The clergy who ran these meetings provided an appealing message in a well-polished style and attracted followers from all denominations. While most organized religious groups and congregations of the time opposed their message, many colonists were attracted to it. Its impact can be seen today in the many charismatic churches and in the contemporary popularity of evangelical Christianity (Lodge, 1964).

It is important to remember that those congregations and the churches they represented were part of the establishment and thus were scrutinized by—and had to demonstrate loyalty to—the British crown. Congregations "subjected themselves," but they were also forced to submit to English authority. Through much of the eighteenth century, some English leaders sought to use the Church of England and its Society for the Propagation of the Gospel in Foreign Parts to increase English control over the increasingly independent colonists. Some colonists welcomed English control as a way of preserving an order they wanted, but other religious groups did not approve of this assertion of authority (Hammack, 1998).

In the era before the Revolution, we see the beginning of the "Americanization" of congregations: the first signs of religious variations and people's choices in how to worship and with whom. Americans who saw that churches—as well as other aspects of life—were governed by European dogma sought more control and involvement in decision-making processes. The fact that members of Christ Church, in Philadelphia, bore the full cost of their church through active participation rather than through regular taxation encouraged them to assume a greater role in deciding who would lead their church. For example, a sizable number of Christ Church members were impressed with the Anglican evangelist William Macclenachen, who came to town in 1759. These members wanted the church to retain his services as an associate minister, but they were opposed by the senior minister of the church, Robert Jenney. A group of 130 members who supported Macclenachen's appointment wrote to Robert Jenney, "rest assure as we pay our Clergy we have right, and shall insist on the services of such who we convince can serve us." The letter went on to say that they did not need the approval of the Bishop (in London) for such appointments. This assertion was in stark contradiction to Anglican Church law that any clergy appointment had to be licensed by the Bishop. On June 18, 1760, Jenney informed the vestry that the Bishop had denied Macclenachen's application to become an assistant minister. The vestry accepted the verdict, but a large group of Macclenachen's supporters decided to secede from Christ Church and to establish a new church, with Macclenachen as the senior clergy. On June 24, they submitted "Articles of Agreement" to form St. Paul Church in Philadelphia.

Within two years, they built the largest church in the city, on Third Street between Spruce and Walnut, with a seating capacity of more than a thousand people. The "Articles of Agreement" defined the church as Anglican but allowed the majority of members the right to choose new ministers without external intervention. The case of St. Paul Church demonstrates two trends that later were to characterize religion in America: the quest for more evangelical and less scholarly religion and the right of taxpayers to participate in decisions about church leadership. St. Paul Church was America's religious Boston Tea Party (Barratt, 1917).

During the period of the Revolution, about two-thirds of the Anglican clergy, who were perceived as associated with the British forces, left America, including the majority of trained clergy. The paucity of religious leaders and sources of religious authority opened the door for unordained clergy to take over. During the war, revolutionary forces destroyed many Anglican churches as symbols of the British oppression. The British forces retaliated and destroyed churches of the rebelling forces. Thus, in colonies where church participation was already low, the war further decimated the role of religion in society, as well as the importance and viability of the congregation in people's lives (Chang, 1993).

After American independence was established, there was significant variation in religious attitude among the new states. New England's Congregationalists were mostly "non-separating" from the Church of England, while German colonists sought to maintain some central control over their Reformed congregations. The Church of England maintained central authority (though this matter is disputed), but the Anglican Church was tarred with charges of "loyalism" toward Britain after the Revolution. The reconstituted Episcopal Church had to prove its patriotism, which gave its leaders a motive to attack the perceived incompetence and ineffectiveness of the Church of England during the colonial period. Presbyterians and other Calvinists had scores to settle, in part by casting aspersions on the pre-Revolutionary actions of the Church of England. Finally, the rapidly increasing numbers of Baptists and Methodists had no reason to honor the Church of England.

The comprehensive church was the first church of America and mirrored much of the European religious scene. Congregations were state dependent and limited their involvement to sacred matters. Congregations were parish based and did not develop unique American traits or theologies until after the Revolution.

The Devotional Congregation

The *devotional congregation* phase (1789–1870) was characterized by the loss of state-church status and by fierce diversification. Several states, such as Connecticut, Georgia, Maryland, Massachusetts, New Hampshire, and South Carolina, first moved to a model of multiple established churches. Rather than supporting one church or abolishing the role of the state in church affairs, these states turned to religious taxation but supported dissenting sects and denominations as well as the institutional church of the colony. This model was not accepted in Virginia; the Virginia legislature repealed most of the legal privileges granted to the Anglican Church (including the collection of taxes for the Church) in 1776 (Levy, 1994). In 1784, a referendum was proposed to adopt a multidenominational model similar to that in other colonies. Thomas Jefferson lobbied against this proposal and suggested instead a "Bill for Establishing Religious Freedom," which forbade taxes for religious purposes and eliminated public support for any kind of worship. The bill passed and later served as the model for the First Amendment in the Bill of Rights. Eventually, the Virginia model prevailed, and all states adopted similar laws. In 1833, Massachusetts became the last of the original states to disestablish its church. In the case of Christ Church, the process was most difficult. Gough (1995) described the shift to disestablishment in the following manner:

> At the same time they had to adjust to the lack of state support, a loss that left the church in an almost continual financial crisis. Just as important, the church had to create a governing structure that worked in the absence of both a resident bishop and the traditional social and political hierarchy that provided stability in England. While, this structural void led to almost continual power struggles and intensified every controversy, Christ Church eventually developed authority structures uniquely suited to the American environment, authority structures that served as the model for the Protestant Episcopal Church. (p. 2)

As a result of disestablishment, today the United States does not have a state religion; nor does it collect or allocate public money to support any religion. Money for maintaining religious services and practices, paying clergy salaries, and repairing and maintaining buildings is solicited from members of the religious groups and is not mixed with public funds.

The post-Revolutionary period was also marked by an influx of immigrants and by the proliferation of ethnic congregations that served as support systems for the newcomers, just as American congregations today serve immigrants from countries like Korea and El Salvador (Warner, 1994). The proliferation of congregations was as impressive as the massive waves of immigration. The number of congregations grew from fewer than 3,000 in 1780 to approximately 54,000 in 1820, an increase that outstripped even the population growth (Miyakawa, 1969). Gaustad (1962) reported that Methodists grew from fifty congregations in 1783 to 2,700 in 1820, and to nearly 20,000 in 1860. The Baptists grew from 400 congregations in 1780 to more than 12,000 in 1860. From the 1780s to the 1860s, the Lutherans grew from 225 to 2,100 congregations, and the Presbyterians, from 500 to about 6,400. Some of this growth can be explained by population growth and some by the migration of African Americans from the South to the North, but most is the result of disestablishment, the active religious leadership of a new type of clergy, the quest for morality, and the unification of society.

Although the primary purpose of the local congregation was still worship, membership began to be distinguished along socioeconomic lines. Rich and poor, even those within the same parish and denomination, began to worship separately. According to Holifield (1994), part of the impetus for this came from Catholic immigrants, who began to use their churches for secular activities as well as for worship.

The busy Catholic parish foreshadowed the future of the American congregation. These Catholic congregations served numerous social purposes because members could not count on public institutions or Protestant churches. Parishes and church organizations offered their members not only worship but relief societies, insurance societies, militia groups (for both protection and entertainment), Societies of St. Paul for welfare and youth work, temperance societies, and schools. For example, Catholics developed separate schools because Protestants controlled public schools and often insisted on Protestant religious practices within those schools, notably daily readings from the King James translation of the Bible, while Catholics insisted on the use of the Douay Bible, with extensive marginal annotations defining Catholic readings of the texts.

Dignan (1933) suggested that the courts and towns treated congregations as voluntary associations and dealt in cases of property and rights between the laity and the clergy as if they were regular voluntary associations. This was the case not only for Protestant churches but also for

Catholic churches and Jewish synagogues. Catholic bishops worked hard from the 1820s on to defeat "trusteeism" within the Catholic community and to secure legislation and corporate charters that would allow them to manage Catholic churches and related institutions in accordance with Catholic practice in Europe—something some American legislatures sought to prevent throughout the nineteenth century. Jews had less trouble, because their congregational and governance practices were similar to those developed by American Protestants. Lynn (1999) said of this period:

> Government subsidies for parishes belonged to a fading past and churches could not rely on the coercive force of the state to raise their much-needed funds. The church was now dependent on volunteerism and the art of persuasion in order to provide support for ministries, religious institutions, and churches. (p. 56)

Lynn further notes that Protestant leaders of the time, fearful that Protestant dominance in America was being threatened by other religious groups (particularly Catholics), told their followers that Christendom's future depended on their support. This led to an important shift away from reliance on few wealthy donors to wider support from ordinary Americans. This shift marked the beginning of a more democratic and influential American church. The sense of Christianity in crisis, along with the call for funds, triggered the formation of many new religious institutions, ranging from foreign missions and Bible societies to Sunday schools and religious education classes. It also saw a new development in church finance: the commissioning of "agents" or fund-raisers by many denominations. The money raised by these agents came for the most part from local parishioners. Agents were used to raise funds for individual Protestant churches, especially large churches in the cities. In addition, Protestant churches and inter-Protestant associations raised funds locally for local charities (notably orphanages, schools, colleges, and clinics) and for mission activities both in the United States and abroad.

The Social Congregation

The *social congregation* phase (1870–1950) was characterized by full disestablishment and enormous social change resulting from major industrialization, urbanism, mass immigration, and scientific progressivism. It was during this time that science began to replace religion as a major force in the public sphere (Turner, 1974), and the Progressive era paved way to the two world wars. As Butler (1997) noted about this era, "At best, theology is brought in as a kind of final rite for Protestantism, the Gilded Age representing the decades when the old marriage of theology and American intellectual life ends in divorce after an increasingly difficult separation" (p. 299). This was also the era of the Social Gospel movement, a Christian response to massive urbanization, alienation, widening class gaps, and the rapid rise of socialism (Dorn, 1993). The Social Gospel movement sought to improve the lives of the masses by introducing the Christian values of just and harmonious living in society (Curtis, 1991).

From the end of the Civil War through the post–World War II era, most American congregations expanded their roles to include social services and community involvement. Holifield (1994) noted, "In the late nineteenth century, thousands of congregations were open for worship but also were available for Sunday school concerts, church socials, women's meetings, youth groups, girl's guilds, boy's brigades, sewing circles, benevolent societies, day schools, temperance societies, athletic clubs, scout troops, and nameless other activities" (pp. 39–40). Congregations, no longer publicly supported, began to take a more active role as the social center of the community. Many congregations became involved in the settlement house movement, either sponsoring or providing volunteer services for settlement houses that helped immigrants and indigent people become self-sufficient and productive citizens. An indirect result of these outreach activities was that congregations became more segregated along ethnic and socioeconomic lines. Various groups of residents who shared similar ethnic and/or socioeconomic backgrounds hired religious leaders, established places of worship, and developed their own local religious congregations. This became easier as more and more people owned cars and were able to travel long distances to attend the congregation in which they felt most comfortable.

Again, to use the example of Christ Church, in Philadelphia, Gough (1995) reported that:

> the twentieth century brought new leadership and a new vision—a vision that saw the neighborhood and the city in general as an opportunity to serve rather than a problem to overcome. As the church's social service activities increased, Philadelphians once again came to see Christ Church as an important part of the city's present and future, as well as its past. (p. 3)

A visitor to Christ Church today will still find pictures from the 1920s and 1930s, when people came to Christ Church to receive hot meals, food, clothing, and counseling. Church data document a period of growth and strength. Moreover, the pictures vividly show that the church assisted both white and black people.

The local congregations in American cities and towns reflected not only diverse religious faiths but also the diversity of the population. While each congregation might have been homogeneous, the combined congregations presented a tapestry of ethnic and sociodemographic groups. For example, Warner and Lunt (1941), in their book *Yankee City* (referring to Newburyport, Connecticut) found many denominations whose congregations were representative of a particular ethnic identity or socioeconomic status.

Warner and Lunt also found a high correlation between congregational membership and the town's social network and power structure. In the 1930s, they found that religious affiliation, more than social or economic status or political connections, was the most important cross-cutting variable that linked the city's secular associations. For example, Warner and Lunt found that members of liberal Protestant groups (Congregationalists, Unitarians, and Episcopalian groups formed before 1930) were more involved in associations than were either conservative Protestants (Baptists and Methodists) or Roman Catholics. The liberal Protestants sat on more boards of civic organizations and were more likely to sponsor organizations such as the YMCA or Boy Scouts, which serve the wider community. In other words, liberal (mainline) Protestants were much more likely to care for the needs of the community as a whole than were conservative Protestants and Roman Catholics or Jews, who were more concerned with the welfare of their own members and with their spiritual needs.

Similar studies in other cities have provided additional insights on congregations of this period. Samuel Lane Loomis (1887), for example, gathered statistics on religious life in Manhattan. He found that there were thirty-one Protestant churches in Manhattan, which then had a population of approximately 360,000, a very low ratio of congregations to residents. A decade later, Walter Laidlaw, executive secretary of the Federation of Churches and Christian Workers of New York City, conducted a study of religious life in New York. Many of his statistical reports were reported in the organization's journal, *Federation*. One key finding was that 50 percent of the Protestants and 80 percent of the Catholics in New York reported regular church attendance. Like many Protestant leaders of his time, Laidlaw had been alarmed by the decline of Protestant influence in urban America. Nevertheless, Laidlaw (1932) later reported that congregational affiliation in New York had risen from 21 percent in 1855 to 40 percent in 1916. Consequently, he revised his opinion about the religious participation of New Yorkers and talked about the contribution of Protestantism to the city.

Congregations, seeking new ways to raise funds, instituted the practice of annual pledges. Members were asked to specify how much they would give and were expected to pay off their pledges by making weekly payments. Sunday collections also became an integral part of the service. Some congregations began using the "duplex" envelope, with one pocket for local expenses and the other for mission support (Lynn, 1999). For most denominations, the catchphrase for giving in this era was "stewardship," and the role of the believer was to be a just steward. To be a just steward of God's bounty meant using money wisely and giving generously. Toward the end of the nineteenth century, tithing became an important concept for congregational fund-raising, even if rarely practiced in full.

The Participatory Congregation

The *participatory congregation* phase began in 1950 and continues today. By 1990, estimates of the number of congregations in the United States ranged from 294,271 (Hodgkinson et al., 1993) to 350,337 (Jackuet & Jones, 1991), averaging one congregation per 350 to 500 residents. These numbers are debatable, as they were based on either Yellow Pages listings in the forty-eight contiguous states (i.e., excluding Alaska and Hawaii) or on records of national denominations (Warner, 1994). Furthermore, according to Finke and Stark (1992), the percentage of United States residents who were actively religious peaked in 1960 and has not dropped since.

While many of the historical trends in congregational development continue today, five new developments are worth noting. First, the denominations that governed religious life until 1950 have become less powerful and have given way to nondenominational charismatic congregations. Second, the rise of new denominations has fostered new forms of religious expression such as "paradigm churches," for whose members the church is the center of their lives, such as the Nation of Islam, the Metropolitan Community Church (a gay and lesbian ministry), and the Vineyard churches (Miller, 1997). Third, it is estimated that there are currently approximately 1,600 denominations in the United States. These range from small fringe religions to national powerhouses such as the Roman Catholic Church and the Southern Baptist Convention (Wuthnow, 1998). Thus, there is widespread variability within many of the traditional denominations, not only in the theological practices and beliefs of congregations but also in the political and social viewpoints of their members. It is not uncommon to find, for example, evangelical Presbyterian congregations, charismatic Catholic congregations, and highly orthodox Episcopalian congregations challenging the authority of denominationally appointed bishops (or other area leaders) whom they consider to be too liberal. Fourth, the rise of mega-churches and storefront churches reflects changing attitudes toward religious participation, particularly as a matter of individual choice. Finally, many people are no longer following the religious tradition of their parents but rather seeking out congregations that meet their own spiritual and social needs. Nancy Eiesland (1999) found that in Gwinnett County, Georgia, "newcomers who were potential members of congregations often seemed less concerned about a congregation's denominational affiliation than they were about its programming for children and whether or not they felt welcome and supported" (p. 12).

This is not to say that congregations are no longer centers for worship and moral guidance. However, the contemporary congregation is a product of the nation's social and historical development, a religious gathering of choice that reflects both the needs of the paying members and changes in society.

Robert Franklin (1997), in a study of megachurches, found that many of the African American members of these churches had been raised in different religious backgrounds. For many, the choice of congregation is based not on denominational ties but on personal desires. He noted:

> It appears that black parishioners have become congregational consumers, using a shopping list of desired characteristics when searching for a church home. The list includes the vibrancy of its worship and music, spiritually fulfilling and intellectually stimulating preaching, safety and attractiveness of the church environment, quality programs for children, programs for single people, and the convenience of scheduling of worship services. (pp. 57-58)

The participatory congregation has also benefited from the complex nexus of transportation and geographical mobility in that it no longer serves as a geographically defined parish but rather as a magnet for people who

wish to worship together. It is not unusual for a local religious congregation to have members who are not residents of the community in which
the congregation is located. Nevertheless, these members invariably have a
sense of ownership or responsibility toward the local community, especially if they have moved to a more affluent urban or suburban neighborhood and return to worship in their former community. However, in the
mega-churches, many members come from a distance but often do not feel
a sense of responsibility toward the neighborhood where the church is located. As a result, megachurches are often more regionally oriented and
less neighborhood oriented.

Modern congregations have undergone a distinct ecological shift. In the
1950s, mainline denominations (such as the Episcopal, Jewish, Lutheran,
Methodist, Presbyterian, and Roman Catholic denominations) dominated
the urban terrain. By the end of the 1990s, many of these urban congregations had closed or relocated to the suburbs. Loizillon and Hughes
(1999) found that by 1999, approximately 60 percent of the historic congregational buildings in North Philadelphia (built before 1940 and designed as a place of worship) housed a denomination different from that
of the original congregation. In most cases, buildings once owned by a
mainline Protestant congregation were now owned by a nonmainline congregation, such as a Pentecostal, Apostolic, or Baptist denomination, or by
an independent congregation.

Peter Dobkin Hall (1998) studied the number and type of nonprofit organizations in New Haven between 1850 and 1990. The number of such organizations grew from forty-two in 1850 to 676 in 1960, with only a slight
decline—from 676 to 630—in 1990. An important finding of this study is
that the number of fraternal organizations, which had risen from one to 257
in the period 1850–1910, dropped to just ten in 1990. During the same period, 1850–1910, the number of congregations increased from twenty-one
to ninety, and then rose even more, reaching 183 by 1990. Hall also found
that the proportion of congregations among nonprofit organizations rose
from 18 percent in 1930 to 33 percent in 1990. Hall summed it up:

> the conventions equating modernism, urbanism, and activist government
> with secularization are not manifested in the declines in the number or
> proportional significance of churches in the population of nonproprietary
> organizations. Indeed, quite the contrary, the number of churches grows
> steadily throughout the whole period of 1850–1990—and in particular in-
> tensity after 1950. (p. 6)

The New Haven study shows that the local religious congregation is thriving and expanding at a time when many predicted that religion would decline or disappear altogether. Thus, while social institutions such as fraternal organizations have declined, organized religion is alive and well at the local level.

Summary

This brief historical review of American congregations demonstrates that congregations are not static but ever-changing and adaptable social organizations. We should keep in mind that congregations were designed to enable people who share similar religious beliefs to practice them together. American society has changed dramatically since the seventeenth century, and so have local religious congregations. The congregation has evolved from a uniform protected arm of the state into a diverse entity that, like public schools, can be found in every community in the United States. Congregations have adapted to the changing needs of the population (and changes in the population itself) because they are financed and maintained voluntarily. Thus, congregations have to adapt to survive.

In the following chapters, we examine congregations at the end of the twentieth century, at the peak of the participatory congregation period. Since we collected data during the years 1996–99, we can report only on congregations from this time period. Nevertheless, their impressive involvement in social services delivery is not a new development. While such social involvement was not characteristic of congregations in the United States prior to the Civil War, over the past 150 years social involvement has become a major part of the activities of many congregations. This story is often ignored and goes untold. Before we proceed to document the stories of the congregations that we studied, we first describe them in detail to establish to what extent they represent the universe of congregations in the United States.

PART II

Congregations Involvement
Empirical Findings

3

The Congregations in Our Study

> To represent the religious history of America statistically and geo-
> graphically is to generalize dangerously and to court disaster openly.
> —E. S. Gaustad, *Historic Atlas of Religion in America* (1962)

Before we discuss the extent and nature of congregational social service delivery, we would like to answer these questions: "Who are
these congregations? Are they old or new? Are they large or small? Are they
stable in their location or planning to leave?" These and many other questions will help us understand the characteristics of the congregations in
our study.

Findings from our study of 251 older and newer congregations in seven
cities (Chicago, Houston, Indianapolis, Mobile, New York, Philadelphia,
and San Francisco) and one small town (Council Grove, Kansas) support
the characterization of America's congregations at the end of the twentieth century as being participatory congregations—diverse and visible entities found in every community, financed and maintained voluntarily by
their willing members. This research builds on our previous study (Cnaan,
1997), which examined the social and community involvement of 111
congregations housed in historic properties.

In the following sections, we document the characteristics of the congregations in our study; demonstrate how the congregations both resemble and differ from one another; and discuss the significance of our findings. It should be emphasized that our study was not fully random, and it
is not certain that we represent all forms of congregations.

The congregational characteristics reported in this chapter follow those
discussed in the literature along with a few that we thought relevant.
Where possible, we compare the characteristics of the congregations in our
study to those found in other studies so that the reader may assess its overall representativeness.

Age of Congregation

The 111 congregations in our original sample (see Appendix) were among the oldest in our study. Many were the original tenants of the historic (built before 1940) properties in which they were housed. To address the potential bias of congregational age, we included more recently established congregations in our expanded study.

The date of establishment for the congregations in the study ranged from 1677 to 1997. Of these, 57.2 percent were established before 1940, 17.6 percent between 1941 and 1960, and 25.2 percent after 1961. The mean age of the congregation was 82.3 years. These numbers are very similar to the national norm. Dudley and Roozen (2001), in a survey of 14,301 congregations that belong to twenty-six different denominations, found that 53 percent were established before 1945. They also found that 39 percent of the congregations in their sample were established after 1965. In other words, we encountered more congregations that were established between 1940 and 1960 than their sample indicates. We argue that older congregations are more likely to be mainline congregations with sizable endowments and with members who are more oriented to "this world" than are members of younger congregations, especially those established after 1960, in which baby boomers are more likely to be members. Indeed, Dudley and Roozen found that the greatest growth in congregations after 1945 came among evangelical Protestants and in Mormon and Muslim congregations. Younger congregations are said to be more concerned with preparing people for the other world and focus on salvation, rather than on helping people in this world. As shown in chapter 6, this was not the case in our sample.

In New York and in Council Grove, all the congregations were established before 1940. It is important to note that the data for New York are somewhat biased, since they came only from the first phase of our study (that of congregations housed in historic properties). In the case of Council Grove, there have been no major changes in population, and thus the congregations that were examined in the first phase of the study are still in operation. However, as is shown in chapter 8, the inter- and intradynamic of congregations is quite active. Among congregations in Houston, Mobile, and Philadelphia, 40 percent were established before 1940. Among congregations in Philadelphia, 46 percent were established after 1961.

Years at Current Location

Of the 251 congregations in the study, only three had no permanent location. For the other 248 congregations, length of time at the current location ranged from six months to 234 years. The mean length of time was fifty-six years. As in the previous section, we found that this mean was influenced by the historic congregations that have been stationary for more than two hundred years.

Only thirty congregations (12 percent) reported that they were planning to relocate. Ten of these congregations reported that their mission required them to remain in an urban area and that they were looking for new space in the same neighborhood. The reason most often given for relocation was the need for additional space, to accommodate either increased membership or increased service provision. Three congregations, however, planned to relocate to a smaller facility. Thirty-four congregations (13.5 percent) reported that they shared space with other congregations. There was little overlap between congregations planning to relocate and those sharing space with another congregation.

With respect to location, we found that the deliberate choice to maintain the property in its current location, coupled with the fact that members, many of whom no longer live in the neighborhood, but are highly concerned with and rooted in the community, makes the religious congregation a natural leader or partner for local coalitions and initiatives. In many ways, the location becomes synonymous with the ties that members have to the congregation and to one another. Once bonded around the congregational property, members feel obliged and related to the local neighborhood and its needs.

Gardner (1994) emphasizes the importance of shared values in regenerating a community at a time when increased mobility erodes the ties that bind people. As places where people who share certain religious and social values come together, congregations help build a sense of community. They also build community by providing services and serving as intermediary structures that link families, neighborhoods, and the government.

Membership

Defining who is a member of a congregation is not an easy task. Bonomi and Eisenstadt (1982), for example, define members as attenders and their children. Many congregations, however, distinguish between communicant members (those who receive communion) and attenders (those who attend services but do not receive communion). Some congregations consider children of members to be part of the membership, while others do not consider them eligible for membership until they become adults. Thus, the issue of measuring membership is not as simple as one would expect because not all attenders are members and not all members attend. Furthermore, unlike clubs where one buys membership, in most congregations people do not pay membership dues (with the notable exception of Jewish synagogues) and are free to come and go as they please. It is also methodologically difficult to account to the people who attend and support the congregation only during major holidays.

For purposes of our study, we used four measures to assess membership. We consistently included children in the membership count, even if the specific congregation did not. We asked the interviewee to count all individuals, including children, in the four categories.

First, we asked each congregation to report its total membership, which we defined as "all those on your mailing list" or "on your rolls." Since this is a broad membership measure, it likely includes people who no longer attend services but who maintain some type of relationship with the congregation, as well as those who attend only during major holidays. It is interesting to note that only one congregation reported eliminating from its mailing list those who did not attend services at least once a year. Although this measure may inflate the number of members, it is indicative of the social network of the congregation. Findings for total membership ranged from a low of nine members to a high of 104,000 members. The mean for total membership was 1,235 members.

Second, we asked each congregation to report the total number of active members, which we defined as those who attend services at least once a month and are known to the clergy and lay leaders. In this category we intended to count those who meet the religious membership criteria, can be trusted to come on a regular basis, and support the congregation. Findings for active members ranged from a low of five members to a high of 14,000 (the latter was not the same congregation that reported total membership of 104,000). The mean for active members was 492 members.

Third, we asked each congregation to report the number of active nonmembers, which we defined as those who attend services at least once a month but who do not meet the religious requirements for membership. This group includes spouses and/or friends of members, neighbors, and others who take part in the worship but either do not wish to join or are unwilling to break ties with their own congregation. One congregation reported 6,000 active nonmembers, while twenty-six congregations (10.4 percent) reported none. The mean for active nonmembers was eighty-seven. Together, the measures for active members and for nonmembers indicate that the congregations in our study have, on average, 579 individuals who attend at least once a month. However, this number is skewed by the significant differences in size between the very small and the very large congregations in the study. In fact, 25.3 percent of the congregations reported membership of fewer than 100 individuals.

Finally, we asked each congregation to report average attendance at nonholiday services. This number fluctuated for congregations that required weekly attendance and for those that were less prescriptive. Findings ranged from a low of five to a high of 7,000. The mean for average attendance at nonholiday services was 387.

None of these measures alone can provide an accurate and reliable tally of congregational membership, but, in combination, they provide a more detailed overview of membership size. What the numbers also show, however, is the wide disparity in congregational size, another indication of the wide diversity among American congregations.

The measure we elected to use in this book is the total number of active attenders: members and nonmembers. Our rationale is that this number most closely reflects the number of people who regularly attend services and upon whom the congregation can rely. As seen in Table 3–1, more than a third of congregations in Mobile, Houston, and Chicago have more than 500 active attenders. In contrast, half of the congregations in Philadelphia and in Council Grove have fewer than 200 active attenders. However, these differences are not statistically significant.

When asked if membership had increased, stabilized, or declined during the three-year period before the interview took place, 55.2 percent reported an increase, 32.3 percent reported no change, and 12.5 percent reported a decline in membership. There were no significant differences among the cities we studied. Hodgkinson and Weitzman (1993) found in their study that 58.2 percent of congregations reported an increased in membership in the past three years, 22.8 percent reported no change, and 18.1 percent reported a decrease, while the rest (0.9 percent) could not answer the question. Given the difference in study methods and time of study, especially the number of congregations reporting an increase in membership, these findings are quite similar to ours. Even closer to our

TABLE 3-1
Congregational Active Membership by City

Congregational size	Chicago (N=21)	Houston (N=24)	Indianapolis (N=54)	Mobile (N=40)	New York (N=15)	Philadelphia (N=63)	S. Francisco (N=27)	C.G. (N=7)	Total (N=251)
0–50	1 (4.8%)	—	3 (5.6%)	1 (2.5%)	1 (6.7%)	8 (12.7%)	3 (11.1%)	1 (14.3%)	18 (7.2%)
51–100	4 (19.0%)	1 (4.2%)	11 (20.4%)	7 (17.5%)	1 (6.7%)	16 (25.4%)	4 (14.8%)	2 (28.6%)	46 (18.3%)
101–200	4 (19.0%)	5 (20.8%)	11 (20.4%)	8 (20.0%)	4 (26.7%)	12 (19.0%)	12 (44.4%)	1 (14.3%)	57 (22.8%)
201–500	5 (23.8%)	9 (37.5%)	19 (35.2%)	8 (20.0%)	6 (40.0%)	12 (19.0%)	6 (22.2%)	3 (42.9%)	68 (27.1%)
501–1,000	2 (9.5%)	3 (12.5%)	6 (11.1%)	12 (30.0%)	3 (20.0%)	8 (12.7%)	1 (3.7%)	—	35 (13.9%)
1,001+	5 (23.8%)	6 (25.0%)	4 (7.4%)	4 (10.0%)	—	7 (11.1%)	1 (3.7%)	—	27 (10.8%)

findings are those by Dudley and Roozen (2001), who found that 51 percent of the congregations they studied reported an increase in the previous five years, 31 percent plateaued, and 19 percent declined.

Congregational Workforce

The work of most congregations is carried out by clergy (paid or unpaid), paid staff, and a cadre of volunteers. Hodgkinson and Weitzman (1993), of the Independent Sector, in their study of the congregational workforce, categorized congregational size as small (fewer than 100 members), medium (100–399 members) and large (more than 400 members). They found a strong association between size and the number of paid staff. They reported that, although 88 percent of respondents overall reported at least one full-time paid clergy, this percentage varied by size of the congregation. For small congregations, it was 70 percent. For medium-size congregations, it was 90 percent. For large congregations, it was 97 percent. A much more dramatic finding was that 53 percent of large congregations had two or more full-time paid clergy, compared with 8 percent for medium-size congregations and 4 percent for small congregations. Similarly, 64 percent of large congregations had at least one paid full-time nonclergy employee, compared with 20 percent for medium-size congregations and 4 percent for small congregations. Hodgkinson and Weitzman also found that volunteers made up 89 percent of the congregational workforce.

Clergy: Of the 251 congregations in our study, forty-nine (20 percent) had no full-time clergy. For some of these congregations, it was a temporary situation; for others, this was a matter of regular practice. The overwhelming majority of these congregations, however, reported that their clergy ministered to the congregation on only a part-time basis and worked at other jobs to support themselves. As Bartkowski and Regis (1999) noted, these clergy are generally paid only a small honorarium. This is typically the case in congregations with limited financial resources, and their clergy are known as bivocational clergy. More than half of the congregations (51 percent) reported only one full-time clergy, the model usually associated with the popular concept of a congregation as a one-clergy sacred property. Finally, seventy-three congregations (29 percent) reported more than one full-time clergy. These were the affluent and, often, larger congregations. It is interesting to note that, although the number of full-time clergy is significantly correlated with membership size, it is even more strongly associated with the size of the congregational budget.

Paid staff: The congregations in our study had an average of 5.2 full-time employees and 3.8 part-time employees (including clergy). However, fifteen congregations (6 percent) had no staff; nine had only one part-time employee, namely the clergy; and twenty had only one full-time employee. For purposes of analysis, we counted two part-time employees as the equivalent of one full-time paid position. By this, we assumed that one part-time position averaged one half-time position, an assumption that we could not study on the basis of our data. According to this method, the number of paid positions ranged from none to ninety-five. The congregation with ninety-five employees is exceptional and supports its own day school and elementary school. The mean number of paid positions was 7.1. Again, the mean is misleading. Three congregations reported at least fifty or more paid positions, while eighteen reported at least twenty or more paid positions. In most cases, these are congregations with schools or large day care centers owned and run by the congregation. When we excluded these congregations from the analysis, the mean number of full-time paid positions dropped to 4.6. In other words, 8 percent of the congregations accounted for a third of the full-time positions.

On average, each congregation employed the equivalent of 1.4 full-time employees as an administrator or secretary. The mean, however, is biased, since one congregation reported ten administrators; another reported fifteen secretaries. Seventy-five congregations (29.9 percent) had no full-time administrative or secretarial positions, while twenty congregations (8 percent) reported more than five such positions. Similarly, on average, each congregation employed the equivalent of 1.05 full-time employees as a maintenance worker or janitor and the equivalent of 0.25 full-time employees as a bookkeeper or treasurer. In most congregations, volunteers performed these services. In some instances, a CPA was hired to audit the annual budget. Other positions, such as program directors, music professionals, teachers, and ministry leaders, were employed at the equivalent of 2.81 full-time positions on average per congregation.

Volunteers as alternative staff: Congregations are known for using volunteers to carry out tasks that in other organizations would be handled by paid staff. However, only eleven congregations (4.3 percent) reported using full-time volunteers as administrators/secretaries. Of these, three reported using more than one full-time volunteer. Five congregations (1.9 percent) used full-time volunteers as maintenance workers/janitors, and eight congregations (3.1 percent) used full-time volunteers as bookkeepers/accountants. Twenty congregations (7.9 percent) used full-time volunteers as directors and organizers of social and religious programs.

The picture changes dramatically with regard to part-time volunteers. Seventy-six congregations (30.2 percent) reported using part-time volunteers as administrators/secretaries. Although these are generally small congregations with low annual budgets, several large congregations reported using three or more part-time volunteers to carry out these tasks. Fifty-one congregations (20.3 percent) used part-time volunteers as maintenance workers/janitors. Eighty congregations (31.9 percent) used volunteers as part-time bookkeepers or accountants. Finally, ninety-seven congregations (38.6 percent) used part-time volunteers as directors and organizers of social and religious programs.

On average, congregations used 3.2 volunteers to carry out tasks at all levels from leadership to maintenance. Once again, the mean is biased. One hundred and one congregations (40.2 percent) reported no volunteer staff, while twenty-five congregations (9.9 percent) reported the equivalent of between ten and forty-one positions filled by volunteers. There was no significant correlation between number of paid positions and number of volunteer positions. In other words, poor and small congregations do not compensate for their lack of financial resources by using more volunteers, and large congregations do not consistently utilize more volunteers, even though they have greater resources, such as members and money, at their disposal. The picture that emerges is one of diversity and singularity. Some congregations have either paid staff or volunteer staff, some have none, and others have both.

Sociodemographic Characteristics of Members

Membership size is not the only indicator of the congregation's stability and ability to provide social services. Members' age, marital status, income, and ethnicity also may have a bearing on the congregation's involvement in social service provision. Given that congregational affiliation is a choice for many people today, we expected to find that congregations develop distinct profiles that indicate that people with certain characteristics tend to congregate with each other.

Age: We asked our interviewees about the percentages of older people (age sixty-five and older) and young people (under eighteen). As might be expected, the findings suggest that many congregations attract older people (24 percent of all congregations members), while the percentage of those under eighteen is lower (22 percent). Thirteen congregations (5.6 percent) reported no elderly, and an additional eleven congregations reported that fewer than 10 percent of their members were elderly. Conversely, twenty-nine congregations (11.6 percent) reported that half or more of their members were elderly.

When asked whether the average age of their membership had increased, remained stable, or decreased during the past three years prior to the interview, 15.9 percent reported an increase in average age; 32.9 percent reported no change; and 51.2 percent reported a decrease in average age. We used decreased age as an indicator that families with children had become members, thereby strengthening the membership base. When this occurred in tandem with increased membership, it was a sign of vitality and growth.

Marital status: We asked congregations what percentage of their membership was single. We used this measure as a proxy for family membership, because our pretest showed that congregations differed from one another in how they defined the term *family*. For some, *family* meant only married couples with children, while others gave *family* the broadest possible interpretation, including single parents and gay and lesbian partnerships. The term *single*, however, posed no problems for respondents. Excluding children who lived with parents in a family unit, we found that 33.9 percent of the congregational membership were single. Anecdotal reports suggested that the majority of these single members were elderly, single parents, and/or gays or lesbians. This is an important issue, since it presents a new picture of congregational membership. In a few congregations, we were told that the congregants target single people in the neighborhood and develop programs to meet their needs. These congregations offer "divorce overcoming groups," "singles outings for Christians/Jews," and "raising children on your own." The congregation is no longer a bastion of families; one-third of the membership is composed of singles who have not joined merely to ensure that their children have a religious education and affiliation. These people join a congregation primarily to meet their own spiritual and personal needs and to find people with similar interests.

Estimated annual income of members: Respondents estimated the annual personal income of their members as follows: the estimated percentage earning less than $25,000 was 28 percent. The estimated percentage earning $25,001 to $50,000 was 32 percent; for those earning $50,001 to $75,000, the estimate was 24 percent. Finally, the estimated percentages earning $75,001 to $100,000 and more than $100,001 were 13 percent and 3 percent, respectively. These findings should be viewed with caution. As Wuthnow (1997) has noted, clergy are usually not privy to the actual income levels of their members, and their estimates often prove inaccurate when compared with the members' own reports. In most cases, respondents in our study based their estimates on the tithing patterns of individual members or the type of job they held. These two measures served as a proxy for the members' real income. Sixty percent of the households in our study reported having an annual income of under $50,000. This large percentage implies that many congregational members have limited means, and their ability to support their congregations is also limited.

Where members live: To distinguish congregations that serve as parishes from those that are magnet or commuter congregations, we asked what percentage of members lived within a ten-block radius or a maximum of one mile from the congregational building. Only nine congregations (3.6 percent) reported that all of their members lived within the vicinity. Most of these congregations were Roman Catholic churches. The percentage of members who lived outside the vicinity ranged from a low of 5 percent to a high of 100 percent, with a mean of 62.1 percent. In other words, the parish model of people living near to the congregational property is diminishing. Most members drive to their place of worship; some travel a few blocks, while others travel significant distances to reach their place of worship. One of our interviewees told us that he drives twenty minutes past ten churches before he reaches the church of his choice.

One question that arises from this finding in regard to our study concerns the extent to which commuting congregants feel obliged to assist the local community and its needy people: will members of the congregations see themselves as invested in the community where the congregational building is housed, will they support the areas where they reside, or will they neglect social and community service involvement altogether?

Ethnicity: Blau and Schwartz (1984) note that constraints on religious choice (sanctions against leaving) may be most potent where social ties are consolidated rather than cross-cutting. These social ties make the ethnic makeup of the congregation an important sociodemographic variable. It is more difficult to leave an ethnic congregation if relatives and neighbors may pressure one to stay. When a congregation's members work in the same place or are members of the same social network, the decision to leave the congregation invariably meets with personal scorn, social pressure, or direct cost. Clearly, religious membership and/or participation levels tend to be highest under conditions of ethnic homogeneity and concentric ties (Blau, Land, & Redding, 1992). It is well known that while Americans work, shop, and eat in multicultural environments, they seldom worship in them.

It is unclear when a certain specific group can be said to predominate a congregation. When all members of the congregation and the clergy are part of the same ethnic group, it is clearly an ethnic congregation. But what is the critical mass of members from one ethnic group necessary to justify calling a congregation an ethnic congregation? If all members except one family are of one ethnic group, does that one family prevent the congregation from being considered an ethnic congregation? We used two indicators to answer this question. We considered a congregation an ethnic congregation if any ethnic group constituted at least 90 percent of the membership. This measure was used to denote the massive predominance of one ethnic group. We applied an additional measure when one ethnic group accounted for at least 75 percent of the membership. This is also a measure of predominance, but it allows for diversity with, nevertheless, one clear influential ethnic group that leads the congregation.

The ethnic composition of congregations in the sample revealed that many congregations were composed solely, or primarily, of people from one ethnic group (Table 3-2). As noted, we used two criteria to determine ethnic dominance; either at least 90 percent or at least 75 percent of the membership came from one ethnic group. Of the total sample, 210 congregations (83.7 percent) reported that three-quarters or more of their members belonged to one ethnic group; 176 congregations (70.5 percent) reported that all or nearly all of their members (90 percent or more) belonged to one ethnic group. In most cases, the dominant group was either African American (27.5 percent and 23.1 percent, respectively) or Caucasian (50.2 percent and 43.0 percent, respectively). Geographical differ-

TABLE 3-2
Congregational Ethnicity by City*

Dominant ethnic group	Chicago (N=21)	Houston (N=24)	Indianapolis (N=54)	Mobile (N=40)	New York (N=15)	Philadelphia (N=63)	S. Francisco (N=27)	C.G. (N=7)	Total (N=251)
Black 75%+	9 (42.9%)	6 (25%)	5 (9.3%)	11 (27.5%)	2 (13.3%)	30 (47.6%)	6 (22.2%)	None	69 (27.5%)
90%+	5 (23.8%)	5 (25%)	5 (9.3%)	10 (25%)	2 (13.3%)	25 (39.7%)	5 (18.5%)	None	57 (23.1%)
Caucasian 75%+	6 (28.6%)	12 (50%)	41 (75.9%)	28 (70%)	7 (46.7%)	13 (20.6%)	12 (44.4%)	7 (100%)	126 (50.2%)
90%+	4 (19.0%)	9 (37.5%)	38 (70.4%)	26 (65%)	5 (33.3%)	9 (14.3%)	10 (37.0%)	7 (100%)	108 (43.0%)
Hispanic 75%+	1 (4.8%)	2 (8.3%)	1 (1.9%)	None	1 (6.7%)	5 (7.9%)	None	None	10 (4.0%)
90%+	1 (4.8%)	1 (4.2%)	None	None	1 (6.7%)	4 (6.3%)	None	None	7 (2.8%)
Asian 75%+	None	1 (4.2%)	None	None	None	3 (4.8%)	1 (3.7%)	None	5 (2.0%)
90%+	None	1 (4.2%)	None	None	None	3 (4.8%)	1 (3.7%)	None	5 (2.0%)
Total 75%+	16 (76.3%)	21 (87.5%)	47 (87.1%)	39 (97.5%)	10 (66.7%)	51 (80.9%)	19 (70.3%)	7 (100%)	210 (83.7%)
90%+	10 (47.6%)	16 (70.9%)	43 (79.6%)	36 (90%)	8 (53.3%)	41 (65.1%)	16 (59.2%)	7 (100%)	177 (70.5%)

* Number/percentage of congregations in which one ethnic group predominates. Top line: number of congregations with 75% or more of members belonging to that ethnic group; bottom line: number of congregations with 90% or more of members belonging to that ethnic group. Congregations in bottom line in each cell are included in the top line, as congregations with 90% or more of members belonging to that ethnic group are included in congregations with 75% or more of members belonging to that ethnic group.

ences were not significant for ethnic dominance. All of the congregants in Council Grove, for example, are Caucasian, because almost all of the residents are Caucasian. In Philadelphia and Chicago, we studied more African American congregations, while in Indianapolis and Mobile, we studied more Caucasian congregations. Regardless of these variations, the overall picture is one of ethnically segregated congregations.

This finding supports previous research that found that congregations are often segregated institutions. That the public frequently uses terms such as the "Korean church" or the "black church" indicates the strong association between congregations and ethnicity. The implications of this finding are many and are elaborated on in later chapters. Hill (1998) found, in a study of congregations in the Baltimore area, that 58 percent were mostly black, 35 percent were mostly white, and only 7 percent were racially mixed. Moreover, this finding of ethnically segregated congregations is consistent with demographic studies that indicate that in many cities almost 90 percent of the residents live in neighborhoods that are populated predominantly by members of their own ethnic group (Farley & Frey, 1994; Massey & Denton, 1993). The segregation by choice of congregations has occurred as far back as the colonial era. Gough (1995) found that, in Christ Church in the 1730s, "a number of Quakers who, as their wealth increased, became tired of strict Quaker lifestyle and turned to the Church of England" (p. 47). These people preferred the religious and congregational proximity of people of similar wealth and social perspective. In this respect, we should also be cognizant of what Ammerman (1997) noted: "The choice of one's congregation is part of the freedom U.S. attenders have long cherished" (p. 35).

Political/theological orientation: To determine the effect of political and theological orientation on congregational involvement in social and community service provision, we asked respondents to characterize their congregations as politically conservative, moderate, or liberal. Of the 251 congregations, 34.8 percent described themselves as conservative, 42.5 percent as moderate, and 22.7 percent as liberal. Concerning theological orientation, 35.5 percent of the congregations described themselves as fundamentalist, 23.5 percent as conservative, 27.1 percent as moderate, and 13.9 percent as liberal. In using the term *theology*, we did not imply support for the so-called Religious Right or for the Christian Coalition but rather a belief in the Bible as the literal word of God and the inclination to spread the word of God. In both instances, the sample tended toward a more conservative (politically) and fundamentalist (theologically) orientation. This trend is representative of organized religious groups, which tend to be less liberal than the general public. We noted that congregations viewed themselves as more politically liberal than theologically liberal. This slant was influenced primarily by African American congregations whose political agenda includes protesting racial discrimination and the belief that government should combat racism. These politically liberal congregations were often theologically as conservative as Caucasian congregations.

Clergy and Lay Leadership

Religious leaders are distinguished from their members by both their responsibilities and their privileges. They are considered to be compassionate people of good character, better educated than most members of the congregation, and knowledgeable about theology. They are viewed not only as religious leaders but also as community leaders in secular organizations ranging from local coalitions to national forums (Cnaan, Yancey, Rodgers, and Trulear, 2002).

Gender ratio: Billingsley (1999), in a study of churches in Atlanta and Denver, reported that, although the membership was predominantly female (93 percent and 90 percent, respectively), males made up 90 percent of the clergy and lay leaders in both cities. Similarly, in our study, 92.3 percent of the clergy were male. Of these, 80 percent were full-time paid clergy.

Although we did not ask about the gender ratio of congregants, we asked how many men and women chaired key committees in the congregation. We used this measure of lay leadership as a proxy for gender distribution within the membership. Of the 827 committees reported, 451 (54.5 percent) were headed by men, 376 (45.5 percent) by women. Compared to the overwhelming number of congregations in our study headed by male clergy, the lay leadership showed a more favorable gender ratio. These two statistics should be considered in the context of the fact that many studies show that more women than men attend religious congregations. In other words, men lead congregations, and men and women serve as lay leaders nearly equally, while women are the majority of members.

Governance: When asked about central committees, which we defined as the administrative/governing body of the congregations, 45 congregations

(17.9 percent) reported three central committees, and 110 (43.8 percent) reported two central committees. Seven congregations (2.8 percent) reported no central committee. On average, this administrative/governing body consisted of 19.5 persons. We also asked respondents how many of these lay leaders were also "leaders in the community," which we defined as people with major responsibilities in local, state, or national organizations that can link the congregation to outside resources. On average, one-third of the governing body, or 6.2 individuals, were identified as leaders in the community.

Congregational Worship

Because worship is the primary purpose of religious congregations, we asked how many worship services were held at the congregational site during nonholiday periods. On average, there are 2.3 weekend services and 3.1 weekday services, for a total of 5.4 worship services weekly. This number was biased, as several mosques reported thirty-five prayer services weekly and some orthodox Jewish synagogues reported fourteen prayer services weekly. When these congregations were omitted from the analysis, the mean was 2.1 weekend services and 1.6 weekday service, for a total of 3.7 services weekly.

Congregational Finances

Giving USA (1995) estimated religious giving in 1994 at $58.8 billion, or 45 percent of all giving by individuals and organizations. Hodgkinson and Weitzman (1993) estimated religious giving to be 63 percent of all philanthropic giving. Nevertheless, the average giving per congregation is much less impressive when compared with the total given by all congregations.

According to the literature, congregations with larger budgets are more involved in social service provision than are those with smaller budgets (see chapter 6 for a more detailed discussion). This is not unexpected, since it is only when income exceeds expenses that a congregation can begin allocating funds to social services. A budget surplus may also account for a congregation's ability to deploy volunteers for social services. Without sufficient staff to provide administrative and maintenance support for the congregation, there is little opportunity for members to engage in social service provision. Thus, the annual operating budget is significantly associated with social service provision.

Annual operating budgets: To determine the operating budget, we asked for all sources of income, excluding capital funds, that is, money raised for new construction or major renovations, and school budgets. Because many congregations were reluctant to reveal their actual operating budgets, we asked respondents to identify the category that most closely matched their annual operating budgets. Twenty-nine congregations (12.1 percent) reported budgets of less than $50,000. Forty-two congregations (17.6 percent) reported budgets of $50,000 to $100,000. Sixty-eight congregations (28.5 percent) reported budgets of $100,001 to $200,000. Sixty congregations (25.1 percent) reported budgets of $200,001 to $500,000. Among the most affluent congregations, twenty-one (8.8 percent) reported budgets of $500,001 to $1 million; ten (7.9 percent) reported budgets of more than $1 million.

When we asked respondents whether their congregation had a budget surplus, a balanced budget, or a budget deficit for the year prior to the interview, 42.6 percent reported a balanced budget, 29.1 percent reported a surplus, and 28.3 percent reported a deficit. Only 42 congregations (17.1 percent) reported themselves as financially strong; 130 (52 percent) reported they were financially sound, and 79 (30.9 percent) said they were struggling. We were surprised to find that the congregational perception of its financial stability was strongly and significantly associated with the congregation's annual operating budget; this association did not occur with regard to whether the annual budget was balanced. In other words, rich and poor congregations alike carried either surpluses or deficits from one year to the next. It seems from the open-ended interviews that the decision to carry over a deficit was based on the financial leaders' willingness to take risks and to assume that a financial solution would be found. Clearly, there were congregations with deficit budgets that were in this situation against their will. However, some congregations with a surplus budget had minuscule surpluses that reflected their financial insecurity and their unwillingness to take risks. Conversely, in some cases a deficit budget reflected the enhanced ministry or building initiatives of strong and viable congregations, while, at other times, it covered unexpected periodic shortfalls.

The financial stability of congregations is important for their social services involvement, because congregations with financial difficulties are more likely to face internal conflicts that stifle the congregation. Dudley and Roozen (2001) found a strong and clear association between congregational financial health and reported level of conflict. When their efforts are focused on the budget and on fund-raising, members have less energy to allocate to helping others who are needy.

Individual giving: In the only study of its kind, Dean R. Hoge and his colleagues found that, on average, congregations receive 90 percent of their income from individuals (Hoge, Zech, McNamara, & Donahue, 1996). Their five key findings were: (1) there is no consistent relationship between congregational size and donations; (2) use of pledges increases donations; (3) family income affects giving to congregations; (4) active members give more than nonactive members; and (5) on average, Catholics contribute less than Protestants.

Pressley and Collier (1999) found that the median annual income of 141 historic black churches was $200,000. About two thirds of this amount —$127,000, or 63.5 percent—came from offerings, tithes, and pledges. Individual giving was, by far, the churches' largest source of income. Community development projects (9.9 percent) was a distant second. Investments, special fund-raising activities, and rental fees together accounted for an additional 7.5 percent. Pressley and Collier also studied the annual spending of these churches. Although their sample was biased toward more affluent and well-established black churches, their findings are of relevance, since this topic has rarely been studied. Of a total median expense of $181,500, only $2,881 was devoted to local and global mission.

Hodgkinson and Weitzman (1993) found that 39 percent of congregational income came from annual pledges (promises by individuals or families to give a specific dollar amount weekly), 59 percent came from collections or offerings (money that is given with no prior commitment, often in plate collections or envelopes), and 2 percent came from dues. The last practice is most commonly used in Jewish synagogues, where monetary dealings are prohibited on Saturday, the traditional day of worship. These authors also found that congregational size hardly matters when it comes to sources of income; most congregations, regardless of size, rely on individual giving in the form of pledges and offerings.

Congregations in our study reported two key sources of income: pledges, possibly tithes, and other offerings. The former method of giving is more reliable: the leadership knows how much has been pledged and therefore can determine annual income more accurately. The latter method is both more common and less reliable, since collection totals may fluctuate from week to week. Both methods rely on the members' willingness to underwrite the cost of congregational operations. In our study, pledges and offerings accounted for 47.3 percent and 31 percent, respectively, of congregational income. Only two congregations (less than 1 percent of our sample) reported no income from pledges or offerings.

Other sources of income: Other sources of support reported by congregations in our study were as follows: rental fees (4.5 percent); fund-raising activities such as car washes, bazaars, bake sales, bingo games, sale of holiday-related items, bus trips, and church suppers (3.4 percent); unrestricted gifts and bequests (3.3 percent); and foundation support (1 percent). Denominational support, on average, accounted for 3.3 percent of income. This percentage was often higher in congregations whose annual budget was less than $50,000, or in changing neighborhoods where denominational support was essential for the congregation to survive. The remaining portion of congregational income (1.9 percent) came from miscellaneous sources such as fees for service, advertisements, royalties, and tuition. Public-sector support (0.3 percent) had little significance as a source of income. Only thirteen (5.2 percent) congregations reported receiving public sector funds, all of which were for service provision.

Hoge and Mead (1999), who studied 257 Presbyterian congregations, found that 89 percent used endowment funds for their operating budget. Furthermore, 81 percent of these congregations reported gifts of more than $10,000 during the past three years. This contrasts sharply with the congregations in our study, whose endowments, if any, were small and which rarely, if ever, received such generous gifts.

External grant support: A third of the congregations (32.3 percent) reported applying for any type of external grant support, including grants from government, foundations, private businesses or corporations, and denominations, during the five-year period prior to the interview. Of the thirty-three congregations (13.1 percent) that reported applying for a government grant in the previous five years, twenty-two (8.7 percent) had received grants. Awards ranged from $750 for a summer camp to $3.5 million for construction of senior adult apartments. Fifty-nine congregations (23.5 percent) reported applying for foundation grants. Of these, eleven had applied to three or more foundations, while thirteen had applied to two. The overwhelming majority of these grant applications were funded, mostly for sums under $5,000. A few (nine congregations, 3.6 percent) received grant support that ranged between $50,000 and $100,000. These awards were usually earmarked for health services or services for the homeless.

Only twenty congregations (8.8 percent) applied for grants from private corporations. Although two congregations received major corporate gifts ($100,000 and $50,000) for their capital campaigns, the rest received small corporate gifts of less than $5,000 for their social programs.

Finally, forty congregations (15.9 percent) received support from their denomination. These grants, which ranged from $500 to $500,000, were used for three purposes: salary support for clergy, building maintenance, and/or support for social services.

The picture that emerges from these findings is that one-third of the congregations applied for external grants, but grants from public sources and foundations were used almost exclusively for the delivery of services for the community and were not used to maintain the congregation or its property. Grants from private corporations and denominational headquarters were used to maintain the congregations, but the grants were often modest in size and did not challenge the assumption that members will shoulder the burden of financing the congregation.

Summary

The congregations in our sample are characteristic of congregations in the United States in most respects. The mean for active attenders (people attending at least once a month) was 579 adults and children. This number may be higher than the national average, although there are no reliable national statistics that can be used for comparison. We found that 25.3 percent of the congregations had fewer than 100 members; 50.2 percent of the congregations had 501 to 1,000 members; and 24.5 percent had more than 1,000 members. Percentages reported by the Independent Sector for these categories were 20.2 percent, 58.1 percent, and 21.8 percent, respectively. Given that our definition of membership differed from that of the Independent Sector (Hodgkinson & Weitzman, 1993) and that of Dudley and Roozen (2001), the parallels between the findings are striking.

We found that 57.2 percent of the congregations in the study were established before 1940; 17.6 percent were established between 1941 and 1960; and 25.2 percent after 1961. The Independent Sector study, which used different categories, found that 47.9 percent of congregations were established before 1930 and 41.4 percent after 1950. Again, there are close parallels between the findings, although our sample is slightly biased toward older congregations. In fact, our sample is closer to that of Dudley and Roozen, which is the largest of its kind.

Our analysis of the workforce indicated that 30 percent of congregations have more than one full-time clergy, 80 percent have at least one clergy, and twenty have no full-time clergy. On average, congregations in our study had 5.2 full-time employees and 3.8 part-time employees. This finding, which includes clergy, is biased by the larger and more affluent congregations, which had many more staff members than the smaller and poorer congregations. We also found that most congregations use volunteers recruited from the membership. On average, volunteers fill the equivalent of 3.2 full-time staff positions.

As expected, congregations attract people from all walks of life: young and old, men and women, rich and poor, married and single. Two findings were of special interest. First, approximately two-thirds of the members live more than ten blocks away from their congregations (and most likely drive to their place of worship). Thus, the congregation model is predominant when compared with the parish model. Second, most congregations are composed of members of one dominant ethnic group. In our study, we found that 43 percent of congregations had only white members. The Independent Sector study found that 49 percent of congregations had a white membership of at least 90 percent or more, while 36.5 percent of congregations had only white members. Our numbers are slightly lower because of the fact that our sample included more urban congregations, which, in turn, reflect urban ethnic diversity. Congregations are also segregated by education level and by political views. We found many ethnically diverse congregations in which members shared a political orientation and worldview. In fact, many ethnically diverse congregations are composed of members who wish to sustain multiethnic relationships and who see this as a priority for themselves. These people sought out ethnically integrated congregations.

Although most clergy in our study were male, the lay leadership showed a more balanced gender distribution. It is no surprise that religious groups based on theologies drafted thousands years ago are slow to change and embrace greater gender equality, though the trend is evident, especially among lay leaders. However, women were still in the minority as clergy and lay leaders, even though they made up the majority of active members. Only one-third of congregational lay leaders were perceived as community leaders who could link their congregations with resources in the community or beyond. Congregations, on the whole, tended to be more conservative politically and theologically than the general population. On average, congregations held 3.7 worship services weekly (2.1 weekend services and 1.6 weekday services). This finding excludes groups such as orthodox Jews and Muslims, who hold daily prayer services.

We found that 29.7 percent of congregations had annual operating budgets of less than $100,000; 28.5 percent, budgets between $100,000 and $200,000; 25.1 percent, budgets between $200,001 and $500,000; and 16.7 percent, budgets of more than $1 million. Balanced budgets were reported by 42.6 percent of the congregations, budget surpluses by 29.1 percent, and budget deficits by 28.3 percent. Only 17.1 percent of congregations reported themselves as financially strong, compared with 52 percent that said they were financially sound and 30.9 percent that said they were struggling.

Finally, money came to congregations mostly from pledges (e.g., planned giving, dues, membership) and offerings (unplanned giving, usually through collection plates). Many other methods of raising funds were reported, but none were as common as these two key methods. Congregations rely heavily on members' support. Few congregations apply to external sources of funding, be it public, private, or endowments. Congregations have emerged as local institutions that attend to their property and financial obligations, as well as sustain a viable community of people. They are visible in every neighborhood or community and attract members into a prosocial environment, while not depending on outside sources for survival.

4

Congregational Involvement I
Areas of Involvement

Preach the gospel all the time, use words if necessary
—St. Francis of Assisi

Gary Trudeau's comic strip *Doonesbury*, known for its ironic commentary on current events, is a telling indicator of how congregational involvement in local communities has become part of our civic culture. A recent *Doonesbury* cartoon depicted a group of congregants planning social and community activities. When one congregant asks about Sunday worship, he is told that it has to be canceled to accommodate all the other social activities. Trudeau exaggerates his point to make us laugh but also to make us think. The point is that many congregational buildings are busy seven days a week, serving the community in numerous ways, from Alcoholic Anonymous meetings to day care centers. New meetings and programs are often scheduled at the expense of other programs or squeezed into the congregation's already busy calendar.

Doonesbury highlights what the *Christian Science Monitor* has called "an emerging brand of Christianity." One *Monitor* article, for example, reported on the growing number of people who are turning to the Bible and to congregational-based programs for help in losing weight. They are shedding pounds by praying to God and not relying on food when they feel a need for comfort. But, as McLaughlin (1998, p. 1) writes, organized religion offers much more: "Weight loss isn't the only everyday issue being tackled by an emerging brand of Christianity. There is a Christian approach to parenting, to public relations, and to doing business. There are Christian career counselors, Christian talent agents, and Christian ministries that cater to college and pro athletes." By the same token, not only Christians recognize that their places of worship ought to be more holistic; all faith communities are acting in similar fashion.

Members of all religious congregations, regardless of their specific faith traditions, set out to influence their communities by performing activities that add to the quality of life in the community. These activities can be subsumed under the term *social ministry*, although this term has a Christian connotation. In this chapter, we use this term interchangeably with *social programs* to denote congregations' involvement in caring for the needs of others regardless of their faith tradition. Unlike *congregations*, which is a faith-neutral term, there is no such across-the-board term to denote the social provisions of communities of faith. In this chapter, we provide an account of the social ministry programs of 251 local religious congregations in our study. We demonstrate that, in addition to their primary religious function, many congregations serve as surrogate community centers and social service agencies and that people in need turn to congregations in the expectation of services that are also available in community centers and social service organizations.

What We Studied

The findings presented in this chapter are based on results from our second questionnaire. The instrument listed about 200 areas of social and community involvement classified under thirteen service areas (see Appendix). We excluded all programs that had religion as their primary purpose, such as bible classes, worship services, wakes, and weddings. We were concerned that this comprehensive list might prove intimidating to respondents. We therefore reassured respondents at the outset that no one congregation provides most of these programs and that most congregations tend to focus their programs within one or a few of the many listed service areas.

The use of a preselected list of social programs proved helpful on two counts. First, we did not need to rely solely on the interviewees' ability to recall all the services their congregation provides. We simply showed them the list and asked whether their congregation did or did not provide each service. Second, we were able to identify many areas of social involvement that interviewees might not otherwise have considered to be social programs.

Since our findings represent *the number of service areas and the type of involvement in these areas*, as opposed to the number of programs and the type of involvement in the program, the results may appear inflated. In essence, one social program/ministry may include several service areas.

Homeless shelters can provide an example of how we differentiated be-tween service areas and programs. A few congregations reported that they provided homeless shelters. In some cases, however, a congregation might also provide the homeless with a soup kitchen, clothing closets, or voca-tional counseling. While the congregation may report this as one social program/ministry, we recorded this program as providing services in four separate social areas. Similarly, a congregation with a program of family support groups may offer both marriage counseling and family counsel-ing through the same program; we recorded this one program as two areas of service involvement. In other words, the results reported in this chap-ter reflect areas of service involvement and not specific social programs.

We asked respondents to identify those services that had been offered in the past twelve months and to omit any that were no longer available. We used a twelve-month time frame to ensure that seasonal programs such as summer camps and heating assistance programs would be included.

If an interviewee responded that the congregation had provided service in a particular area during the past year, we then asked him or her to iden-tify the type of involvement—its formality, the sponsorship, and the loca-tion of service, according to the following categories:

1. *Informal services.* This type of involvement refers to service areas that are addressed by clergy or other members as the need arises. For example, a congregation may not have a domestic violence program, but, should a member need assistance, the clergy or a member with the appropriate skills may intervene or refer the member to a professional agency. Involvement of this kind included assisting others in moving, babysitting, and information sharing. Harris (1998) has called this type of service "informal care." Al-though this type of service is seldom listed in congregational literature, it is clearly available to congregational members and, at times, to people in the community. This type of service may also be considered pastoral care be-cause it includes such activities as marital counseling, visiting the sick, and crisis intervention counseling (Ewalt & McMann, 1962).

2. *On-site congregational programs.* This refers to programs that are sponsored by the congregation and operated in-house. The congregation has ownership of the program and provides the service on site in its own facilities. Examples include latchkey programs, food pantries, and clothing closets.

3. *Off-site congregational programs.* This refers to programs that are run by the congregation but do not use congregational facilities. For example, a congregation in Staten Island, New York, travels fifteen miles each week

to feed homeless people at another church in Manhattan. Similarly, in Oakland, California, a congregation adopted a nearby nursing home, and members of the congregation visit the elderly residents and help them as needed.

4. *On-site noncongregational programs.* This refers to programs sponsored by other organizations but held on congregational property. The congregation provides the space but has little or no control of the program. At times, these programs may be run by congregants, but in their capacity outside the congregation. Examples include Alcoholics Anonymous and other twelve-step groups; some day care centers, especially Head Start programs; and Boy Scout/Girl Scout troops.

5. *Support for non-congregational programs.* This refers to congregational support for other programs, whether local, national, or international. Examples include support for local coalitions, community development corporations, and Habitat for Humanity, as well as support for denominational social ministries and international relief efforts.

Our findings primarily correspond to categories 2 through 5, that is, formal social and community involvement. However, the informal programs offered by congregations are an important part of the hidden safety net of our society. Consequently, we devote a special section in this chapter to the nature and importance of informal care offered by American congregations.

We first discuss those congregations that are not involved in any social service area. We then examine trends suggested by the data and identify formal and informal social services offered by congregations in our sample cities. Next, we show how our findings present a distinct profile of the social and community involvement of congregations in the United States. We conclude by discussing geographical variations.

How Many Congregations Get Involved?

The first step in our analysis was to determine how many of the 251 congregations in our sample had no involvement in any formal service. We defined those services as those found in categories 2–5. Only four congregations (1.6 percent) reported no involvement in any of the thirteen listed service areas. Almost all of the congregations provided at least one service, either through their own program or in collaboration with another congregation or organization. The range of involvement was between none and 175 service areas of involvement. The mean number of areas of involvement was thirty-nine, with a standard deviation of 26.4.

As previously discussed, a program/ministry may span several service areas. For example, a transitional housing facility for women might include a meal program, child care services, parenting classes, case management services, health services, and vocational training. Such a comprehensive program is costly. Thus, the number of service areas per congregation is not an accurate indicator of the number of formal social programs, but it is an important measure of the congregation's commitment to social and community involvement. We use this measure in chapter 6 to determine what type of congregation is more likely to be more active in social and community service provision.

What Programs Do Congregations Offer Most Frequently?

The area in which at least one-third of the congregations were actively providing service include:

Program for children and youth
1. Recreational and educational programs for children and youth
2. Summer day camps for children and youth
3. Scholarships for students

Programs for the elderly and disabled
1. Recreational programs for the elderly
2. Visitation—"buddy" programs for sick and homebound people
3. Hospital visitation

Programs for homeless and poor people
1. Clothing closets
2. Food pantries
3. International relief—both in-kind and monetary

Community-oriented programs
1. Music performances
2. Supporting neighborhood associations
3. Supporting and participating in interfaith coalitions
4. Holiday (nonreligious) celebrations
5. Community bazaars and fairs
6. Athletic activities

These programs, which focus primarily on the poor, children, and the elderly, as well as the community at large, are those most often provided by congregations in the United States. Congregations also provide many other services, some of which address unique and specific needs. Examples range from medical, law, and dental clinics to building projects, credit unions, and midnight basketball. While these programs are important to their communities, they constitute only a small percentage of the services provided by congregations.

Our findings on congregational involvement are similar to those of recent studies (Cnaan 1997; Grettenberger & Hovmand, 1997; Jackson, Schweitzer, Cato, & Blake, 1997; and Printz, 1998; Hodgkinson et al. 1993). One study, of about 1,000 congregations in California, found that each and every one of them was engaged in at least one form of social service provision (Silverman, 2000). One study, however, did not support our findings. Chaves (1999) found that only 57 percent of the congregations in his study were involved in social service, whereas we found that 93.2 percent of the 251 congregations in our study were involved in at least one social or community service. In his study, Chaves (1999) used the 1998 General Social Survey of the National Opinion Research Center in Chicago, with approximately 4,000 interviewees, to identify their religious leaders. In a follow-up study, Chaves called these religious leaders. Of the 1,236 religious leaders identified, he interviewed approximately 80 percent, a remarkable response rate. Chaves's study is clearly more representative of smaller unlisted congregations than any other study to date. He defined *social program* narrowly, however, and did not elicit information about informal, but often meaningful, benevolent activities. The congregations in Chaves's study were more involved in food services (31 percent), housing (15 percent), and services to homeless people (7 percent). He also found that fewer than 5 percent of congregations were involved in services related to health, substance abuse, domestic violence, tutoring/mentoring, or work issues. Our findings, presented in this chapter, show higher percentages in each category. We believe that methodology accounts for the difference in findings between Chaves's study and our own. That we found greater involvement in service among congregations is a result of the fact that we conducted lengthy face-to-face interviews. The interviews, together with the study instruments, provided a comprehensive context that enabled interviewees to relate their social ministries/pastoral care to the activities that we described as social and community services. For example, some congregations that provide day care centers, neighborhood cleanups, or visitation to the sick were quick to dismiss these activities as a service to the members or "just something that they do." By spending extra time to learn about the background and history of the congregation and providing the inventory list, we were able to identify the wide spectrum of service areas in which clergy, lay leaders, and congregants were involved.

Informal Care

The congregation is often the only or most visible social institution in the community. Members and nonmembers alike expect the clergy and the congregations to be able to meet their needs, even the most idiosyncratic ones. Most clergy reported that people approach them with needs that the congregation is not equipped to meet. Often an ad hoc solution or counseling is offered, along with a referral to a professional provider. The areas in which congregations offer informal help most commonly are counseling, one-time financial assistance, and referrals. However, clergy in this study told us about helping people who are stranded on a highway, helping to fill out college applications, and feeding the livestock when one farming family went on vacation.

Counseling: Clergy are viewed as leaders who are able to provide wisdom and guidance for their members in religious, moral, and family issues. In addition, many clergy have been trained in the seminary to serve as counselors. Since it is common for congregational members to seek advice from their religious leaders, we expected to find that many clergy provided informal or pastoral care to congregation or community members on an as-needed basis. Thirty-nine percent of Americans who have a serious problem solicit help from a member of the clergy, more than the percentage who seek help from human and health services professionals (Veroff, Douvan, & Kulka, 1981). For example, Gelles and Straus (1989) found that victims of domestic violence often tend to approach a clergy for help when no one else is willing to help. However, some of these victims noted that the clergy's intervention also made things worse at home, which indicates that many clergy have little training in handling domestic abuse.

Most clergy in our study reported few formal counseling programs but extensive informal counseling. For example, only thirty-eight congregations (15.1 percent) reported formal couple counseling programs. In contrast, an additional 194 clergy (77.3 percent) reported that they had provided couple counseling on an as-needed basis during the previous year. For the same period, 196 clergy (78.1 percent) reported informal family counseling, whereas only forty-three congregations (17.1 percent) reported formal family counseling programs. Despite the fact that fewer than 25 percent of congregations in any city reported formal family counseling programs, the overwhelming majority of clergy reported they were involved in informal family counseling.

While clergy are considered authorities on family issues, they are seldom viewed as advisers on secular issues per se. Few clergy reported that people asked their advice on legal or vocational issues. This corresponded with other findings. Wuthnow (1997), for example, found that only 13 percent of his sample would talk with their clergy about major ethical dilemmas related to their workplace, whereas 56 percent would discuss their concerns with their supervisor; 36 percent would talk with coworkers; and 20 percent would prefer to read something about the problem. In other words, clergy are perceived as authorities in religious, marital, and familial issues, but their authority is often limited to those domains. However, they are often asked to counsel in areas in which their training is limited, such as serious mental health problems, substance abuse, domestic violence, developmental disabilities, and career changes.

Most clergy are not trained to counsel in these areas. Nevertheless, their congregants expect them to have knowledge that goes beyond seminary training (Cnaan, Yancey, Rodgers, & Trulear, 2002). However, various studies indicate that clergy are not well trained in identifying serious mental health problems, and only a few of them tend to refer people in need to professional mental health settings (Mollica, Streets, Boscarino, & Redlich, 1986). Often they use their experience, compassion, and intuition when dealing with mental health issues (Taylor, Ellison, Chatters, Levin, & Lincoln, 2000). Many clergy told us that when they confront an area that requires special expertise they tend to refer the requesting congregants to specialized services run by the denomination, the government, or even private, for-profit organizations. In fact, many clergy we met had an informal directory of potential referrals that they used when asked to help in areas in which they felt inexperienced or uncomfortable. In this respect, clergy serve as mediators between congregants and the formal network of services delivery.

Financial assistance: Clergy and, in some cases, staff members are often empowered by the congregation to financially assist poor and homeless people. A number of our interviewees reported that when those in need asked for help, the clergy or staff member would conduct an interview and provide the necessary support, whether it be money, a food voucher, rent, or some other basic need. Only 29.8 percent of the congregations reported formal cash-assistance programs, but close to 75 percent reported some mechanism for assisting the poor. Ninety-eight (39 percent) congregations assist the poor financially on an informal basis or when asked to help. Of the seventy-five congregations with formal programs, forty congregations (15.9 percent) offer informal scholarships for adults. Twenty-seven congregations (10.8 percent) provide informal scholarship support for children and youth. It is important to note that these funds, distributed on an as-needed basis, are one of the most critical elements in our social safety net. It is to local congregations that those in acute need most often turn. These clients include those who have yet to seek formal public assistance, those who have been rejected by public agencies, and those who need to supplement their welfare assistance.

Congregations generally consider these informal and formal financial assistance programs to be benevolent activities, rather than distinct social ministries or programs. When we inquired, we were often told that such informal financial support is only the "discretionary fund" of the clergy. Our study does not explain who is most likely to turn to religious congregations in times of need or the extent that such help alleviates need in a systematic manner. What is evident is that the nation's congregations are serving in some cases as the first line of the last frontier of social care for those desperate for something to eat, a safe place to sleep, or care for their children.

Many congregations support members in time of loss by providing meals in the congregational building. For example, one Catholic church in Indianapolis reported that whenever there is a funeral, congregants prepare a meal and bring it to the church, where the family and friends of the deceased come after the funeral. The interviewee wasn't sure when the dinners began; she suspects that they date back to the founding of the church in 1891. In this church, which is quite large (about 1,000 members), approximately sixteen people help prepare the dinners, which take place, on average, once a month. Between twenty-five and fifty people attend each such dinner. The dinners take place in the church hall, a meeting room adjacent to the kitchen. The dinners last ninety minutes; two clergy members attend. All the food is prepared at the congregants' homes, and they donate nearly all of it. Occasionally the church donates some meat. This church was not the only one to hold such meals at times of loss. When people are facing the greatest pain, their fellow congregants, even those who do not know them well, come together to assist and support.

Referrals: Referrals are another important form of informal service provided by congregations. Many interviewees in our study reported that people often come to them with problems that they cannot address. Some congregations are so familiar with such requests that they have developed a list of professional contacts to meet a wide range of needs. This informal role makes the clergy and congregations in the United States brokers between the service system and the local residents. In some cases, clergy and congregants invite public officials and professionals to the congregation to address issues, solve problems, or establish collaborations. In one case, a pastor of a congregation in a poor Philadelphia neighborhood invited the sheriff to come and pray with the congregation. As the result of the invitation, the sheriff and his staff opened an office in the church building for one afternoon. In the course of that afternoon, four house titles were cleared (houses that passed as inheritance but were not declared as such due to unpaid property taxes), and three city-owned houses in need of renovation were sold for one dollar each to three single mothers from the congregation with a congregational commitment to assist these mothers in renovating the houses within a year. This is indicative of the power and importance of many informal linkages that congregations provide to their community, even if they do not represent a distinct program.

> And in every community, congregations of every shape and color provide spaces of sociability, laboratories for civic participation, places of moral guidance and nurture, and points of contact with transcendent powers that can work transformative miracles small and large. (Ammerman, 1997, p. 3)

When one considers the informal care and small acts of service, the spectrum of help provided by congregations may be even larger than the one we describe in this book. For example, Bartkowski and Regis (1999) found many instances in which clergy checked "no" in all the categories in their study. When they visited these clergy, however, they found that the clergy were assisting many people, not as part of an organized program but on an as-needed basis.

The full range of flexible, ad hoc, and as-needed assistance provided by congregations is not documented in our study. Our findings, therefore, underrepresent the true extent of their contribution to society. However, by providing a comprehensive list of social services, with a range of responses for social and community involvement, including informal activities, our study comes closer than previous studies to understanding the scope of social service provided by congregations.

Health Care

Congregations are heavily involved in health care services, especially among the poor. Seventy congregations (27.9 percent) reported formal health screening programs, and a similar number reported health education programs. Sixty-three congregations (25.1 percent) reported programs for HIV/AIDS. These ranged from education to active support, including food service and counseling. In addition, three out of every ten congregations participated in a blood drive in the year prior to our visit. More than half of the congregations reported formal programs for the visitation of the sick, whether members of the congregation or members of the community. A few well-established congregations provided a health or dental clinic. These congregations usually have volunteer professionals who offer their services on the congregation's property once or twice a week free of charge. In other cases, the congregation joins a local coalition that supports a free medical or dental clinic, and the congregation contributes space, volunteer professionals, and funds to pay for the clinic's operation. In many cities, these are the major sources of health care for the very poor and for uninsured families.

For many people in the community, the visitation services are their primary contact with the outside world. Many congregations we studied have an organized visitation program to help shut-ins emotionally, practically, and spiritually. A typical program has volunteer congregants and/or clergy visit sick people, some of whom may be noncongregants. The visits usually take place once a week, on a designated day, at the homes of the sick, at hospitals, and at nursing homes. The program costs little or nothing to run but takes time from paid clergy and volunteers. The focus of these visits is both religious and social. Communion or other religious services are brought to the shut-ins, as well as news from the congregation and community. Visitors also bring items the shut-ins want or need, such as food baskets, clothing, or books. The importance of these visits goes beyond the social and religious contributions. Supported sick people tend to recover faster, and those shut in tend to stay longer in the community rather than be transferred to a nursing home.

One example of a congregational focus on health issues involves the New Covenant Church of Philadelphia. The church developed a program called Health Team Ministry. The team delivers basic medical assistance, educates the congregation about health and safety issues, and promotes wellness. Its Summer 1997 newsletter, for example, featured brief articles, written in layperson's terms, concerning the use of over-the-counter medications, domestic violence, quitting smoking, and the connection between religion and health care. The team's newsletter is the major, if not the only, source of health education for many members of the congregation. Most important, it comes from trusted sources; the editors of the quarterly newsletter are two medical doctors who are also members of the congregation.

New Covenant Church became involved in this ministry because many congregants work in the health profession and were willing to use their skills and knowledge to assist members and others in the community. The health care team provides services that complement formal health services, as well as services not available from formal health care providers. The team is trusted and trained to handle issues as sensitive as domestic abuse. In order to be successful, members use "African American culture" to speak with local residents in their own language. Thus, they have been successful when "the larger society have routinely turned a blind eye to this issue." These volunteer professionals, for example, write newsletter articles that use scientific data to demonstrate the devastating consequences of domestic violence on children and adults alike. Team members also assist in linking the church volunteer-based services with three professional organizations that help victims of domestic abuse.

Another example is a Methodist church in Indianapolis. In 1993, the church contracted with the Indiana University School of Nursing to open a wellness center on the congregational site. The program helps people of all ages with both acute and chronic illnesses. There are three nurse practitioners, an outreach worker, a secretary, and a director. The center also has an agreement with a general practitioner and a pediatrician, who help with some cases. There are eight people from outside the church who work at the center. By 1996, 530 people had been helped, only twenty-six of them were members of the church. The center has an advisory committee, which is required to be at least one-third church members and one-third community members, with the remainder of board made up of health professionals. The center operates two days a week, for eight and a half hours on Tuesdays and for seven hours on Fridays. It is housed in four congregational rooms: two offices and two examination rooms. The annual cost of running the center is $82,000. The money is provided by various sources, including the Robert Wood Johnson Foundation, the Indianapolis Foundation, the Health Foundation, and the Indiana State Department of Health. The center asks a fee of $2 to $5 for each visit, but no one is turned away if he or she cannot afford it.

Social Change Efforts

Congregations are, as a rule, highly involved in service delivery that helps people solve personal problems and meet material needs. They are less involved in efforts to bring about social and political change. As we previously noted, only 22.7 percent of our interviewees characterized their congregations as politically liberal. Even among these congregations, involvement in social change efforts results more from theological orientation than from political orientation. For example, many clergy alluded to a holistic ministry theology that called upon them to help people in every aspect of their daily lives. More on this is discussed in chapter 12. What is important to note here is that congregations tend to focus more on helping and even changing the person in need than on changing the environment in which the person lives.

Only a few clergy mentioned a theology of social justice that called upon them to change the power structure or economic distribution in society. For example, participation in boycotts or protests was reported by fewer than 10 percent of the congregations. However, four of fifteen congregations (26.6 percent) in New York reported engaging in such activities. However, this finding seems to overrepresent the real involvement of congregations, since our New York sample is the least representative of any in the cities we studied. Similarly, Chicago, New York, and San Francisco were the only cities in our sample in which at least 25 percent of the congregations were involved in gay and lesbian issues. The following advocacy issues were not addressed by congregations at the 25 percent level in any of the cities studied: mental retardation, mental illnesses, school choice, and firearm and gun control.

Social change issues addressed by congregations in our study include voter registration (eighty-two congregations, 32.7 percent) and racism (eighty congregations, 31.9 percent). With the exception of interfaith relations, most congregations support the work of other organizations in these areas rather than initiate and sponsor their own programs. On the basis of a survey of 600 African American ministers, Robert Franklin (1997) noted that "in response to questions of political attitudes, 54.4 percent believed that preachers should run for political office; 83.1 percent believed it is appropriate during worship to urge people to register to vote" (p. 81). However, our interviewees reflected a lower level of involvement in efforts to bring about political and social change

An example of how congregations link with a national effort to effect social change is the campaign to support the United Nation's global-warming treaty, negotiated in Kyoto, Japan, in December 1997. In 1998, the National Council of Churches (NCC) initiated a national campaign to engage Christian congregations to write letters in support of ratification of the treaty by the U.S. Senate. The NCC launched its campaign in partnership with the U.S. Catholic Conference and the Evangelical Environmental Network. The campaign attempted to enlist the support of 100 million Americans in 67,000 congregations. Many congregations responded by printing appeals in church bulletins and urging congregants to write and call their senators in support of the Kyoto treaty. Nevertheless, it was not a hot topic in many congregations, and the initiative failed to stir enough public opinion to bring about the desired ratification.

In our study, only thirty-eight congregations (15.1 percent) reported formal environmental programs. Many more clergy, however, reported that, in their weekly sermons, they often discussed environmental issues and the need to protect the environment for future generations. Some congregations are active in a number of efforts to save the environment, ranging from supporting the Kyoto agreement and lobbying against nuclear testing to opposing toxic dumping in their regions.

Collaboration for Service Delivery

Some social service programs are carried out by congregations in collaboration with other congregations, their denominations, or other organizations. These are usually costly programs (e.g., homeless shelters) that require considerable volunteer and professional support. Only eighteen congregations (7.2 percent) have their own homeless shelters, that is, run programs on site. Fourteen congregations (5.5 percent) have shelters for men, and seven congregations (2.7 percent) have shelters for women. However, six congregations have shelters for both men and women on site, and thus the total is not twenty-one but eighteen. A homeless shelter is very expensive and requires a large space, and there are numerous requirements for zoning and certification. Although few congregations have their own shelters, at least 25 percent of congregations provide support for shelters run by others. For example, of the seventy-one congregations (28.3 percent) involved with providing a homeless shelter for women, sixty-four are collaborating with another provider to implement the program. That 7 percent of congregations are operating an on-site homeless shelter and that more than a quarter of congregations assist in running homeless shelters is impressive.

A similar phenomenon is evident with soup kitchen programs. Again, these are difficult programs to deliver, especially in comparison with food pantry programs that serve the same function. Soup kitchens require cooking, serving, and cleaning within in a short period of time, whereas food pantries can be organized ahead of time and require minimal personnel to distribute food to eligible people. Thus, while two-fifths of congregations (39.4 percent) have their own food pantries, only one-sixth (13.9 percent) have their own soup kitchens. However, 11.6 percent of congregations support soup kitchens, and an equal number of congregations reported they supported soup kitchens run by someone else.

What the examples of homeless shelters and soup kitchens teach us is that even when congregations cannot provide a costly and complex program on their own, they may collaborate with or support others in the delivery of such a program. The power of congregational collaboration to assist other providers or to enrich the community network of support is a topic we have only started to unravel and that requires further research.

Use of Space

One of a congregation's greatest assets is its property. Many American congregations own a large building where congregants gather for weekend worship services. Were it not for social programs, these buildings would be unoccupied and unused during the rest of the week. However, these large facilities, centrally located in urban neighborhoods, equipped with classrooms, bathrooms, kitchens, dining halls, auditoriums, or gymnasiums, make a congregation a hub for social and community activities, even if those activities are not organized by the congregation. We found that the rooms most frequently used for social and community programs were the parish or fellowship halls, classrooms, basements, and sanctuaries.

Programs most often reported as using congregational space were scouting programs, twelve-step programs, and day care centers. In our study, we found that seventy-nine congregations (31.5 percent) housed a scout troop, while only thirty-nine congregations (15.5 percent) sponsored a scout troop. Thus, scouting programs used congregational space, regardless of whether the program was run under congregational auspices or was independent of the congregation. Many congregations reported that they had a designated scout room that was kept locked and not used for other purposes. Similarly, seventy-six congregations (30.3 percent) housed a day care center in their building; two-thirds of these day care centers were sponsored by the congregation. In addition, forty-four congregations (17.5 percent) housed a nursery school. One can only wonder what working parents would do were these congregations to close their doors and disappear from the neighborhood. Reliable day care in our society is already scarce and would be even more so were it not for congregations. A third of all day care in the United States is housed in congregational properties. This makes the religious community the largest provider/host of day care in the country and potentially a key participant in the campaign of "welfare to work" (Lindner, Mattis, & Rogers, 1983; Trost, 1988).

Twelve-step programs are often housed in congregational property. These programs include Alcoholics Anonymous (AA), Narcotics Anonymous (NA), Sex and Love Addiction Anonymous (SLAA), Overeaters Anonymous (OA), ALANON, and ALATEEN. In our study, sixty-nine congregations (27.4 percent) housed at least one twelve-step program. Two congregations also housed Gambling Anonymous programs based on the twelve-step model. Alcoholics Anonymous was the program most often reported as using congregational space. Seventy-one congregations (28.3 percent) housed AA programs. Only thirteen congregations directly (5.2 percent) sponsored AA programs. Forty-eight congregations (19.1 percent) housed NA programs, while only twelve congregations (4.8 percent) directly sponsored an NA program. Eighteen congregations (7.2 percent) housed OA programs, while only three congregations (1.1 percent) directly sponsored OA programs.

People who needed a twelve-step program are seldom treated sympathetically by our society, which tends to view them as deviant, if not dangerous. The mere fact that they are welcomed in a religious space and that they can find a safe haven is testimony to the contribution of local religious congregations throughout the United States. They know that a call to a local congregation or clergy will provide them with information about where and when a group meets. The association between twelve-step programs and congregations has become so well known that it is not unusual to find it depicted in movies, novels, and even songs.

Congregations provide space for a host of other community-related programs. For example, sixty-three congregations in our study (25.1 percent) provided space for regularly scheduled police and community meetings, whereas sixty congregations (24 percent) did so on an as-needed basis. Given the issues that often arise between police and community regarding public safety, crime, and police brutality, the local religious congregation becomes the de facto headquarters for collaborative efforts to improve the quality of life in the neighborhood. Similarly, 114 congregations (45.4 percent) provided meeting space for local neighborhood groups and associations. Twenty-four congregations (9.5 percent) had their own community theater; an equal number provided practice and performance space to nonmembers. The use of congregational space by aspiring actors and other artists was most significant in New York City, where space is most expensive. Although no congregation in New York had its own community theater, six congregations (40 percent) provided space, often at no charge, to community theater groups. One congregation whose building was destroyed by arson and was unable to be rebuilt chose to use its space for a community garden. This congregation currently meets in the community center that was originally created by the congregation and that is now a separate entity. This was a unique use of space among those we encountered.

Joint Use of Congregational Space and People

The use of space by outside groups and individuals is only one aspect of congregational involvement. Many congregations also give themselves when they deem an initiative worthy of their support. One such example is a blood drive. Seventy-seven congregations (30.7 percent) reported participating in blood drives. In these instances, members of the congregation, friends, and neighbors volunteered to give blood to an external organization while using the congregational space, usually on the weekend following worship services. This is an example of joint use of space and people: the building was used as a station for the bloodmobile, and congregants volunteered as a group to support this initiative.

In Philadelphia alone, there are more than 100,000 school-age children who are facing problems that will severely limit their ability to become self-sufficient adults. For example, nearly half the city children are poor, and more than 40 percent of the public school students will not graduate. The local United Way, along with other local organizations, established the Greater Philadelphia Mentoring Partnership to link adult volunteer mentors with pairs of public school students (one adult to a pair of students) who have been deemed "at-risk." The mentors help youth develop socially, academically, and spiritually. The program attempts to recruit from congregations, and participating congregations have mentoring coordinators to oversee mentors. In 2000, seventy-three churches provided mentoring services to 700 youths. The mentors meet the youth in school, in the congregation building, and in the community. They help with homework and serve as positive role models. It is through the congregations that the Greater Philadelphia Mentoring Partnership was able to recruit so many dedicated volunteers. In order to help congregations get involved in such programs, a special manual was developed (United Way of Southeastern Pennsylvania, 1999). Indeed, in our study we found that ninety-eight congregations (30.1 percent) were involved in the provision of tutoring services, directly or in conjunction with other organizations. To encourage congregations in Philadelphia to develop afterschool tutoring programs, the Board of Education reimburses congregations for expenses related to these educational programs.

Congregations were also involved in providing space and volunteers for neighborhood cleanups. In many instances, the congregation provided space (as the headquarters and meeting place) and members as volunteers. Sixty-eight congregations (27.1 percent) were involved in neighborhood cleanups that ranged from park restorations and landfill removals to the removal of graffiti. This type of activity, although it may take place only once or twice a year, demonstrates the congregation's willingness to be an anchor for community efforts to bring together people from all walks of life. Such efforts create social bonds that may later benefit the community and the congregation.

Many congregations reported involvement in the Habitat for Humanity program, which builds affordable housing for low-income families. Seventy-five congregations (29.9 percent) provided volunteers and, in some instances, made space available to the program. In this respect, Chaves (1999) noted that:

> The results reported here suggest that congregations tend to participate in social service activities in a distinctive way. They seem most apt to organize small groups of volunteers to conduct relatively well-defined tasks on a periodic basis—having 15 people spend several weekends renovating a house, having 5 people cook dinner at a homeless shelter one night a week, having 10 young people spend two summer weeks painting a school in a poor community, and so on. It probably is not an accident that the highest levels of congregational involvement are in arenas—such as food and housing—where organizations have emerged that are able to take advantage of congregations' capacity to mobilize volunteers to carry out well-defined and bounded tasks. (p. 9)

In chapter 13, we discuss the group dynamics of congregations and their power over individuals. At this point, it is sufficient to note that a group of people who hold common beliefs and enjoy being together are likely to join forces and commit to a cause with which they empathize. The following anecdote is indicative of how this group effort operates. One of our interviewees told us that a representative of a small charity had approached the congregants and requested their support for a silent auction. After a short discussion, it was agreed that the congregation per se could not make a donation but that members would be asked to participate. Half the members attended the auction, and their purchases helped the charity raise the needed funds. This was not a formal program. Nevertheless, it illustrates how a formal approach to the congregation can give a charitable organization access to a large group of caring individuals who often are delighted to do good deeds collectively.

Regional Differences

As noted earlier we found wide geographical differences in terms of services offered. One explanation for these differences may be that the cities themselves reflect historical and socioeconomic trends that, in turn, influence the type of services provided by local congregations. Philadelphia, founded in 1682 by the Quaker leader William Penn, has its own culture and a way of doing business that differs from the practices in Mobile, Alabama. Mobile was founded in 1702, and there was a very strong Catholic influence in its formative years. Other regional differences range from population size to political orientation. For example, Chicago is a much larger and more cosmopolitan city than Indianapolis. Philadelphia and Houston have approximately comparable populations, but Philadelphia represents a more consolidated urban region and has the most "in-city born" of any region or city in the country. San Francisco is known for its liberalism and for its prosocial attitudes, while New York is known as the financial and performing arts capital of the country. The question then is whether these and other regional differences influence congregational involvement in social service delivery, or whether congregations are similar regardless of regional location. Our findings regarding the small town of Council Grove, Kansas, are discussed separately in chapter 8.

Congregations in Indianapolis, on average, provide fewer services than congregations in other cities. Most of these services are programs for children and youth, the elderly, and family counseling. Indianapolis, however, has one of the most active congregations in our study. The Tabernacle Presbyterian Church provides a legal clinic and a health clinic for local residents and employs a full-time youth worker to work with neighborhood children. However, congregations in Indianapolis are less likely to be involved in adult education, community security, community economic development, arts and culture, community organizing, or social issues. In fact, there is no area of social or community service in which at least 25 percent of the congregations in Indianapolis are currently involved.

Congregations in Mobile resemble those in Indianapolis in that they provide fewer services. However, congregations in Mobile provide more "Mothers' [of preschoolers] Morning Out"; meals on wheels; art classes; film series; and services to youth offenders (along with Chicago), people with physical disabilities, and people with developmental disabilities (along with San Francisco) than do congregations in other cities. Mobile congregations are also involved in programs to increase neighborhood security, such as crime watch, community policing, and cooperative efforts with police.

Chicago congregations, compared with those in other cities, provide the most services in areas related to social change, as well as less traditional areas of service. For example, Chicago is the only city in which 25 percent or more of the congregations had consumer counseling programs, most of which were run by the congregations on their own property. Congregations in Chicago and Houston have the most exercise programs for seniors. Congregations in Chicago and San Francisco are the most involved in communal meals and health care for the elderly. Chicago and Houston also have the highest percentage of congregations that provide nursery schools for young children.

Chicago is the only city in which more than 25 percent of the congregations are involved in parish or regional health programs. A congregational-related regional health program is often costly and difficult to operate, and these programs indicate a comprehensive approach to meeting needs, rather than a policy of referring people to existing private health providers. Given this commitment to health care, it is not surprising that congregations in Chicago rank highest in health screening and health education programs.

Chicago congregations also rank highest in the area of community economic development. These programs include recruitment of new businesses to the neighborhood, job training, job counseling, and job placement. Programs such as these are characteristic of congregations involved in social and economic advocacy on behalf of their communities, as opposed to those congregations whose primary goal is to help individuals in need. Chicago and New York had the most congregations involved in low-income housing, particularly new housing initiatives; collaboration with the Community Development Corporation (along with San Francisco); and advocacy for housing.

New York congregations are relatively less engaged in services to seniors and youth. Although four congregations have recreational programs for seniors, few New York congregations are involved in feeding, transporting, or caring for the health of elderly people. Furthermore, New York is the only large city in which fewer than 25 percent of the congregations operate summer day camps. New York congregations rank highest in support of art and culture. They support the cultural life of the city by holding art exhibits, providing space for community theaters and music performances, and sponsoring book clubs and choral groups. As noted previously, New York is the national center for the performing arts, and many aspiring actors and musicians perform in congregational space before making it to the professional stage. In addition, New York congregations rank highest in social action activities, such as protests, boycotts, and environmental action projects.

Congregations in San Francisco are similar to those in New York in that both are involved in housing projects and both support services for the homeless. San Francisco congregations, however, provide more health care and mental health services for the homeless than do congregations in other cities. San Francisco ranks highest (along with Chicago) in programs for runaway children and in programs for refugees and immigrants.

Philadelphia congregations provide many support services to individuals and families but do not engage in social change issues. Philadelphia is the only city in which at least 25 percent of the congregations provide couple counseling and bereavement counseling (the latter was also reported in Council Grove). Philadelphia ranks highest in latchkey programs (after-school homework preparation programs for children of working parents). While many congregations are involved in prison ministry, a large percentage of the congregations in Philadelphia run their own prison programs. Philadelphia also ranked highest in providing assistance to prisoners' families and educational opportunities for adults. Like those in Mobile, Philadelphia congregations have many programs aimed at increasing neighborhood safety and security.

Houston, the city with the largest Hispanic population in our study, has a high percentage of congregations that provide English as a Second Language (ESL) programs. Many congregations in San Francisco also provide ESL programs, but in collaboration with other groups, whereas most Houston congregations run their own ESL programs on their own property. Houston and Mobile, the two southern cities in our study, have more congregations involved in prochoice or prolife advocacy than do the other cities.

There are significant regional differences among the urban congregations in our study. Some of these differences can be attributed to the local history and ecological conditions; other reasons are not readily discernible. It may be that when one congregation in a city develops a unique social program, other congregations in the same city are likely to learn about it and replicate the program. This may explain the popularity of latchkey programs in Philadelphia and "Mothers' Morning Out" in Mobile. Local culture is influenced both by specific local needs and by the success of a particular congregation in meeting a specific need, thereby setting an example that can be replicated by other congregations. A key factor in the provision of service is that congregations will adopt only those programs that are of interest to members and that constitute a good fit with their environment and local expectations. Congregations are not corporate franchises, all serving the same product in the same package. Each congregation is free to develop whatever services it wishes to provide its members and the community. To an external observer, the decision may seem illogical, but, to the congregation, the decision is logical because it is based on community needs, local norms, implicit expectations, the congregation's resources, and members' preferences. It may be that a trend in one city, such as latchkey programs, will spread to congregations in other cities. Program replication, however, will depend on whether the program is suitable in a different local context and culture.

Summary

In this chapter, we provided data regarding the areas of service in which congregations are involved and discussed the significance of these data, as well as levels of service. On the basis of our study of 251 congregations, we identified several characteristics of congregational involvement. First, congregations, with few exceptions, provide some form of social and community service delivery. These services range from large, formal programs to small, informal services. Second, the areas most frequently addressed by congregations are services that benefit children, the elderly, the poor and the homeless, as well as the community at large. The latter including programs such as neighborhood cleanup, provision of space for community meetings, and representing the community in dealings with public authorities. Equally important are services that range from support groups to large-scale housing projects. To understand the contribution of congregations to society, we must observe and consider their activities as a whole. It is only when we examine the ecology and specific needs of a local neighborhood and the unique contribution of local congregations to their members and the larger community that we can begin to appreciate the full impact of congregational involvement. While some congregations provide similar programs, often within a particular geographical area, each provides different services. These programs, when combined, address a wide range of human needs and social problems. Nevertheless, congregations tend not to collaborate and/or systematically plan how to meet all or most needs in their areas. In fact, one congregation may be unaware of what others in the same neighborhood are doing. When clergy or members observe certain human needs they assume are unmet, they are likely to organize the congregation to help. In the planning process, they are likely to assess what is available locally and attempt to meet a need unattended by other congregations. Thus, it is likely that a congregation will encounter problems or needs not being addressed by a neighbor congregation or community organization (see chapters 8 and 9 for a discussion and findings regarding this issue). This is not to say that congregations are unsophisticated in their planning. In many cases, congregations conduct full-scale needs assessments and develop strategic plans based on their mission; the match between what is needed and what services are available in the community results in needed social programs. Our point is that, despite the lack of an organized planning process, congregations meet a wide range of human needs in most urban neighborhoods and towns. Were such services to be consolidated under one roof, they would rightly demand the recognition and support of many secular social service agencies.

To understand the unique and full contribution of services provided by congregations, we must consider not only large, formal social services programs but also informal activities. To appreciate the full scale of congregational social and community involvement, we must start at the level of clergy pastoral counseling, informal care, and referral and then move toward the distinct and formal 501(c)3 incorporated agencies (Jeavons & Cnaan, 1997). The informal support provided by congregants and clergy is rarely addressed in the literature. Those most in need know to knock on congregational doors and ask for help, whether money, food, or simply a sympathetic ear. This access, in and of itself, constitutes a major source of immediate support and serves as a network of social care and referral. Given the large number of congregations throughout the United States, we can only imagine how many people daily knock on the doors of congregations to ask for assistance or advice.

Congregation members assemble for the primary purpose of worship and religious practice. They collectively practice their faith by caring for those in need and combating social injustices. Congregations provide yet another function as one of the few community venues where people can interact with others whom they trust and care for. As communal settings, congregations provide a forum for publicizing and discussing community, municipal, state, national, and international issues. The congregational spectrum of concern has ranged from health education and voter registration to pressuring corporations to withdraw investments in South Africa in the days of apartheid. Given the decline of other social institutions, it is not surprising that many health intervention advocates and politicians address congregations as a means of bringing public attention to their cause. Congregations also serve as the "bully pulpit" for clerical activists concerned with initiating social change and increasing members' participation in civic and political campaigns. The voluntary coming together of people as a group in a respectful and reflective manner distinguishes the congregation as a unit of social intervention from any other institution in the community.

Given the voluntary nature of congregations and the autonomy of members in the governance of congregations, the finding of regional differences among congregations is not surprising. As we show in chapter 12, the impetus for social programs comes from the congregation itself, and programs are not begun in response to an external challenge. Because these programs are initiated by members and clergy who are aware of local needs and local standards of service, it is logical that the types of programs vary from city to city. For example, one finds more aspiring artists in New York and more homeless people and runaway youth in San Francisco than in other cities. The vast majority of programs come into being because members and staff tell the congregation what they have witnessed, and the congregation agrees to help. Some programs remain unique to the region; some spread beyond the region; still others meet basic needs that are found in every region of the United States.

One way to understand congregational involvement in social and community services provision is to imagine the United States without congregations. Without congregations, one-third of the children now in day care centers would have no place to go. Most scout troops and twelve-step groups would have no meeting place. Many food cupboards, soup kitchens, and homeless shelters would disappear, leaving a large number of people hungry and on the streets. New immigrants and refugees would lose their strongest supporters and their anchor as they move into mainstream American life. Numerous old and sick people would be neglected, and the waiting list for institutionalized care would double. The list goes on and on, underscoring the important fact that the absence of congregations in the United States would create a significant social void, along with the loss of the religious, spiritual, and social support provided by congregations.

5

Congregational Involvement II
Characteristics of Service and Financial Value

> As government on all levels pulled back from providing or funding services, many congregations have been active in picking up the pieces, providing shelter for the homeless, food for the hungry, and support for the unemployed.
>
> —Kim Zalnet, *Economic Home Cookin'* (1989)

Congregations are often labeled social clubs (Smith, 1993) or member-serving organizations. This school of thought assumes that the sole beneficiaries of congregational activities are the members. Our findings suggest the opposite, namely that congregations are a major force in sustaining the quality of life in the community and that they are essential for social stability in urban neighborhoods. As we show in this chapter, there is compelling evidence in support of the argument that congregations are community-serving organizations.

In determining the social importance of congregations, does it matter whether a congregation serves its members or others? We believe that it does, for two important reasons. One concerns the fiscal value of congregational social service programs; the other, the benefits that the wider community receives from these programs. Consider the case of low-income, minority-dominated neighborhoods that lack banking services and whose residents are often unable to obtain loans. If a congregation establishes a credit union that serves more than 200 local families who are also members of the congregation, is this not a major social service for the community? In fact, the National Federation of Community Development Credit Unions (1997) reports that 40 percent of its organization members are faith-based credit unions. Consider also the case of a congregation that provides in-home support services for elderly members and parents of members. If these services prevent or delay nursing home entry, does this not represent a conservation of limited resources for the wider society? Or consider the summer camp that offers swimming, arts, sports, and films, as well as religious education. Does this camp not represent a recreational alternative for neighborhood youth that benefits the community?

These examples indicate that even those congregations that serve only their members benefit the community. Thus, congregations classified as member-serving are as relevant to our discussion of community involvement as are congregations with social ministry programs.

In this chapter, we discuss the ratio of congregational members to people in the wider community who are served by congregational social programs. We then assess the fiscal contribution of congregations to social services by assigning monetary replacement value to the services and financial support provided by the 251 congregations in our study. First, we estimate the percentage of the annual congregational budget allotted to social services programs. We then assess the imputed economic value of the 1,005 programs reported in our study, that is, how much it would cost to replace a faith-based service with a similar secular social service. To determine these costs, we assess the dollar value of clergy/staff/volunteer hours; the value of space used by the program; the value of utilities; and the value of in-kind support. These indirect costs, together with the actual dollar support, are used to determine the average fiscal value of the programs reported in our study. By determining the fiscal contribution, we are able to establish a measure of the congregational investment to social programs and community service.

Focus of Our Study

Interviewees were asked to identify the programs that best represented their social and community involvement. We limited the number of programs to a maximum of five to meet the time constraints of the study. In many cases, we interviewed both the clergy and the person in charge of the congregational program. This often required separate visits, weeks and even months apart.

Interviewees were asked to report detailed information for each of the programs they selected (see Appendix, Specific Program Form). We used this questionnaire to collect the following information: who provides the service; who benefits from the service; operating budget; percentage of budget for social ministry; clergy hours; staff hours; volunteer hours; financial support for program; in-kind support; cost of utilities; and value of space. Responses to the questions about who provides the service and who the beneficiaries are enabled us to assess the ratio of congregational members to members of the community who are assisted by the congregation. The annual budget and percentage of the annual budget allocated for social programs/ministries were used as indicators of the congregation's commitment to social services. Clergy/staff/volunteer hours, financial support for the program, in-kind support, cost of utilities, and value of space were used to determine the imputed economic value of providing social programs. Although this method provides a reasonable estimate of the financial replacement value of a congregation's social and community programs, it underestimates the real value of all of their programs. For example, a congregation that reported five programs valued at $10,000 may also have had a sixth program valued at $3,000. Because the number of programs was limited to five, the latter would not have been included in the analysis.

Those Who Serve/Those Who Are Served

As discussed in chapter 4, congregations are highly effective in attracting members to volunteer as a group to carry out social programs. Members' enthusiasm and the nature of the work often attract additional volunteers from the community. We were therefore interested in the ratio of community members to congregants among those involved in social services provision. It should be noted that, in two cases, the term *community members* includes teachers, group leaders, and community professionals. The first case concerns the use of congregational facilities by others; the second concerns congregational assistance to others in carrying out a program. One final note is necessary before we present our findings. Several congregations reported programs such as community fairs and Habitat for Humanity projects that involved more than a thousand volunteers. Because we considered these types of programs to be outliers, we excluded them from our analysis.

Of the 1,005 programs reported, 102 programs (10.1 percent) involved no congregational members. Such programs, for example, included AA groups that met on the congregational premises but were not affiliated with the congregation. In contrast, 589 (58.6 percent) programs used only congregational members to provide the service. The number of congregational members providing service ranged from none to 500, with a mean of seventeen (SD = 36.7).[3] The number of people from the wider community involved in providing service ranged from none to 600, with a mean of 11.7 (SD = 50.7). Comparisons of these findings led to two conclusions. First, congregational programs that involve nonmembers tend to be larger in size. When we ignore the zeros in both groups, programs using only congregational members have a mean of 18.9 providers, while in programs including people from the wider community, the mean jumps to 28.3. Second, when we use the original two means that apply to the 1,005 programs (including cases where no providers were reported), the ratio of congregational members to people from the wider community involved in congregational programs is 1.45 to 1 in favor of congregational members. In other words, congregations serve to attract civic activities by members and nonmembers alike.

The more interesting finding concerns the beneficiaries of congregational programs. For example, interviewees who reported large-scale programs such as voter registration and civic protests estimated that more than 100,000 people in the wider community benefited from these programs. In another instance, a campaign to improve health services for children was reported as benefiting some 200,000 children. To avoid bias, we limited the number of beneficiaries to 5,000. We found that, on average, a congregation's social program serves 181.8 persons each month. This is a larger number than that found by Hill (1998) in the Baltimore area. Hill reported an average of 120 persons served each month by the social programs.

Compared with people in the wider community, significantly fewer congregational members benefited from these programs. When we look at programs that serve only congregational members or those that do not serve congregational members at all, an interesting contrast emerges. Of the 1,005 programs, 340 (33.8 percent) had no congregational members as beneficiaries. In other words, one-third of congregational programs benefit only people from the wider community. Only one-quarter of the programs (240; 24.0 percent) benefited no people from the wider community.

A complementary analysis concerns the average number of congregational members who benefit from the social programs and the average number for people from the community who benefit from the social programs but are not members of the congregation. The mean number of congregational members who are beneficiaries of these programs was

39.5, with a standard deviation of 120.4. The mean number of beneficiaries from the wider community was 142.3, with a standard deviation of 379.0. Comparison of the means for these two groups of beneficiaries reveals that the ratio of those in the wider community to congregational members is 3.6:1. It should be noted that Jackson and his colleagues (1997), in Michigan, found that 70 percent of reported programs were open to every person in the community regardless of congregational affiliation, 18 percent were open only to members of the community at large (no congregational members), and only 13 percent were exclusively for members of the congregation. Regardless of the different categories used in counting, their findings are similar to ours in that they too suggest that congregations emphasize service to others, rather than limiting service exclusively to members.

As we have shown, members are the key providers of congregational programs, and the overwhelming majority of beneficiaries are nonmembers from the wider community. In this respect, congregations should be viewed not as social clubs or member-serving organizations but as community-supporting organizations. It is evident from the findings so far that congregations in urban America are highly involved in providing services to their communities and beyond. What still must be established is the fiscal value of these services.

Percentage of Congregations with Social Programs

Of the 251 congregation in our study, seventeen (6.8 percent) reported no formal social programs, although eight of them reported provision of social services on an as-needed basis. The remaining 234 congregations, 93.2 percent, reported at least one social program. Of these, seven congregations (2.8 percent) reported only one program; twelve (4.8 percent) reported two programs; thirty-three (13.1 percent) reported three programs; thirty-five (13.9 percent) reported four programs; and 147 (58.6 percent) reported five or more programs. As we had limited the number of reported programs to five, we do not know how many congregations had more than five programs, although we were informed that a large congregation in Houston currently provides twenty-six social programs.

Our finding that a high percentage of congregations provide at least one social and community service is in line with a host of other studies.[4] Chaves (1999), however, found that only 57 percent of the congregations in his study, containing 75 percent of religious service attenders, reported participating in or supporting social service projects. The distinction between the 57 percent and 75 percent is that the former indicates the actual number of congregations and the latter, the percentage of the total membership of congregations; larger congregations are more involved in social services provision. Chaves obtained his sample of congregations by calling people at random and asking them whether they were a member of a congregation and, if so, to identify their clergy. The congregations identified and contacted via this survey method are presumed to be a more representative group of congregations than those obtained in our study. However, his method is less efficient in obtaining information about social programs and is likely to underrepresent the real number of social programs provided by congregations. In Chaves's study, eliciting information about social and community programs was done using telephone interviews without appropriate probing. In this study, we used in-depth personal interviews of clergy and lay leaders and probed deeply by using the list of recognized programs/ministries. In this respect, we should reiterate Heidi Rolland Unruh's (1999) experience:

> While it might seem that identifying social ministries would be the easiest part of this study, we encountered more ambiguity than we expected. Ministries that had been reported on the initial pastoral survey disappeared when we actually went to observe them, and conversely, after spending six months with a church, we would discover a program that no one had told us about. (p. 5)

Nevertheless, we recognize that bias is possible in both methods and that identifying congregational social programs is a difficult task.

Another indication of the methodological problem inherent in asking for social ministries/services is reported by Pearson and Anhalt (1993). They studied eighty black congregations in Denver. They report that "to the question 'Is your church involved in community service outreach program?' 48 of the 80 interviewed senior ministers responded affirmatively." This rate implies only 60 percent of the studied congregations. However, when asked for specific programs, sixty-seven congregations (84 percent) reported having a food program. In other words, recalling programs when the question is too general results in omission of some actual programs, while responding to a list of recognized programs increases the chance of accurate recall.

The 251 congregations in our study reported a total of 1,005 programs for an average of four programs per congregation. Again, this underestimates the number of programs, as we limited the number of programs to a maximum of five per congregation.

Social Program Provision as Percentage of Operating Budget

The cost of social and community service provision as a percentage of the annual operating budget is a crude measure of congregational commitment to help others. To determine the cost of service provision over the past twelve months, we asked the congregations to include not only the designated budget for benevolence (or equivalent term) but also special collections for projects such as flood relief, international relief, any discretionary budget for the homeless and poor, and costs of providing congregational space at no charge for community meetings and programs.

In addition, we asked them to factor in the percentage of the clergy salary allotted for social ministry. The following example illustrates the monetary value of this service. One of the clergy in our study reported that he served two days each week as a pastoral counselor at a local children's hospital. Given that the congregation pays the clergy's salary, the congregation is underwriting his two-day commitment. Were he a corporate employee serving two days a week at the local United Way, the corporation could write off 40 percent of his salary as a charitable contribution. Hodgkinson and Weitzman (1993) found that, on average, clergy (paid and volunteer) spent 38.5 hours a month on nonreligious activities, most of which correspond to our category of social and community care. This significant investment of time by the clergy equals a full workweek per month, or one quarter of a full-time position.

Of the 251 congregations in our study, seventeen congregations did not answer our question regarding the percentage of their budget allocated to social service provision. Of the remaining 234 congregations, five (2 percent) allocated none of their budget to social service provision, and four (1.7 percent) allocated 0.5 percent of their budget. On the other hand, twenty-eight congregations (12 percent) allocated more than 50 percent of their annual budget to social programs. The rest ranged from 1 percent to 50 percent of their annual budgets. The mean percentage of social and community service provision as a percent of the annual operating budget was 22.6 percent, with a standard deviation of 18.7.

The percentage of the annual budget allocated for social programs was significantly associated with only two background variables. The first variable was the congregation's financial status. As expected, wealthier congregations reported higher percentages of their annual budget allocated for social services ($r = .14$).[5] Clearly, congregations with budget surpluses can afford to spend more to help others. The second variable significantly associated with the percentage of annual budget allocated to social programs was the percentage of Caucasians in the congregation. This was an inverse correlation ($r = -.15$). In other words, the lower the percent of Caucasians in the congregation, the higher the percent of the annual operating budget allocated to social programs.

The size of the congregation was not significantly correlated with the percentage of annual budget allocated to social programs. Thus, we can assume that, regardless of size, congregations allocate 22.6 percent of their operating budgets on average to social services. The Independent Sector's (Hodgkinson et al., 1993) *From Belief to Commitment* estimates the annual budget of small congregations at $54,000, of medium-size congregations at $108,000, and of large congregations at $432,000. On the basis of these 1992 estimates, we conclude that the financial contribution of congregations for social services is as follows: $12,204 for small congregations, $24,408 for medium-size congregations, and $97,832 for large congregations. While these numbers are based on our sample and correlated with data from another source, we believe they are useful in assessing the extent of congregational financial support for social programs.

Chaves (1999), on the other hand, reported that congregations allocate approximately 3 percent of their "total budget" to social service and community programs. While Chaves's definition of budget is much narrower than ours, his finding of 3 percent differs markedly from our finding of 22.6 percent. This difference is due to methodology. Because Chaves's telephone interview method involved little probing, it is likely that his respondents reported their benevolence budget but ignored all other fiscal contributions to social service, particularly the salary of clergy or staff for designated services.

It is important to note that in our sample as a whole and for each city, the mean percentage allocated to social programs (22.6 percent) was higher than traditional tithing (10 percent). Although tithing is a dictum directed at individuals, rather than at organizations, we use it here as a baseline measure of charitable giving. But tithing is not the only measure of charitable giving. The United Way of America, for example, asks individuals to "Give

Five," or 5 percent of their income, whereas American corporations, on average, designate only about 1 percent of their pretax net income for charitable contributions (Galaskiewicz, 1997). By any of these three measures, congregations can be considered the most charitable in supporting social programs that benefit the community.

Calculating Imputed Economic Value of Congregational Social Services—The Replacement Value

Rationale

Any attempt to assess the imputed economic value of a congregational program must necessarily go beyond dollar expenses, since these are only a small part of the congregation's contribution. In addition to money allocated to the program, congregational support ranges from donated labor (clergy, staff, and volunteers), in-kind support, and cost of utilities to program space that is provided free of charge. The key question is: What is the estimated replacement value of all the social and community programs provided by local religious congregations? It is our assumption that the programs developed and carried out by local religious congregations contribute to the quality of life throughout America. These programs enable the public sector to devote fewer resources to underwriting social programs and eventually reduce the tax burden.

If tomorrow the doors of all congregations were to close and a secular, possibly public, provider were called upon to replace these lost social programs, how much would it cost to build a similar tapestry of social services? In the following paragraphs, we explain how to calculate the replacement value.

Congregational donated labor has three components: clergy, staff, and member volunteers. First, the clergy is often the full-time paid leader of the congregation and may spend time on the social program at the congregations's expense. For example, four-hours-a-month service at a soup kitchen by a given clergy may go unnoticed, yet this service helps ensure the survival of the program. These hours are equivalent to four professional hours given to social service provision. For purposes of this study, we assessed the value of a clergy hour at the lowest scale of professional work: $20 per hour.

Second, members of the congregational staff often provide the same services as the paid staff of a secular service provider. For example, the congregational secretary may schedule meetings, process forms, answer phone queries, and perform office tasks essential for the program. Similarly, the choir director may help plan a holiday celebration for the children in the community. Thus, time spent by the congregational staff on social programs should also be factored into the congregation's contribution. For purposes of this study, we assessed the value of staff time at $10 per hour. This estimate reflects the fact that staff often receive benefit packages, as well as an income above minimum wage.

Finally, congregations have their own volunteer cadres that provide invaluable program support (see chapter 11 for a detailed discussion of congregational volunteers). From running food distribution centers to building homes with Habitat for Humanity, congregational volunteers provide the same services at no charge as do the paid staff of secular providers that cannot attract sufficient numbers of volunteers. Hill (1998) noted that "volunteers accounted for the overwhelming majority of staff members carrying out church outreach programs" (p. 34). Several authors have tried to assess the financial contribution of volunteer hours (Brown, 1999; Clemens & Francis, 1998; Hodgkinson & Weitzman, 1993). For purposes of our study, we used a single hourly wage rate. Our decision was based on findings that volunteers, regardless of their skills and income, were perceived to incur equal opportunity costs (Handy et al., 1998). We therefore assessed the value of congregational member-volunteer time at $11.58 an hour. This figure accords with the average hourly rate computed in 1992 by the Independent Sector and supported by an economic analysis carried out by Brown (1999).

Estimating the value of in-kind support is complicated because congregations provide numerous types of in-kind support. These include, but are not limited to, publicity, postage, printing, transportation, telephone use, food, art supplies, computer analysis, and refreshments served at meetings. Interviewees in our study were asked to consider these examples of in-kind support and to assess the extent to which each program used these goods. Since not every one was able to assess in-kind support, some did not answer the question, and others gave incomplete answers.

Congregations provide important subsidies for programs housed on their property. One such subsidy is the underwriting of utility costs. In many cases, the congregation must heat or cool the building at specific times to enable the program to take place. Another is the underwriting of insurance, which enables congregational space to be used for programs and meetings. Congregations also underwrite maintenance costs for wear and tear caused by the programs that use their space. Again, we asked our interviewees to assess the cost of these subsidies, but, again, many failed to answer or gave incomplete answers.

The final element in determining the true cost of a program is the value of space used by the program. To determine this value, we asked what it would cost to rent similar space in the private market. For example, if the program were a day care center, then a private secular provider would have to rent a facility that had classrooms, kitchen, toilets, and a playground. Provision of space at no charge is a congregational contribution that is seldom acknowledged.

Methodological Note

Some readers may consider the imputed economic (replacement) value of congregational programs generated by our analysis to be exaggerated. We ask readers to consider the following points. First, the goal of our analysis was to assess *imputed value* of the in-kind support, labor, space, and subsidies that congregations provide without charge to programs. To do this, we calculated what these same services and labor would cost a secular provider. We did this because we believe that congregational support, in terms of labor and/or services, merits both fiscal evaluation and discussion.

Second, our analysis of imputed (replacement) value is a conservative one. As we have noted several times, we limited the number of programs per congregation to five. Many congregations could have reported more than five programs. This, in turn, would have increased the estimated monetary worth of programs per congregation. Conversely, we assigned the value of zero to programs in which interviewees failed to answer questions regarding specific costs. Furthermore, we did not include any informal programs, such as those discussed in the previous chapter; nor did we include the time clergy or other staff members contributed to social causes in the community. These clearly add to the congregational support of its community, but we did not include them in our analysis of replacement value. Finally, there are congregational members who volunteer to various social causes outside the church as individuals and not as representatives of the congregation, yet do so because of their church affiliation. Again, this support was not measured as part of the replacement value.

Third, if a congregation reported uncharacteristically high support for a program, such as a $200,000 gift by a Philadelphia congregation to a community sports program, we omitted the data from further analysis as biased. Similarly, if a program reported thousands of volunteers, we also omitted this program from further analysis. Such statistical outliers represent real cases, but we were worried that they would bias the results in the direction of overly high values.

Finally, we used traditional economic analysis to determine the average monetary value of the monthly support for a congregation program. We assumed that respondents had reported the total value of each program's operation on all dimensions (e.g., financial support, value of space, value of volunteer work, in-kind support). To calculate the *average monetary value of each item*, we took the total estimated values reported for all programs and divided that by the total number of programs, including programs with no reported values. For example, only 498 (49.6 percent) of the 1,005 programs estimated the value of the space used by the program. For these 498 programs, the mean value per month was $1,458.70. Thus, the total mean space value cost per month was $726,434.10 ($1,458.70 x 498 programs). To obtain a conservative cost estimate that would be applicable for all programs, we assumed that programs that reported no costs for the value of program space had zero costs. We therefore divided the total average value of space per month ($726,434.10) by the total number of programs (1,005). This gave us an average monthly space value cost of $722.82 per month for all 1,005 programs, compared with $1,458.70 for the 498 programs for which estimated space costs were available.

The Findings

To determine the economic value of congregational contributions to social programs, we assessed seven variables: clergy hours, staff hours, volunteer hours, financial support, in-kind support, cost of utilities, and value of space.

Clergy Hours

Clergy initiated many of the programs (39.2 percent) reported in our study. Involvement in social ministry requires considerable time and effort on the part of American clergy, who bear the moral and administrative responsibility for the activities of their congregations. A clerical presence ensures that service is provided in a principled and respectful atmosphere even if the clergy themselves do not take an active role in the program.

As mentioned earlier, we used the value of $20 per hour of clergy time per program. Again, this is an imputed economic value and assumes that clergy hours devoted to social ministry are, in fact, underwritten by the congregation that pays the clergy's salary. In contrast, a secular or public provider would have to pay a qualified professional to take this leadership role. It is important to note that, of the seven variables used to assess the economic value of congregational programs, the value of clergy time is most underrepresented. Many clergy told us that they were involved in more than five social service programs, including coalitions and interfaith or interdenominational reconciliation or advocacy groups. Because we did not consider the latter to be congregational programs, we did not include them in our study.

Of the 1,005 programs reported, 405 (40.3 percent) had no clergy involved. The majority of these programs were carried out on congregational property by an external provider, such as Alcoholics Anonymous. In these cases, the congregation served as host, rather than as provider. For all 1,005 programs, the estimated contribution of clergy was $507.40 per program per month. This estimate varied significantly across our study sites. New York and Council Grove reported the lowest values for clergy time ($144.80 and $62.60, respectively), while Indianapolis reported the highest value ($870.80). These differences were statistically significant.[6]

Staff Hours

As noted in chapter 3, each congregation employed, on average, the equivalent of 1.4 full-time administrators/secretaries; 1.05 full-time maintenance workers/janitors; 0.25 bookkeeper/treasurer; and 2.81 full-time directors of education, social programs, and music. Several wealthy congregations also employed a full-time social service coordinator or youth worker. Social programs rely on these staff people, from the secretary who mails out program notices to the janitor who sets up and cleans the meeting room. According to Hodgkinson and Weitzman (1993), each staff member, on average, spends 38.5 hours per month on social and community services provided by the congregation. Given the ratio of clergy to staff members, it is not unexpected that the staff members spend twice as many hours on social programs as do the clergy.

Salaries of congregational staff range from full salaries with benefits to minimum wage. Since no previous estimates have been reported in the literature, we decided to use half the value of a clergy hour ($20), or $10 per staff hour. Poor or small congregations are unlikely to have paid staff in addition to the clergy; therefore, the finding that 549 programs (54.6 percent) used no paid staff was not unexpected. In some cases, interviewees underestimated staff involvement, as in the case of a Chicago clergy who reported: "My secretary helps the program, but it really doesn't take her a lot of time so I'd rather say no paid staff helped in this program."

The estimated average value of staff work per month per program was $563.90. New York, Mobile, and Council Grove reported the lowest values ($272.10, $242.50, and $35.30, respectively). Indianapolis and Chicago reported the highest values ($1,188.30 and $844.60, respectively).

Volunteer Hours

Volunteer hours represent the congregation's most important resource in social service provision. According to Hodgkinson and Weitzman (1993), each volunteer gives, on average, 4.6 hours per month. Taken as a whole, volunteer hours account for half of all hours spent in social service provision by congregations.

Of the 1,005 programs, 217 programs (21.6 percent) reported no use of volunteers. These were programs that were run by others on the congregation's property or programs, such as international relief, and received only financial support from the congregation. The remaining 788 programs (78.4 percent) reported using volunteers. This percentage is similar to that reported by Jackson and his colleagues, who found that 70.8 percent of the social programs provided by black churches in Michigan used volunteers. As previously noted, we used the Independent Sector value of $11.58 to assess the value of one hour of volunteer work.

The estimated average monetary value of volunteer work per month per program was $1.754.72. New York, Mobile, and Council Grove again had the lowest values ($1,213.58, $697.27, and $365.12, respectively). Chicago and Indianapolis had the highest values ($5,270.87 and $2,226.14, respectively).

Financial Support

A congregation's support for its social service program often includes cash assistance, as well as noncash support. In some instances, financial support by a congregation was limited to cash assistance, such as helping poor families pay their rent or helping the denomination pay for its international relief program. About half the reported programs (472 programs, 47 percent) were financially supported by the congregations. In some cases, the support was minimal and mostly symbolic in nature; however, at times major financial support underwrote a very impressive ministry/program. We identified eleven programs, such as housing projects and homeless shelters, that received significant monthly financial support from wealthy congregations. To avoid bias, we excluded any congregational financial support that exceeded $10,000 a month from our analysis.

Of the 1,005 programs, 502 (50 percent) received financial support from the congregation. The mean was $497.26 per program per month. There were no significant differences among the study sites.

In-Kind Support

In-kind support was often underreported because many interviewees found the concept difficult to grasp. Of the 1,005 programs, 623 programs (62 percent) reported no in-kind support. This can be explained, in part, by the fact that some programs receive only financial assistance. However, the report of no in-kind support for most programs is indicative of a congregational culture that underwrites these costs, such as postage, telephone use, or photocopying, but fails to understand the implications of this support.

In-kind support averaged $97.52 per month per program. Although there were no statistically significant differences, Indianapolis and Council Grove reported the lowest values for in-kind support ($39.91 and $29.17, respectively), whereas New York and Mobile reported the highest value ($198.46 and $174.46, respectively).

Cost of Utilities

Estimating the value of utilities, insurance, and maintenance provided in service provision proved difficult for interviewees. As a result, they failed to answer the question regarding these costs for 644 (64.1 percent) of the programs.

The estimated average utility costs for all 1,005 programs was $142.16 per program per month. There were no significant statistical differences. Council Grove reported the lowest value for utility costs ($8.33); Indianapolis reported the highest ($232.34).

Value of Space

Space provision by congregations is extremely important because most neighborhoods have few, if any, facilities available to community organizations at little or no cost. Furthermore, few local facilities have kitchens where food can be prepared for the hungry, the elderly, or children in day care. Congregations often have the combination of kitchens, meeting rooms, classrooms, offices, sanctuary, and playground space that is preferred for day care centers, programs for the elderly, local theater groups, educational programs, and community organizations. Such facilities are expensive, and few owners are willing to make them available at little or no cost.

When we consider the replacement value of congregations' social services, we should keep in mind that the unique structure of churches, which were built to serve a religious purpose, meets the needs of many community groups and organizations quite well. In some cases, the congregation charges rent to users, and these sums, as discussed later, were deducted from the total replacement value.

Of the 1,005 programs, 498 (49.6 percent) estimated the value of the space used by the program. Council Grove, where there is abundant space available, reported the lowest rate for value of space ($53.34). New York, where space is costly, reported the highest rate ($1,474.54). It should also be noted that New York has many large-scale programs that require the full use of a congregation's facility.

Total Estimated Value of Congregational Contributions to Social Programs

As shown in Table 5-1, the average total estimated value of congregational contributions was $4,285.78 per program per month. However,

TABLE 5-1
Assessed Average Monetary Monthly Value of an Average Program by City

	Chicago	Houston	Indianapolis	Mobile	New York	Philadelphia	S. Francisco	C.G.	Total
Clergy hours (@ $20 hr.)	$307.80	$509.80	$870.80	$510.40	$144.80	$330.80	$230.20	$62.20	$507.40
Staff hours (@ $10 hr.)	$844.60	$678.60	$1,188.30	$242.50	$272.10	$402.70	$411.20	$35.30	$563.90
Volunteer hours (@ $11.58 hr.)	$5,270.87	$1,087.01	$2,226.14	$697.27	$1,213.58	$1,432.33	$1,082.27	$365.12	$1,754.72
Financial support	$351.33	$491.17	$432.09	$434.95	$492.38	$590.90	$650.91	$513.00	$497.26
In-kind support	$87.11	$100.92	$39.91	$174.46	$198.46	$121.64	$87.62	$29.17	$97.52
Cost of utilities	$96.98	$81.77	$232.34	$105.97	$173.59	$110.24	$193.30	$8.33	$142.16
Value of space	$965.72	$812.26	$392.06	$708.40	$1,474.54	$493.20	$1,332.71	$53.34	$722.82
Total	$7,924.41	$3,761.53	$2,423.06	$2,873.95	$3,969.45	$3,481.81	$3,988.21	$1,066.46	$4,285.78

this number does not take into account an important fact of congregational life: some congregations earn money or offset costs by charging
rent or participation fees or by seeking external grants. Thus, we needed
to address the issue of program income/external support received by congregation in conjunction with their social ministry.

The first and most important finding is that most programs reported
no income through their social ministries/programs. This finding supports
those of Pearson and Anhalt (1993) for Denver. They report that most of
the identified programs in their study were funded exclusively by the
church. We found that in 943 programs (93.8 percent), no cash support
was awarded to the congregation from any source—that is, only sixty-
three programs generated any income. Similarly, no in-kind support was
given to congregations from 866 programs (86.2 percent). Only 119 programs (11.8 percent) provided in-kind support.

To assess what congregations gain from their social programs we calculated the sums reported and divided them by the total number of programs reported by all congregations. The mean cash income to the congregations from the 1,005 programs was $59.80 and from in-kind support,
a value of $399.30. The total value was $459.10 per program per month.

We deducted the estimated combined monthly mean of the cash income and in-kind support accrued by the congregations ($459.10 per pro-
gram) from the estimated monthly total cost ($4,285.78 per program) to
the congregations (as shown in Table 5-1) to determine the net value of a
congregational program. We found that the estimated total net value of
congregational contributions averaged $3,826.68 per program per month.
Given that the average congregation in our study had four programs, the
total net congregational contribution averaged $15,306.72 per month.
Over a year, the average total net congregational contribution to social services provision was approximately $184,000 per congregation.

Summary

In this chapter, we have shown that congregations in urban America function not as exclusive clubs but as social institutions that meet the needs of
others in the community. Although the majority of congregations serve
primarily their members, member-serving congregations also contribute
to the quality of life and civility in the community as a whole. The ratio
of people from the wider community to people from the congregation

who benefit from congregational social services is 3.6:1. These numbers suggest that the awarding of tax-exempt status to congregations was a wise legislative decision.

While congregations function primarily as gathering places for collective worship, they also function as social safety nets. The findings reported in this chapter and in chapter 4 indicate that numerous people in need approach congregations for assistance and that congregations, in turn, are actively involved in providing assistance and support for those in greatest need.

To determine the overall imputed value of congregational contributions to social and community, we calculated the value of clergy/staff/volunteer hours; cash support; in-kind support; cost of utilities; and value of space. We found that, on average, the net value of congregational contributions was $3,826.68 per program per month. Given that the average congregation has four programs, the total net contribution averaged $15,306.72 per congregation per month, or approximately $184,000 per congregation per year. This contribution takes the form, for the most part, of volunteer hours and other noncash support. The magnitude of this congregational contribution to social services provision can best be appreciated by comparing it to the costs incurred by secular providers who must pay for in-kind support that congregations provide at no cost.

When local authorities reconsider the justification to exempt local religious congregations from various taxes they should keep these findings in mind. These impressive fiscal values are only one side of the picture. They do not represent moral and social contributions. These contributions are qualitatively assessed in the third part of this book, chapters 8 to 10.

6

Which Congregations Tend to Get Involved

Like the society they serve, American congregations are diverse. They range from megachurches to storefront places of worship. Some have significant financial endowments; others struggle for daily survival. Some are fundamentalist in their beliefs; others are liberal. This diversity raises an important question: do congregational characteristics explain and predict congregational involvement in social services provision?

Determining the congregational characteristics associated with social and community services provision is of critical importance on two counts. First, such knowledge provides congregations with a means of comparing themselves with others, determining whether change is required to facilitate further social and community involvement, and identifying the type of social services that they are most capable of providing, independently or in collaboration with another organization. Second, understanding the connection between congregational characteristics and social services provision helps congregational leaders to identify the potential of congregations whose current involvement in social service provision is minimal. Furthermore, politicians and civic leaders who wish to encourage congregational social services provision will, with such knowledge, make better decisions when choosing partners for service provision or will know what areas of change are necessary to enhance congregational involvement.

There are many ways to measure the extent to which a congregation is involved in social and community services provision. One can measure the number of people who benefit, the number of volunteers, or the number of programs provided by the congregation. We chose not to use these measures in this chapter because, as previously noted, our data were limited to a maximum of five programs per congregation. Instead, we have used three other complementary measures to determine the extent of involvement in social and community services provision: (1) the number of areas of involvement reported by the congregation (see chapter 4); (2) the percentage of annual budget allocated to social services; and (3) the financial value of a congregation's programs (limited to five programs) as reported in chapter 5.

The Measures of Social and Community Involvement

As noted in chapter 4, interviewees were given a list of approximately 200 areas of social services and asked to identify those areas in which their congregations were most involved. It is important to note that our method allowed for double counting, since one program could involve several service areas. For example, a homeless shelter program might also provide a soup kitchen, clothing closets, and vocational counseling. While the congregation might consider this as one social program, we recorded this program as involvement in four service areas. Similarly, we recorded a family support group program that offered both marriage counseling and family counseling as involvement in two social service areas. In addition to double counting, the problem with this method is that it does not measure the degree of involvement. For example, a one-time contribution of $100 to a program is counted as equal to the daily provision of volunteer labor for the same program. The degree of involvement signified by the volunteer service far outweighs that of writing a check. Finally, it is important to note that large, multifaceted programs are more expensive and difficult to maintain. Thus, recording them as representing more than one area of service is logical because it is indicative of greater congregational involvement

Keeping in mind these limitations, we used *the number of formal social and community areas of service* as an indication of the congregation's level of overall involvement. Those with the highest scores were the most active congregations in social services provision; those with the lowest scores, the least active. As noted in chapter 4, the areas of involvement ranged from none to 175. Four congregations (1.6 percent) reported no involvement in any service areas. Three congregations reported the highest number of areas of involvement (175, 136, and 104, respectively). The mean number of areas of involvement was thirty-nine, with a standard deviation of 26.4.

Our second measure of congregational involvement was the *percentage of the annual budget allotted for social programs*. This is an important measure because it concerns percentages, rather than dollar amounts. For example, a congregation that allots $50,000 (50 percent) of its $100,000 budget for social services is demonstrating a much greater fiscal involvement that a congregation that allots $50,000 (5 percent) of its million-dollar budget. In other words, the percentage is a relative measure of the congregation's commitment to social and community care relative to budget size. Moreover, this is not a measure of actual fiscal investment, unlike our next measure, which assesses the dollar value of social program. As noted in chapter 5, seventeen congregations (6.7 percent) did not answer this question. Of the remaining 234 congregations, five congregations (2 percent) reported that none of their budget is allocated to social service provision; and four (1.6 percent) reported an allocation of 0.5 percent of their operating budget. The mean percentage of the annual budget allotted for social and community service provision was 22.6 percent, with a standard deviation of 18.7.

Our third measure of community involvement was the *average monthly fiscal value of the congregation's social programs* (limited to a maximum of five). The method we developed to calculate this measure is discussed in detail in chapter 5. This measure is indicative of the value of the congregation's commitment to society. Congregational size is a factor in this measure, unlike the measure that uses a percentage of the annual budget allotted for social services provision. The advantage of this measure is that it assesses the magnitude of aid generated by the congregation to improve the quality of life of people. Again, it must be stressed that congregations with more than five programs are underrepresented in this measure. These congregations are better represented by the previous measure. Conversely, congregations that invest most of their resources in only a few programs are better represented by this measure.

In determining the fiscal value of social programs per congregation, we also took into account possible income from programs. We found a few instances in which congregations either profited from the programs or made no contribution to the programs. These included struggling congregations with declining membership that rented space at commercial rates to balance their budgets, as well as three congregations whose grant awards generated monthly income that ranged from $270 and $2,800 a month. In addition to these congregations, twenty other congregations (8 percent) reported no cost of social programs. These were either congregations that provided no organized programs or congregations that provided organized programs but assessed their contribution at zero.

Each of these three measures—the number of social and community areas of service, percentage of the annual budget allotted for social programs, and monthly fiscal value of the congregational social and community services in no more than five programs—has limitations. Nevertheless, these three measures, when taken as a whole, compensate for the individual measures' limitations. The number of areas of involvement indicates the breadth of involvement but is biased by the degree of involvement and by the duration of the service, which may range from daily to seasonal. The percentage of the annual budget allotted for social programs is a fiscal indication of congregational involvement that favors smaller congregations. The monthly fiscal value of social programs is indicative of congregational contribution to society but favors congregations that can provide one or two large-scale programs. Thus, the measures are interrelated in that each measures a different dimension of the overall congregational contribution to society.

We expected these three measures to be moderately correlated, that is, that congregations with many services would score high on all three measures and that those with few or no services would score low. Our expectations proved to be wrong. The correlations among the three measures were both insignificant and low. The highest correlation was between the monthly fiscal value of the programs and the number of programs. However, it was only .061 and not statistically significant. Thus, the data indicate that the three measures of congregational commitment to society are disparate and unrelated.

What Explains Congregational Involvement?

The literature provides many suggestions for explaining congregational involvement (Iannaccone, Olson, & Stark, 1995; Billingsley, 1992; Dudley & Van Eck, 1992; Mock, 1992). Nevertheless, a variable that might explain the number of areas of involvement might not necessarily explain the percentage of annual budget allotted for service, and so forth. We therefore identify and discuss a list of variables that may be of relevance in explaining the three measures of involvement and then study their effect on each measure separately.

Most congregations have a congregational norm (Cnaan et al., 1999) for social and community involvement. These norms do not themselves generate active participation and hence must be considered in conjunction with other factors. These factors are generally congregation membership, leadership, financial resources, and the congregational characteristics (Iannaccone, Olson, & Stark, 1995; Billingsley, 1992; Dudley & Van Eck, 1992; Mock, 1992). We considered aspects of each of these four factors to determine their significance as predictors for congregational involvement in social services provision.

Congregation Membership

To determine the significance of leadership in congregational involvement, we considered the following five variables: *size of congregation, membership growth, percentage of congregants age sixty-five years and over, change in age of congregants in past three years,* and *percentage of single adults.*

Size of congregation: For the purposes of our study, we used *size of the congregation (number of active attenders)* as an explanatory variable. Size of membership has often been used as a measure for the available volunteer pool of a congregation (Ammerman, 1997; Thomas, Quinn, Billingsley, & Caldwell, 1994; Ward, Billingsley, Simon, & Burris, 1994; Billingsley, 1992). Similarly, the National Council of Churches of Christ (1992) found that congregation size is a key predictor of the number of community outreach health programs offered by a congregation. It is assumed that large congregations have more member volunteers, more financial and technical resources, and ample facilities to hold programs and that they can attract professionals to help plan their social and community services.

The size of the membership has been defined as the number of members who regularly attend religious services (Iannaccone, Olson, and Stark, 1995).We expanded this measure of congregational size to include all persons who attend the congregation at least once a month (see chapter 3). It is this core group of members and nonmembers that contributes financially to the congregation and that serves through, and for, the congregation in social and community services. As Chaves (1999) has noted, the size of the congregation is associated with congregational involvement in social service provision:

> The first finding is unsurprising, but its importance is such that it should be clearly stated: larger congregations do more than smaller congregations. . . . Half of the congregations with 75 or fewer regularly participating adults have social service programs of any sort compared with 86% of the congregations with more than 900 regularly participating adults. The

pattern is equally strong for most of the specific activity types. Considering that the median congregation in the U.S. has only 75 regularly participating adults, only about 10% have 250 or more regularly participating adults, and only about 1% have 900 or more, these results make clear that the minority of large congregations do the bulk of the social services carried out by this organizational population. (p. 10)

Because we expected that congregations whose memberships were increasing would be more active in social and community service provision, we used *membership growth* to measure any changes in congregational size. Interviewees were asked to report the size of their current membership and to indicate whether the number of members had risen, remained stable, or declined over the three previous years. In our analysis, we compared congregations with increased membership to those whose membership had declined or stabilized.

Age of congregants: Ammerman (1997) has suggested that the age of the congregation's members is an important factor in congregational social involvement. In her discussion of congregations in communities that experienced major demographic and/or economic changes, she stated:

> By the time the current changes were underway [*sic*], they were already so depleted in human and material resources that their primary objective was to survive from one month to the next. About 15% of the congregations we surveyed reported that their membership was primarily elderly, that they had few, if any, younger adults or children, and that their attendance was less than a hundred (usually less than 50) and shrinking. Many of these congregations are able to sustain no programming beyond Sunday services. (p. 74)

The age variable used in our study measures the *percentage of members who are sixty-five years of age or older*. We also asked whether the average age of the membership had decreased, increased, or remained stable over the three previous years. In our analysis, we compared congregations whose membership age had decreased with those whose membership age had increased or remained the same. Like Ammerman, we assumed that the higher the percentage of elderly, the less likely that the congregation would be involved in social and community service provision. It is expected that older people have less energy and fewer disposable financial resources to invest in serving others. Conversely, younger people are expected to have greater disposable incomes and more energy to invest in congregational activities, particularly those that are compatible with their individual or family needs. Taken together, the variables for change in congregational size and the age of the congregation serve as measures of the dynamism and rejuvenation that are characteristic of increased social and community involvement by a congregation.

A related variable is *change in age of congregants in the past three years.* This variable not only measures the exact age of the members but the dynamics of membership. Stagnating congregations tend to get older because they do not recruit new members, resort to old routines, and generally fear change. Congregations that became younger are often characterized by recruitment of families and concerned members willing to involve themselves in developing new ministries/programs. Thus, we used the variable *congregations which in membership became younger in the three years preceding the interview.*

Another measure of congregational involvement in social services provision is the *percentage of single adults.* We assumed that single people would either be elderly, single parents, or young adults. It is likely the elderly and single parents would have less time, energy, and resources to assist others in need, compared with young single adults. In this analysis, we used the *percentage of single adults* as a measure of those who have the interest, time, and resources to get involved with social services.

Leadership

To determine the significance of leadership in congregational involvement, we considered the following two variables: *number of paid clergy* and *number of paid staff.*

Previous research has found that congregations with paid clergy and other paid staff offer significantly more social and community services (Thomas, Quinn, Billingsley, & Caldwell, 1994; Ward, Billingsley, Simon, & Burris, 1994). The clergy play a critical role in social service provision. They are instrumental in initiating new social programs, and they are personally involved in three of every five programs. Thus, we used the *number of paid clergy* as a measure of congregational involvement in social services provision. As another explanatory variable, we used the *number of paid staff.* Staff size is indicative of the resources of the congregation, as well as its ability to provide services.

It is reasonable to assume that a congregation that must depend on part-time clergy, unpaid clergy, and volunteers for its operation will find it difficult to initiate and maintain congregational social programs. Thus, the number of paid clergy and paid staff is a measure of congregational leadership that is highly associated with involvement in social service provision. It should be noted that we used only the number of paid clergy as an explanatory variable in the final model.

Financial Resources

To determine the significance of financial resources in congregational involvement in social services provision, we considered the following three variables: *annual operating budget, fiscal status,* and *income of congregants.*

We used the *annual operating budget of the congregation* to determine the financial strength of the congregation. This variable measures the money available to the congregation over a year. The higher the annual budget, the more likely it is that the congregation will have the financial capacity to support social programs, assuming that there are no outstanding maintenance and property expenses.

To counter the influence of congregational size on the annual operating budget, we also used *fiscal status* as a measure of a congregation's ability to invest in social services. In our analysis, we compared congregations that reported their fiscal status as strong with those that reported their fiscal status as either sound or struggling. Because of the high association between annual budget and fiscal status, we excluded the latter from our final analysis.

Another measure of congregational resources is the *income of congregants.* Chaves (1999) found that congregations with more middle- and upper-class members provided more social service programs than did congregations with less affluent members. The more affluent the members, the more likely the congregation is to be involved in social and community services provision. Thus, we used *income of congregants* to measure the percentage of households in the congregation whose annual income was $75,000 and higher. It should be noted that the variables *annual budget* and *income of congregants* are not necessarily associated. Larger congregations of less affluent members may have annual budgets that are higher than those of small congregations with wealthy members. As Ammerman (1997) reminded us, wealthy people tend to give a lower percentage of their income to the congregation than do poorer people.

Congregational Characteristics

To determine the significance of congregational characteristics on congregational involvement in social services provision, we considered the following five variables: *age of congregation, percentage of white congregants, political orientation of congregation, theological orientation of congregation,* and *percentage of congregational members who live with one mile radius of the congregation.*

An issue of interest in the literature is whether new congregations are as likely to engage in social and community service provision as older congregations. It has been suggested that, compared with older congregations, new congregations are more likely to serve individuals seeking personal gratification, to be nondenominational, and to be led by clergy who have less formal education and who are less concerned with social problems (Roof & McKinney, 1987; Wuthnow, 1988). Pearson and Anhalt (1993) found, in a study of eighty black churches in Denver, that "on average, churches with outreach programs had been in operation 38 years as compared with 27 years for the churches without community outreach" (p. 28). New congregations are also more likely to spend more of their resources and energy in establishing their religious community, which limits their capacity to provide services for others. Farnsley (1997) has further suggested that long-established mainline congregations are more concerned with the welfare of others, while newer congregations are more concerned with personal spiritual welfare.

Hill (1998) found, in the Baltimore area, that younger congregations were more likely than older congregations to have program coordinators. On the other hand, "older churches were more likely than younger churches to collaborate with other churches" (p. 14). However, predominately white churches also tended to be older than predominately black churches.

We have therefore used *age of congregation* as an explanatory variable for congregational involvement in social services provision. We should stress the study of congregations in New Haven, Connecticut, by Peter Dobkin Hall (1996). He found that the character of congregations established after 1930 differed from that of congregations established prior to 1930. The newer congregations were mostly nondenominational (64 percent). Almost all were located in black or Hispanic communities and followed theologically conservative Baptist, Methodist, or Pentecostal faith traditions.

The literature suggests that white and black congregations differ in the types of social services that they provide (Lincoln & Mamiya, 1990; Chaves & Higgins, 1992). For example, Bartowski and Regis (1999) found, in their nonrandom sample of Mississippi congregations, that black churches and white churches did not provide the same services: "Black churches . . . provide emergency relief (i.e., cash assistance, temporary shelter) as well as educational or skill-based programs targeted at youngsters (e.g., tutoring, after-school programs) with greater frequency [than white churches]" (p. 17). White congregations, however, were more active in supporting people with rent, utilities, and grocery assistance. Chaves and Higgins (1992) also found that services provided by black congregations differed from those provided by white congregations. Similarly, Hill (1998) found that "black churches provide more outreach services than predominately white churches" (p. 27).

Hence, we used *percentage of white congregants* as a measure of members of the majority group in the congregation. In so doing, we grouped all minority groups, including African Americans, Hispanic, and Asians, into one non-majority group.

A congregation's political and theological orientation affects its involvement in social and community services provision (Billingsley, 1992; Dudley & Van Eck, 1992). Politically conservative and/or fundamentalist congregations are less likely to provide social services and more likely to evangelize and proselytize. Roozen, McKinney, and Carroll (1984) characterized evangelistic churches as "otherworldly" in that they emphasize "salvation for the world to come" and make "a relatively sharp distinction . . . between religious and secular affairs" (p. 34). Clydesdale (1999) and Mock (1992), however, questioned whether the allegation that fundamentalist or evangelical congregations disdain worldly affairs and social care would hold up under empirical scrutiny.

It should be noted that some scholars have found no significant relationships between theological stance and involvement in caring for the needs of people in the community. Ammerman (1997), for example, noted that, "If ideas about the Bible can be taken as rough theological indicators, theology does not predict responses to change. Congregations with a predominantly conservative view of Scripture differed a little from congregations with a predominantly liberal view" (p. 342).

To determine the effect of political and theological orientation, we used two dichotomous variables. One compared politically conservative congregations with moderate or liberal congregations. The other compared theologically conservative or fundamentalist congregations with theologically moderate or liberal congregations.

The invention of the automobile in the early 1900s has had a long-term effect on congregational membership. Whereas members once lived within walking distance of their congregations, they are now able to choose their place of worship on the basis of personal preferences, rather than geographical proximity. The traditional parish model in which membership consisted of local residents is long gone, with a few notable exceptions, such as orthodox Jewish communities and Catholic parishes. Many people currently attend congregations outside their neighborhoods. This raises the question of the extent to which commuter congregations are involved in social and community services provision. To determine the effect of nonresident membership on congregational involvement, we used the variable *percentage of congregational members who live within a one-mile radius of the congregation* as a proxy for members who live within the congregation's geographical boundaries.

Results

To perform a regression analysis that considered fifteen variables as potential factors in explaining variability in congregations' involvement in social services provision, we first had to ensure that there were no strong correlations among the variables. If any set of variables was too strongly correlated (a problem of multicolinearity), then the measurement of their effect on involvement would be distorted. Thus, we carried out a series of analyses to determine the intercorrelations among the fifteen explanatory variables.

We found the variable *fiscal status* to be significantly correlated with nine other variables. The strongest correlations were with *number of paid clergy* (r = .375, p<.001); *percentage of families with annual income of $75,000 or above* (r = .254, p<.001); *annual operating budget* (r = .232, p<.001); and *number of active members* (r = .217, p>.001). So many strong intercorrelations pose a major source of bias to the analysis. We therefore omitted *fiscal status* from further analysis.

We also found *number of paid staff* to be significantly correlated with nine other variables. The strongest correlations were with *annual operating budget* (r = .565, p<.001); *number of paid clergy* (r = .532, p<.001); *number of active members* (r = .390, p<.001); and *percentage of families* *with annual income of $75,000 or above* (r = .297, p<.001). We therefore omitted *number of paid staff* from further analysis.

Our analyses showed a strong and significant correlation between congregations with a majority of politically conservative members and those with a majority of theologically conservative or fundamentalist members. We therefore created a new variable, *conservative ideology,* in which politically and theologically conservative congregations were considered as one group. This group included seventy-two (29.1 percent) of the 251 congregations in our study. *Conservative ideology* was significantly inversely correlated with *percentage of single adults* (r = .-247, p<.467). Because these two variables measured two distinct phenomena, we retained both in the analysis.

Thus, three of the original fifteen explanatory variables were excluded from final analysis due to problems of multicolinearity. Of the twelve remaining variables, several showed significant and strong correlations. We nevertheless retained them because they measured important domains of congregational life. *Number of paid clergy* and *annual operating budget* were significantly correlated (r = .595, p<.001). Percentage of members sixty-five years of age or older was significantly correlated with *age of congregation* (r = .309, p<.001) and negatively correlated with *membership growth.*

Our first regression analysis tested the impact of the twelve remaining explanatory variables on the number of areas of involvement of congregations. While the explained variability was significant (R^2 = .214),[7] only one variable—*annual operating budget*—was significant as a predictor of congregational involvement in social services provision. As shown in Table 6-1, *annual operating budget* was the only significant variable in the equation, and its Beta was at least five times that of any other variable.

We used two target variables that measured financial commitment of the congregation: *percentage of operating budget designated for social programs* and *fiscal value of the congregation's programs.* When we regressed the twelve independent variables to assess their ability to explain variability in these two target variables, each regression model yielded a very small explanatory model to account for the variability. In the case of the percentage of operating budget allocated for social and community services, the model yielded an insignificant result (R^2 = .035, p<.05). In other words, the twelve explanatory variables combined could not explain more than 3.5 percent of the variability in the target variable of percentage of operating budget allocated for social and community services.

TABLE 6-1

Regression Models Explaining Congregational Social and Community Involvement

Variable	No. of programs B (St. Error)	Beta	% of budget B (St. Error)	Beta	Fiscal value B (St. Error)	Beta
Constant	11.75 (6.905)		36.328 (51.169)		16761.56 (23165.5)	
Number of active attenders	.0007 (.001)	-.040	.003 (.009)	-.026	1.332 (4.358)	.023
Income of members (% with $75,000 +)	.07 (.078)	-.065	-.412 (.567)	-.055	-456.31 (262.749)	-.125
Annual operating budget	7.953 (1.716)	.409***	7.651 (12.60)	.061	9626.34 (5757.58)	.158
Number of paid clergy	1.755 (1.658)	.082	-3.801 (12.05)	-.028	-3943.29 (5563.89)	-.059
% 65 years or older	.006 (.100)	.004	.933 (.74)	.100	-779.14 (334.73)	-.172*
Membership growth (past 3 years)	-2.552 (3.551)	-.048	42.697 (26.33)	.124	5030.23 (11911.8)	.030
Membership got younger (past 3 years)	1.646 (3.382)	.031	-30.970 (24.98)	-.114	3400.04 (11344.9)	.021
% of whites	.002 (.043)	-.033	-.124 (.315)	-.031	283.30 (143.06)	.146*
Conservative ideology	4.751 (3.892)	-.082	-19.804 (28.72)	-.053	10070.97 (13056.1)	-.056
Age of congregation	.001 (.032)	.030	-.004 (.233)	-.001	91.51 (106.97)	.066
% living within a mile from the congregation	.0006 (.053)	.008	-.366 (.394)	-.066	102.69 (177.43)	.038
% single adults	.006 (.076)	.061	-.384 (.566)	-.051	435.97 (254.1)	.126
Variance explained	$R^2 = .214$		$R^2 = .035$		$R^2 = .096$	

* Significant at the .05
*** Significant at the .001 level.

In the case of the financial value of the congregation's programs, the model accounted for less than 10 percent of the variability ($R^2 = .096$). The independent variables that statistically contributed to this model were *percentage of white members* and, inversely, *percentage of members sixty-five years of age or olde*r. In other words, white and younger congregations tend to provide programs that have a greater financial value, but, while the power of this model is significant, it is very weak.

Implications

The findings presented in this chapter can be viewed as either disappointing or encouraging. The disappointing news is that while we searched the literature and came up with three promising models, the results indicate weak explanatory power. On the other hand, the fact that the independent variables unexpectedly failed to explain the levels of involvement in social and community services provision suggests the existence of a more generic explanation that we mention here and present later on in the book.

Clearly, our statistical models did not tell us much. The finding that the annual operating budget has an effect on congregational involvement in social services provision was not surprising and tell us too little. We were surprised that none of the other fourteen variables made a contribution to explaining variability in the three studied target variables. This means that we cannot predict which congregations are more or less likely to provide and to remain committed to social services by using organizational and member-related characteristics of the congregation. In other words, regardless of the budget, history, size, theology, and demographic makeup of congregations in the United States, most congregations are involved in social and community services provision.

Of course, not all congregations are equally involved in social and community services provision. Nevertheless, we found that the overwhelming majority are involved in social care, even if at a very modest level. While we followed social science tradition by studying the impact of independent variables on the phenomena we wished to explain, the weak results suggest that a different approach is required. We need to look at what congregations are doing and why in the context of the American society and with respect to their historical and social development as described in chapter 2.

The encouraging news is that social and community service provision is not an outcome of the congregation's membership or size but rather seems to be an outcome of a deep-rooted and serious commitment to serve others. What the data suggest, and a point on which we elaborate in chapters 13 and 14, is that social and community involvement is a *congregational norm* and not an activity undertaken only when the means are available and members are young and innovative. The decision to engage in social and community services provision is rooted in the very nature of America's religious communities, and the annual operating budget explains only the number of program areas in which the congregation may be involved. Given that most congregations are involved in at least one social service program, the distinction between the high performers and the low performers is not mediated by budget, size, membership, or theology. Rather, it is mediated by the congregation's commitment to faith-based action and a tradition of congregational care. We suggest that, through the years in the United States, social concern and care by local religious congregations became an expected behavior, almost a standard. Clergy and congregants assume it is their role and responsibility, needy people expect help from congregations as part of the natural order of things, and politicians and the media view this as the American way of life, as if no other way could exist.

7

Comparing Neighbors
Canada and the U.S.A.

It is one thing to claim, as we have, that congregations in the United States are unique in their involvement and impact on the quality of life of individuals. It is quite another to substantiate this claim. We have demonstrated in previous chapters that local religious congregations constitute a significant part of the nation's social safety net. In chapter 2 we have also shown that, compared with congregations in the United States, congregations in Europe are only minimally involved in social and community services provision. But the question remains: are congregations in the United States truly unique in their involvement in social service provision? To answer this question, we need to compare them with congregations in countries similar to the United States.

We attribute congregational social and community involvement in the United States to several factors: the unique separation of state and church, a pluralistic ethnic society, and the market economy of religion in the United States. If these factors explain the impressive involvement of local religious congregations in helping people in need and in enhancing quality of life in the community, is it uniquely American?

We chose Canada for comparison, specifically the province of Ontario. Although the Ontario provincial government fully supports some parochial (Catholic) schools, it does not favor any particular religious group. Furthermore, the government provides no public support for clergy or congregations. Unlike the United States, which does not require congregations to register or file income tax, Ontario requires congregations to register with Revenue Canada. This is actually a minor difference, given that congregations in the United States and Ontario receive no support from the public sector but are eligible for reduced taxation. Furthermore, both the United States and Canada have pluralistic societies, composed of numerous ethnic, cultural, and religious groups.

In a cross-national comparison of congregational involvement in social and community services, it is important to remember that people's needs in one country may differ from those of residents in another country. In Canada, for example, every citizen is eligible for national health care, whereas, in the United States, 14 million children are without health insurance. Canada, which experiences severe winter weather, is also far more involved in providing public housing than is the United States. As a result, homelessness is less of a problem in Canada than it is in the United States. However, under the leadership of former prime minister Brian Mulroney, Canadian national policy in the late 1980s and 1990s began to follow in the footsteps of Ronald Reagan's antiwelfare philosophy and weak central government. While Mulroney and the Conservative party were defeated and almost erased from the political map, in the last years of the twentieth century, in Ontario, Premier Mike Harris moved the province by leaps and bounds into devolution and retrenchment. As a result, Ontario provides fewer social services now than in 1990, and the needs of people in the province are becoming more like those of urban residents in the United States.

It is also important to note that, in Canada, income tax and all other taxes are much higher than in the United States. This is important for two reasons. First, average disposable income is lower in Canada. Second, the people expect the government to produce more public goods than they do in the United States.

Finally, Canada has one important cultural and political distinction: a strong collectivist identity and orientation. In general, the Canadian government allocates rights and privileges to groups (including churches), rather than to individuals (Lipset, 1990). In contrast, the United States is distinguished by individual rights, economic individualism, personal competition, and fewer collectivist arrangements. Although a group may obtain special status as a compensatory mechanism for previous injustices, the U.S. government is committed to equal treatment for all groups that can then act on their own behalf. Canadian history and politics are replete with struggles and attempts to achieve unity by balancing competing claims of different groups (Francophones versus Anglophones, the West versus Ontario and Atlantic Canada, the Inuit and other natives versus Ontario and the Québécois), religious groups included.

Given that Ontario in particular, and possibly Canada as a whole (excluding Quebec), manifests many characteristics similar to those of U.S. cities, it is reasonable to ask whether Canadian congregations are similar to those in the United States. Do they also help people in the community, and do they have a similar impact on the quality of life of people in their communities and beyond?

Religion and Religiosity between Two Neighboring Countries

Before comparing Canadian and U.S. congregational involvement in social and community service delivery, a few words of caution are in order. Our aforementioned question has two components. First, we seek to understand the behavior of congregations and their relationships with people in need. Second, we seek to understand the social policy implications of such findings. Given that calls for congregational involvement in social and community service delivery have been heard in the United States (Cnaan, Wineberg, & Boddie, 1999), and given that Ontario is following in the devolutional footsteps of the United States, it is imperative to understand whether the impact of congregations and religion is similar in both contexts. In other words, if the conditions that have fostered congregational involvement in social and community services delivery are the same in both contexts, and if Ontario congregations are shown to provide social and community services similar to those provided by their neighbors to the south, then it would be logical to expect them to play the same social role as U.S. congregations. A critical step in answering this question is to compare religious participation and contribution to congregations in the United States and Canada, with special reference to the province of Ontario.

In 1994, there were 71,413 charities registered in Canada. Of these, 36 percent (25,458) were classified as "places of worship," making them the single largest category of charities.[8] Of all places of worship in Canada, 9,253 (37 percent) are registered in Ontario, making them the single largest category of charities in the province. Despite their predominance among Canadian charitable organizations, congregations account for only 6 percent of the $90.5 billion revenues received by all registered charities. Overall, charitable organizations receive a sizable portion (60 percent) of their revenues from the government, but congregations receive only 1 percent. Congregations receive the bulk of their revenues from private giving (81 percent) and the remainder from earned income (18 percent). Congregations receive a higher percentage of their budget from private giving than any other type of registered charity (Hall & McPherson, 1997).

In the United States, as we have noted previously, the exact number of congregations and the amount of money generated are not known. Estimates of the number of congregations range from 250,000 to 400,000, with an accepted estimate of 350,000. The fact that congregations in the United States do not need to register or report their income and are less dependent on public authorities makes them more difficult to study.

In 1994, the United States had a population of 260,602,000 people; Canada had a population of 29,619,000 people. On the basis of these figures, the United States has one congregation per 745 residents; Canada has one congregation per 1,163 residents. These numbers indicate either that Canada has larger congregations or that fewer Canadians participate in organized religious life. As we show, Canadian congregations are smaller in size, and religion plays a lesser role in the life of Canadians.

Canadian churches are more hierarchical than those in the United States, which tend to be more congregational in nature (Lipset, 1990). What is most astonishing is that almost 90 percent of Canadians who reported themselves as religious belong to one of the three mainline Christian denominations: Catholicism, Anglicanism, and the United Church (Lipset, 1990). None of these churches can be viewed as fundamentalist and/or anti-institutional. Thus, the rate of prescriptive congregations in the United States is higher than that in Canada. The implication is that, in Canada, most of those affiliated with religious congregations are members of congregations that have a "this-world" orientation, as compared with the United States, where many people are members of congregations that have a "next-world" orientation. The former are more likely to engage in social and community care, while the latter are more likely to focus on evangelism and proselytizing. In a survey conducted by the Angus Reid Corporation, in 1996, 3,000 Americans and 3,000 Canadians were asked about their social and religious involvement. The findings indicate that Americans are much more religious than Canadians, at a ratio of almost 2:1. For example, 40 percent of Americans reported regular or frequent congregational attendance, compared with 20 percent of Canadians (Smidt, Green, Guth, & Kellstedt, 1998). While 22.5 percent of Canadians agreed with the statement that "the concept of God is an old superstition," only 9.6 percent of Americans agreed. The authors concluded that, "Regardless of whether one examines belief in God, specific beliefs related to the Christian faith, or relative significance of a particular religious faith, Americans were significantly more likely to provide 'religious' answers to the questions than were Canadians"(p. 7). Although Canada and the

United States are similar in many ways, Canada is significantly less religious than the United States.

The meaning of religion to people also differs in the two countries. In the United States, religious education implies a moral obligation to do good (see chapter 13). In Canada, the link between the church and good deeds is weaker and is moderated by the state's responsibility to help those in need. Congregations are assumed to be secondary in the quest to help those in need, even by their own members (Lipset, 1990; McRoberts, 1993).

One of the few studies that has measured participation in voluntary activities is the World Value Survey. This survey, a cross-national study of twenty-two countries, done between 1981 and 1983, was designed to compare values and behaviors (Inglehart et al., 1990). Using these data, Curtis, Grabb, and Baer (1992) compared voluntary participation in the United States with that in other countries, particularly Canada. When all types of voluntary activity were combined, they found that people in the United States were much more active in voluntary associations (72.7 percent as compared with 58.2 percent in Canada). However, when congregational participation was excluded from the analysis, the two countries showed striking similarities in voluntary participation: 47.1 percent in the United States and 44.3 percent for Canada. In other words, the United States's vaunted voluntary participation is frequently rooted in active religious participation. These authors noted that "our data indicate that 55% of Americans have church or religious memberships. Except Northern Ireland at 52%, every other nation is at least 20 percentage points below the American figure . . ." (p. 145). These findings tell us that Americans not only feel more religious and pray more often but also are more likely to belong to an organized religious community, most commonly a congregation.

Harvey Lipman (1999) compared the financial giving practices and the memberships of Americans and Canadians affiliated with Protestant churches. On average, members in the United States contributed $498.47, compared with CAD$288.17 in Canada. It should be noted that value of the Canadian dollar is approximately two-thirds that of the U.S. dollar. Lipman also reported that, in 1997, in the United States close to 50 million people were registered church members, compared with 2.5 million in Canada. This gives a membership ratio of 25:1, whereas the population ratio is only 9:1. When population size is controlled for in the analysis, membership in and financial support for U.S. Protestant churches is four times that of Canadian Protestant churches.

Finally, in the mid-1970s, Fallding (1978) found that there were 223 different religious denominational bodies in the United States, compared with only sixty-three in Canada. A later review, based on the *Yearbook of American & Canadian Churches: 1997*, found that, in the mid-1990s, there were 203 different religious denominational bodies in the United States, compared with eighty-five in Canada. Findings from these two different time frames indicate that organized religion is much more diverse in the United States than in Canada.

The literature shows that, compared with Canada, the United States has more people who belong to local religious congregations and that these people, on average, contribute at least twice as much to their congregations. Thus, the combined potential impact of congregations in Canada on their society is likely to be less than that of congregations in the United States. Regardless of their scope and potential impact, we now move to test our key question by assessing and comparing the impact of congregations in the United States and in Ontario, Canada.

Methodological Note

Our Ontario, Canada, study was an in-depth survey of forty-six local religious congregations in three urban areas: Kingston, London, and Toronto. To identify the congregations in each city, we used the local phone directory and a list provided by the local Council of Churches. We combined the lists for the three cities and generated a random list of congregations to be studied. The Ontario sample included fifteen congregations in Kingston, fifteen congregations in London, and sixteen congregations in Toronto.

Demographics of the Ontario Congregations

Membership varied widely among the samples. The mean membership for the Ontario sample was 328 members, whereas in the United States the mean membership was 571, but this difference was not statistically significant. Size of membership varied considerably. The number of members in the Ontario sample ranged from a low of thirty-nine to a high of 5,500 (S.D. = 599), compared with a low of ten and a high of 14,400 (S.D. = 1368) in the United States. United States congregations were not only larger in size but also attracted significantly more people for weekend prayer services. On average, 387 people in each congregation in the United States attended a weekend service, compared with 225, per congregation in Ontario.

The ethnic composition of congregations in Ontario replicated findings for congregations in the United States (see chapter 3). Many congregations were composed solely, or primarily, of people from one ethnic group. In the Ontario sample, thirty-eight congregations (82.6 percent) reported that three-quarters or more of their members belonged to one ethnic group; sixteen congregations (34.8 percent) reported that nearly all of their members belonged to one ethnic group. In both the Ontario and the United States samples, the dominant group was Caucasian. However, the United States sample included sixty-nine (27.5 percent) congregations with 75 percent or more African American members, while the Ontario sample included only one (2.2 percent) such congregation.

Comparison of the two samples showed no significant differences in political and theological orientation, except for theological fundamentalism. Forty percent of congregations in the United States reported themselves as theologically fundamentalist, compared with 25 percent of the Ontario sample. When conservative and fundamentalist orientations were combined, the percentages were similar (56.2 percent in the United States and 58.2 percent in Canada). Politically, the United States sample was slightly more liberal than the Ontario sample. This difference, although not statistically significant, is explained by the higher frequency of African American congregations in the U.S. sample. Having endured continual discrimination, African Americans in the United States tend to be more supportive of publicly funded social programs and less individualistic in their ideology.

Most congregations in both samples were old congregations. The mean date of founding was 1925 in Ontario, compared with 1908 in the United States. This difference was not statistically significant. Most congregations in the sample reported that they have been at the same location for many years. The average number of years for a congregation at the same location was 50.4 years for Ontario, compared with 56.1 years in the United States. This difference was not statistically significant.

As expected, the Ontario sample included a higher proportion of Anglican and United Church of Canada congregations. In the United States sample, no one denomination dominated. Because no one denomination occurred with great frequency in the U.S. sample, denomination-based analysis was not possible.

Although congregations were often housed in buildings that are costly to maintain, only a few congregations were considering relocating. When asked "Are/were there plans for a relocation of the congregation from its current building?" only three of forty-six (6.5 percent) congregations in Ontario answered affirmatively, compared with thirty congregations (12 percent) in the United States. These low percentages are a strong indication that congregations in both the United States and in Ontario consider themselves a permanent part of their communities. In an era of high urban mobility, congregations have become the most stable community institutions and are often viewed as part of the neighborhood. Even non-believers can identify local congregations as part of their personal space and communities.

There was no significant difference in annual operating budgets (excluding building funds and school budgets) between the two samples. An overwhelming majority of congregations (93.6 percent) in Ontario reported annual budgets between $50,000 and $500,000, compared with 71.2 percent of congregations in the United States. Most notably, 16.7 percent of congregations in the United States reported annual budgets of more than $500,000, compared with 4.3 percent of congregations in Ontario. It is important to note that the Canadian budgets were measured in Canadian dollars, the U.S. budgets in U.S. dollars. During our study, the rate of exchange for the Canadian dollar ranged from $1.35 to $1.50 per U.S. dollar. In our comparative analysis, we did not take the exchange rate into account, instead using the face value of the dollar amount. We did this for two reasons. First, given the volatility of the exchange rates during the two years (1997–1998) of the data analysis, determining the exchange rate was problematic. Second, there was minimal flow of income or goods and services between the two countries, and the revenues collected were spent within the local boundaries. Thus, by making the assumption that currencies were at par with each other, we simplified our analysis, but we did not bias the results of the comparative analysis.

The number of full-time paid clergy is another indicator of congregational strength. There were no statistically significant differences between the Ontario and the U.S. samples, although only 15.2 percent of the congregations in Ontario reported no full-time staff, compared with 20 percent in the United States. A significant finding was revealed when we compared the number of full-time paid clergy positions in the two samples. On average, congregations in the United States had 1.63 paid clergy positions, compared with 1.17 positions in Ontario. This indicates that, in addition to having higher operating budgets and receiving greater financial support from their members, congregations in the United States also employ more clergy. This is critical in explaining the following findings on social and community involvement.

Social Service Delivery

As discussed previously, we used three methods to determine the extent to which congregations provided social and community services.

First, we asked interviewees whether their congregation had provided, within the past twelve months, any of the 200 programs listed in our (first) questionnaire. Note that this approach measured only: (1) areas of service in which congregations were involved; (2) whether the program was held on congregation property or elsewhere; and (3) whether the congregations ran the program alone, ran it in cooperation with another provider, or only provided space for the program.

We then asked the congregations what percentage of their annual budget was allocated to social programs and helping others.

Finally, we asked each congregation to identify up to five programs that were most representative of its social and community involvement. For each of these programs, respondents were asked to explain the nature of the program, how it was funded, who the beneficiaries were, where it was carried out, and whether the congregation derived any income from the program. (See chapters 4, 5, and 6 for more detail on the survey methods.)

Areas of Congregational Social and Community Involvement

Of the forty-six congregations in the Ontario sample, all (100 percent) provided at least one formal program. Of the 251 congregations in the United States, four (1.6 percent) provided no formal program. This indicates that, with very few exceptions, congregations in Ontario and in the United States provide a minimum of one program either on their own or in collaboration with another congregation or organization.

The number of service areas in which the United States sample was involved ranged from none to 175, with a mean of thirty-eight areas per congregation. The number of service areas in which the Ontario sample was involved ranged from two to seventy-two, with a mean of thirty-four areas per congregation. These differences are not significant. These high percentages of involvement are similar to those found by the Gallup organization (Hodgkinson and Weitzman, 1993).

In the areas of counseling and programs for families, there were a few statistically significant differences between Ontario and the United States. Ontario congregations were more involved in intergenerational programs and in loss-of-spouse support groups, while U.S. congregations were more engaged in single-parent programs. This is a result of the fact that the United States has a higher proportion of single parents than does Canada.

In terms of services for the elderly, there were no significant differences between Ontario and the United States. However, there were significant differences regarding services for children and youth. Ontario congregations offered significantly more programs that allowed mothers of young children to socialize, whereas U.S. congregations offered significantly more afterschool programs for children and teens. The programs in the United States may be a response to the higher rate of single parenthood and to the need to provide safe, supervised afterschool care for children during hours when many parents are still at work. In Ontario, the concept of the unsafe neighborhood is less common, hence parental concern for their children's safety is less of an issue. In the areas of services for homeless and poor people, both Ontario and the United States had high rates of congregational involvement. However, the congregations in Ontario reported significantly higher rates of involvement with children than did those in the United States.

It is interesting to note that fourteen (5.5 percent) of the congregations in the United States provide services to seasonal workers, compared with none in Ontario. Conversely, Ontario congregations are more involved in programs for refugees and with support for international relief, compared with those in the United States. The reason may be that concern for group rights, including those of refugees and immigrants, is higher in Canada than in the United States, where a more individualistic ideology prevails.

In the areas of health services, U.S. congregations were much more involved in health programs than were Ontario congregations. The most likely explanation is the difference in public health coverage in the two countries. Canada's national health system meets the health needs of most citizens. In the United States, however, many hospitals and foundations work with the community through congregations for health education and promotion.

U.S. congregations were significantly more involved in diet workshops and programs than were Ontario congregations (19.5 percent and 2.2

percent, respectively). The trend in the United States toward using congregational building space as centers for the community was reported by McLaughlin (1998), who reported on diet programs offered by congregations and found them to be sensitive to the needs of people. A similar trend is shown for immunization programs, which occur significantly more in the U.S. congregations (36; 14.3 percent) than in congregations in Ontario (one congregation). Finally, eleven congregations in the United States (4.4 percent) had an artist-in-residence, compared with none in Ontario.

In the area of security, U.S. congregations were more active than those in Ontario. Again, this may reflect need. Given the higher crime rate, especially for violent crime, in the United States, many congregations tend to be involved in community safety issues (DiIulio, 1997). Twenty-three (9.2 percent) congregations in the United States were active in efforts to prevent police brutality, compared with none in Ontario. Similarly, forty-nine congregations (19.5 percent) in the United States were involved in community policing, compared with two (4.3 percent) congregations in Ontario.

In the area of community organizing and development, U.S. congregations were more involved in civic beautification and improvement projects, neighborhood cleanups, sport activities, and interracial collaboration than were those in Ontario. Similarly, U.S. congregations were more involved in social issues such as racism, civil rights, and voter registration. The latter trend seems to be unique to the United States, a country in which the right to vote is not automatic but requires an act of registration. In Canada, the right to vote is guaranteed by the state, and voting certificates are automatically mailed to all citizens.

Compared with the United States, Ontario provides not only more extensive public health provision but also more housing support, even after the retrenchment under the Mike Harris government. The American notion that the "government is not in the business of housing" is not prevalent in Canada, where poor people, despite insufficient housing and long waiting periods, can expect public housing. U.S. congregations (fifty-six; 22.3 percent) reported significantly more building initiatives than did congregations in Ontario (three; 6.5 percent). Homeowner/tenant repairs were organized by fifty-five (21.9 percent) U.S. congregations, compared with five (10.9 percent) congregations in Ontario. Similarly, greater involvement by U.S. congregations was reported in connection with zoning appeals, provision of loans for housing, and advocacy for housing. More than 25 percent of U.S. congregations were involved in house renovation, Habitat for Humanity, and housing coalitions. With the exception of work done with Habitat for Humanity, a significantly smaller percentage of congregations in Ontario were involved in these activities.

What emerges from these findings is that, in many areas, congregations, regardless of region, are socially active. The areas in which Ontario congregations were more involved than those in the United States were helping the homeless, provision of loss-of-spouse programs, international relief efforts, and provision programs for refugees. We discuss these areas later in the chapter. In all remaining areas, U.S. congregations were equally or significantly more active compared to their counterparts in Ontario. U.S. congregations were more active in helping single parents; in providing afterschool and health care programs; in supporting community security and neighborhood organizing efforts; in supporting neighborhood cleanup and beautification efforts; and in renovating housing. The data show that U.S. congregations are more active in areas where need for services has increased due to decreased government service provision and where people in the community are in need. That is, we observed a phenomenon of crowding in where congregations fill out the void created by public entrenchment.

Over the course of our study, it became evident that programs supported by the congregation but carried out by another provider represent a lesser commitment by the congregation. For example, a denominational office may request financial support for a certain campaign, or a local social service agency may ask for volunteers to assist in a seasonal project. In these cases, the congregation makes a deliberate decision to assist but has no control over or ownership of the program. Temporary or minimal support of another's program requires the least amount of work and investment from the congregation. Thus, we wanted to determine whether U.S. congregations and Ontario congregations were more likely to carry out their own social and community programs or to assist in programs carried out by others. For example, if in Ontario sixteen congregations reported being formally engaged in marriage encounters but eleven of them are only supporting the work of others, then 68.8 percent are not providing the service by themselves or hosting it on their property.

We limited our analysis to sixty-seven areas of social and community involvement in which more than 25 percent of the congregations in at least one sample were involved. Of these sixty-seven areas, only in ten cases (14.9 percent) did U.S. congregations report higher percentages of helping others' programs, while for the other fifty-seven areas, Ontario congregations reported that they did not provide the service themselves but only assisted others. Clearly, more U.S. congregations own their programs than do Ontario congregations. When we tested these sixty-seven differences using Chi Square tests of association, only twelve comparisons yielded a significant difference.[9] In eleven of these twelve comparisons, the U.S. congregations tended to take a more direct role in carrying the programs and/or to act as host on their own property.

This accords with our understanding of U.S. congregations as suspicious of cooperating with secular or government organizations, even if they are active in the same social field. Moreover, the U.S. ideology that favors economic individualism and isolationism explains the desire of congregations to own their programs. In contrast, Ontario congregations adhere more to the European tradition of wanting the government to take responsibility for people's needs. In the United States, a congregation's independent help seems feasible and desirable, while, in Ontario, congregations wish for the government to contribute its fair share and are more willing to support larger arrangements without feeling that they may betray their cause or their religious independence.

For example, twenty-four of twenty-six involved congregations in Ontario (92.3 percent) reported that their services for the homeless were not independent programs but rather took the form of support provided to programs run by local coalitions. The comparable figure for congregations in the United States was fewer than 70 percent.

Each of the 200 programs in our original list was reported by at least one congregation. However, some programs were offered by only a few congregations. These programs reflected either a minority interest or a service, such as a dental clinic, that only a very rich or a very large congregation could provide. Data from the U.S. and the Canadian samples confirm that there are wide variations in types of programs offered by congregations in different cities.[10] This finding supports the premise that congregations meet unique and specific needs within their communities by implementing a wide spectrum of programs. It is also probable that congregations that choose to be socially active in their community carry out a local needs assessment and develop programs to fill existing voids. Thus, services offered by congregations in different need areas cover a wide range of human needs and together form an impressive network of social services.

Percentage of Operating Budget Dedicated to Social and
Community Care

The cost of social and community service provision as a percentage of
the annual operating budget is a good indicator of congregational commitment to helping others. This measure includes benevolence (or an
equivalent term), designated budget, support for others' social programs,
collections for special projects such as flood relief and international relief,
clergy discretionary budgets for the homeless and indigent, and indirect
costs of providing space for social and community meeting and programs
at no charge. Also included in this measure, where applicable, is the percentage of clergy salary earmarked for social services. The salary paid to
the clergy by the congregation enables him or her to provide service for
hospitals, nursing homes, prisons, and other community organizations.
Recall that Hodgkinson and Weitzman (1993) found that, on average,
clergy (paid and volunteer) spent one week per month in community services. This is equivalent to a quarter of a full-time position.

As noted previously, seventeen of the 251 congregations (6.7 percent)
in the U.S. sample refused to report the percentage of their budget allocated to social care. Of the remaining 234 congregations, five (1.9 percent)
allocated none of their budget to social service provision. The mean percentage of social and community service provision as a percentage of the
annual operating budget for U.S. congregations was 22.6 percent (S.D. =
18.7). Of the forty-six congregations in the Ontario sample, one congregation refused to answer this question. The mean percentage of social and
community service provision as a percentage of the annual operating budget for the Ontario congregations was 20.2 percent (S.D. = 13.4). This difference was borderline significant (t = 3.4, p = .067).[11] Even if the Canadian and the U.S. dollar were given equal value, the average dollar support
by U.S. congregations for their community would still be higher than that
of the Ontario congregations. Since there are more congregations in the
United States than in Canada, U.S. congregations collectively infuse more
support into their communities than do Ontario congregations.

Representative Findings

Programs/services: The forty-six congregations in the Ontario sample reported a total of 190 programs, with a mean of 4.13 programs per congre-

gation. The 251 congregations in the U.S. sample reported a total of 1,005 programs, with a mean of 4.0 programs per congregation. Every congregation in Ontario reported at least one program, whereas seventeen (6.8 percent) congregations in the United States reported no programs. If we consider only the 234 U.S. congregations that reported at least one program, the mean number of programs would be 4.30 programs per congregation. The difference between the two samples is not statistically significant.

Who benefits: To determine whether a congregation's programs were intended primarily for its own members or for those in the larger community (nonmembers), we asked respondents to indicate for each program: (a) the total number of individuals served monthly and (b) the total number of nonmembers served monthly. We also asked for the numbers of members and nonmembers involved in providing each service. The analysis in this section is per program and not per congregation.

For the Ontario sample, the average number of participants per program provided by and/or housed in a local religious congregation was 142.2; for the U.S. sample, the average was 181.8. The average number of members benefiting from a program was 27.1 in Ontario and 39.5 in the United States. The average number of nonmembers benefiting from a program was 115.1 in Ontario and 142.3 in the United States.

The largest number of beneficiaries in both samples were nonmembers. For the Ontario sample, the ratio was 4.2:1 in favor of serving others; for the U.S. sample, the ratio was 3.6:1 in favor of serving others. The differences between these two ratios, which are statistically insignificant, indicate that many programs offered by local religious congregations are primarily designed to benefit the community at large. The explanation for why Ontario congregations helped more nonmembers may in part be attributed to the larger percentage of their programs that are in support of others and hence serve people outside the congregation.

Program Replacement Values

Program costs incurred by congregations in the Ontario sample varied widely. As in the United States, we asked the respondents to assess monetary support by the congregation; type of space used; its assessed value; in-kind support; and total hours worked by clergy, staff, and volunteers. The results for the two samples are reported in Table 7-1.

TABLE 7-1
Assessed Averaged Monetary Monthly Value of a Social Program and of Congregation by Context

	Ontario/ per program	United States/ per program	Ontario/ per congregation	United States/ per congregation
In-kind support	$79.45	$97.52	$328.13	$390.08
Cost of utilities	$76.46	$142.16	$315.78	$568.64
Financial support	$321.21	$497.26	$1,326.60	$1,989.04
Clergy hours (@ $20 hr.)	$103.22	$507.40	$426.30	$2,029.60
Staff hours (@ $10 hr.)	$233.98	$563.90	$966.33	$2,255.60
Volunteer hours (@ $11.58 hr.)	$1,708.79	$1,754.72	$7,057.30	$7,018.88
Value of space	$478.37	$722.82	$1,975.67	$2,891.28
Total	$3,001.48	$4,285.78	$12,396.11	$17,143.12
Cash support	$43.97	$59.80	$181.60	$239.20
In-kind support	$35.43	$399.30	$146.33	$1,597.20
Total support	$79.40	$459.10	$327.93	$1,836.40
Net value	$2,922.08	$3,826.68	$12,068.18	$15,306.72

In-kind support: The most commonly reported types of in-kind support were food purchases/donations; use of phone; transportation; materials for classes (such as books, papers, notebooks, crayons, and chalks); printing/photocopying services; and postage.

For Ontario, in-kind support for the 190 programs averaged $79.45 per program per month. For the United States, in-kind support for the 1,005 programs averaged $97.52 per program per month. When we multiplied these means by the mean number of programs per congregation (4.13 in Ontario and 4.0 in the United States), the difference between the means decreased. For Ontario, in-kind support averaged $328.13 per congregation per month; for the United States, in-kind support averaged $390.08 per congregation per month.

Cost of utilities: We asked respondents to assess monthly utility costs. For Ontario, the mean utility cost per month was $76.46. For the United States, the mean cost of utilities was $142.16 per month. Utility costs of programs in the United States were twice those in Ontario. One reason for this difference is that many programs in Ontario are not provided on site or are carried out in collaboration with others. When we multiplied the mean cost of monthly utilities by the mean number of programs per congregation (4.13 in Ontario and 4.0 in the United States), the difference between the means narrowed slightly. For Ontario, utility costs averaged

$315.78 per congregation per month; for the United States, utility costs averaged $568.64.per congregation per month.

Financial support by congregations: Again, we treated the Canadian and U.S. dollars as of equal value and considered only formal programs in our analysis. In Ontario, financial support by a congregation averaged CAD$321.21 per program per month; in the United States, financial support averaged $497.26 per program per month. When we multiply the mean financial support by the mean number of programs per congregation (4.13 in Ontario and 4.0 in the United States), the difference between the means narrowed. For Ontario, financial support averaged CAD$1.326.60 per congregation per month; for the United States, the average was $1,989.04 per congregation per month.

Clergy and staff hours: For the Ontario sample, clergy hours per program per month averaged 5.16; staff averaged 23.40 hours. For the U.S. sample, clergy hours per program per month averaged 25.37; staff, 56.4 hours. In other words, Ontario clergy are involved in more programs, but they invest significantly less time per program than do clergy in the United States.

As described in chapter 5, we valued a clergy work hour at $20 and a staff work hour at $10. In Ontario, the value of clergy hours averaged $103.22 per program per month; in the United States, the average was $507.40 per program per month. In Ontario, the value of staff hours averaged $233.98 per program per month; in the United States, the average was $563.90 per program per month. These figures indicate that U.S. clergy and staff spend more time in social and community services provision, even though they are involved in fewer programs. When we multiplied these means by the mean number of programs per congregation (4.13 in Ontario, 4.0 in the United States), the means for Ontario were $426.30 for clergy work and $966.33 for staff work per congregation per month; means for the United States were $2,029.60 and $2,255.60, respectively.

Volunteer work: Our findings show that volunteers are an important resource for congregations in providing community service. For the Ontario sample, 165 (86.84 percent) of the 190 programs used volunteers. For the U.S. sample, 788 (78.41 percent) of the 1,005 programs used volunteers. In Ontario, volunteer hours averaged 147.64 per program per month. In the United States, volunteer hours averaged 151.53 per program per month. These figures indicate a high rate of volunteer participation in community service by congregation members in both samples.

As noted in chapter 5, we valued a volunteer work hour at $11.58 (Hodgkinson & Weitzman, 1993; Brown, 1999). For Ontario, the mean value of volunteer work was $1,708.79 per program per month; for the United States, $1,754.72. When we multiplied these means by the average number of programs per congregation (4.13 in Ontario, 4.0 in the United States), the difference between these means narrowed. In Ontario, the mean value of volunteer work was $7,057.30 per congregation per month; in the United States, $7,018.88.

Space provision: In Ontario, 129 (67.9 percent) of the 190 programs were solely on site; nine programs (4.7 percent) were both on site and off site, for a total of 72.6 percent. In the United States, 828 (82.4 percent) of the 1,005 programs were solely on site; sixty-four programs (6.4 percent) were both on site and off site, for a total of 88.8 percent. The difference between the two sample indicates that Ontario congregations are more likely to support programs provided by others than are U.S. congregations.

To determine the monetary value of the space provided by congregations for social and community service, we asked respondents to assess the market value of the space that they provided for the programs. For Ontario, the value of space provided averaged CAD$478.37 per program per month; for the United States, the average was $722.82 per month per program. When we multiplied these means by the average number of programs per congregation (4.13 in Ontario, 4.0 in the United States), the difference between the means decreased slightly. For Ontario, the mean value of space provided was CAD$1,975.67 per congregation per month; for the United States, the mean was $2,892.28. Higher property values in the United States may account for this difference: two-thirds of the Ontario sample came from smaller cities, while most of the U.S. sample came from large urban centers where property values are higher.

Average monthly value of congregational programs: To assess the monetary value of social programs per congregation per month in each of our samples, we summed up the seven items associated with the overall cost of social service provision (see Table 7-1). For Ontario, the monetary value of congregational involvement in social and community care averaged $12,396.11 per congregation per month; for the United States, the average was $17,143.12. These impressive figures indicate a major contribution and commitment by North American congregations to their communities. They also indicate that for every four dollars provided by U.S. congregations for social and community program, three dollars are provided by Ontario congregations. It is important to note that we measured imputed values, or the equivalent cost of what congregations can give at no or low cost.

These statistics indicate that congregations are actively and generously supporting their communities by providing services. It is therefore legitimate to ask what they receive in return. With the exception of intrinsic rewards such as "fulfilling our mission"or "serving God," congregations receive little material benefit in return. Few programs generate any income for the congregation. To assess the net congregational contribution to society, we deducted the total average monthly income from the total average monthly costs (see Table 7-1). For the Ontario sample, the value of a congregation's social and community care averaged $12,068.18 per month, or $144,818.16 per year; for the United States, the average was $15,306.72 per month, or $183,680.64 per year. When income to the congregation is taken into account, we find that for every five dollars provided by U.S. congregations for social and community programs, four dollars are provided by Ontario congregations. In other words, the gap between the congregations in Canada and the United States narrows. However, one can also suggest that congregations in the United States are more active in obtaining resources to support their efforts, compared to the Ontario congregations.

Summary

In this chapter, we assessed the involvement of United States and Ontario congregations in social and community services. Using data on a sample of three cities in Ontario and seven cities and one town in the United States, we attempted to ascertain whether local religious congregations in the United States and Canada differed in the ways that they served their communities.

We noted that Ontario is similar to the United States in some key respects, such as the disestablishment of church (no public support for churches) and the existence of a diverse cultural and ethnic society. We also noted that, compared with Canada, the United States is more religious. In addition, the United States has a much greater diversity of organized religion, with more fundamentalist groups; a less developed public welfare system; less public trust in government; an inclination to pursue citizen's initiatives through nonprofit arrangements; lower taxes; higher rates of disposable income; and more public safety issues.

Given these similarities and differences, it was our hypothesis that religious congregations in both Canada and the United States would be significantly involved in social and community service provision and that the level of involvement would be higher in the United States. Our hypothesis was supported by the data presented. We found that congregations in Ontario were actively involved in many aspects of social and community services provision. Given the collectivist nature of Canada and its national and provincial government's involvement in the health and social arenas, we were surprised by the amount of social care provided by Ontario congregations. Every congregation in our sample was involved in at least one social program, and most were involved in many more. In this respect, we suggest that in societies where congregations are disestablished and clergy are agents of transformation, involvement in social care is common. It is evident that when a congregation must support itself, as well as make itself a viable place for members, the congregation will venture outside the religious realm into the social life of community and attempt to make itself more relevant to people's lives and needs.

We also found consistent evidence that U.S. congregations are more involved in social and community services provision, compared to Ontario congregations. These findings are not surprising, given that the U.S. government is less involved in welfare provision and that the national ideology supports economic individualism. Congregations in the United States reported, on average, more areas of involvement, allocation of a higher percentage of their annual budget to social programs, and a higher rate of involvement in social services provision. In all three measures of involvement used in this study, U.S. congregations reported higher involvement, even though the differences were not statistically significant in all cases. The implication is that we are not comparing a society in which congregations are giving to their communities and a society in which congregations withdraw from social life. Our findings show that congregations in both societies are involved in social and community services provision but that in one society, the United States, the level of involvement is considerably higher than it is in the other, Ontario.

U.S. congregations are more involved in social service provision than are Ontario congregations for several reasons. One reason is that federal, state, and local governments in the U.S. are less involved in welfare provision than are the comparable governments in Canada. As a result, U.S. congregations are particularly active in the areas of health care, community security, and housing—areas that receive minimal attention from the U.S. government. Each of these fields poses a greater problem in the United States than in Ontario, so there is no real need for Ontario congregations to become involved in them. However, the data also suggest that U.S. congregations are more inclined to provide their services independently, whereas Ontario congregations are more inclined to partner with external groups, including their denominations and the government. In London, Ontario, for example, congregations that reported being involved in helping the homeless all supported a secular coalition to assist the homeless. In the United States, thanks to the ideology of individualism, most citizens view federal, state, and local governments with suspicion. Congregations in the United States tend to echo this sentiment and avoid collaboration with the government so that they can control their own programs.

Another key issue is that compared with Canada, the United States citizens more often express a belief in God, have higher rates of congregational membership, and form more congregations. These findings indicate that Ontario is more secular than the United States. Moreover, the influence on and the contribution to social and community service by congregations in Ontario has less impact, because there are fewer congregations and smaller memberships on those that do not exist.

PART III

Congregations for Society
Additional Studies

8

Small-Town Congregations
The Case of Council Grove, Kansas

Congregations can be studied as closed systems or as open systems. The closed-system approach focuses on the intradynamic and organizational structure of the congregation and does not consider the ways in which the congregation influences or is influenced by its environment. We used this approach in studying, among others, St. Gabriel's Church, in Philadelphia (see chapter 10). The open-system approach focuses on the congregation as an interdynamic organization that influences and is influenced by other religious and secular institutions. We used this approach in our study of congregations in Council Grove, Kansas.

The open-system approach to the study of congregations requires careful consideration of intercongregational networks and their impact on individuals and organizations within a given geographical locale. The examination of these networks is important for two reasons. First, congregations do not operate as self-contained entities but rather interact with other congregations, as well as with other religious and secular organizations. Second, the congregation itself is influenced by members who are active in other civic, political, social, and economic organizations in the community. These members, in turn, influence the community and its organizations by applying congregational norms and culture to their personal and professional lives. Warner and Lunt (1941) described the dynamics of these personal interactions in their pioneering study of congregations in Bridgeport, Connecticut. They found that people who interacted with one another in congregations also interacted on boards of organizations and that these relationships led indirectly to links between religious and secular interests.

Ammerman (1997) described the interrelationship among congregations, members, and other organizations as follows:

Just as a congregation can supplement its own material resources with help from outside, so it can supplement its human resources through the networks in which it and its members are embedded. Co-workers, neighbors, and co-participants in other community organizations are thereby indirectly connected to the congregation. They become potential recruits for the congregation's activities, potential contributors to the congregation's causes. (p. 50)

She further suggested that the congregation itself is also embedded in a network of organizations that are potential resources in its work. Her approach is similar to an open-system approach in that she views the congregation as an integral part of the community. This is also the perspective of the *institutionalist* theory, namely that an organization and its functions are influenced not only by its own internal culture but also by its interactions with similar organizations and their key personnel.

Mesch and Schwirian (1996) studied the effectiveness of neighborhood associations in Columbus, Ohio. They tested several hypotheses to determine which best explained the type of neighborhood association that is most effective in informing residents about threats to the community, influencing policy makers, and representing local residents. They found that the more effective neighborhood organizations were those that collaborated with local business and congregations. They suggested that one explanation may be that congregations and local businesses provide resources (meeting space, office supplies, and human resources), legitimacy, and access to residents. In other words, neighborhood representation is most effective when people from diverse groups collaborate on an ongoing basis, rather than on a time-limited, immediate-need basis. The authors defined this process as "neighborhood embeddedness."

Neighborhood embeddedness is an umbrella term that includes all the ways, including coalitions, by which people in the community come together and exchange information. It is the process that produces norms, local culture, and patterns of interaction, and it is the sum of all formal and informal exchanges outside the family domain. It is argued that the more such exchanges take place, the greater the organizational power of the community. For example, when a congregation is considering a community need, members and clergy first discuss the issue among themselves and reach a consensus. The agreed-upon message is then communicated by members of the congregation to a few individuals or groups. This may be done formally, socially, or in the workplace. In this way, the congregation's position is elaborated and widely communicated and influences local decision making and policies.

In the course of our national study, we found that many congregations had formal and informal collaborations with other congregations and organizations. In some cases, it was a local coalition that focused on specific issues. In other cases, it was the tacit recognition that, if one congregation was already involved in a certain social program, other local congregations should not compete but should concentrate on meeting other human needs. To determine the extent to which intercongregational networks affected the relationship between congregation and community, we conducted a substudy in which we interviewed clergy of all congregations in the small town of Council Grove, Kansas.

We first describe the history, the people, and the key institutions of Council Grove. We then discuss the local congregations and their involvement in social and community services provision. Next, we examine local coalitions and the provision of faith-based social care. Finally, we interpret our findings and discuss the role of "servant churches" and the ways by which congregations, individually and collectively, are crucial in preserving the quality of life for the residents of Council Grove.

Council Grove, Kansas

History: Council Grove, a small town in the center of Kansas on the banks of the Neosho River, is known as the "Rendezvous on the Santa Fe Trail." The term reflects the town's historical claim to being the last trading post and the last civilized town on the Santa Fe Trail during the westward migration in the nineteenth century. Each year, traders loaded down with supplies would flock to Council Grove, where other traders were waiting to outfit their wagon trains for the long trek west.

Council Grove got its name from the historic 1825 treaty council between the Osage tribes and the U.S. government concerning the government's desire to survey the Sante Fe Trail. In 1846, the government signed a treaty with a small tribe called Kansa or Kaw, for whom Kansas is named. The treaty required the tribe to relocate to the upper valley of the Neosho River, not far from Council Grove. The following year, two traders, licensed to trade with the Kansa tribe, established a trading post at Council Grove and made Seth M. Hays their permanent representative. Hays, who later got his own license to trade with the Kansa, was an ambitious entrepreneur. He built the first house and the first store in Council Grove, in 1847. By 1867, he had opened two supply stores for travelers on the Santa Fe Trail, a hotel, and Hays House, a restaurant that is still in operation.

In 1851, a few years after Hays's arrival, the Methodist Episcopal Church established the Kaw Mission in Council Grove. The purpose of the Kaw Mission, which was supported by government funding, was to educate the Kaw tribal members, introduce them to modern ways, and integrate them into the white Christian society of traders and settlers. The school closed in 1854 because it was deemed impossible to educate the Kaw in the "Christian way." The Kaw people refused to be assimilated and to assume the Western way of work and thinking. The building was later used as a school for the children of the settlers and traders. The Kaw Mission now serves as a state-operated historic site to tell the history and cultural heritage of the Kansa and other native cultures.

In 1858, Council Grove held its first term of court and appointed its first sheriff. In 1869, the Missouri, Kansas, and Texas (Katy) Railroad was built, and soon trains were bringing new citizens to Council Grove. In 1873, the Kansa Indians were again removed from their land and relocated to Indian Territory, now Oklahoma. The Indian land was opened to white settlers. With the lure of easy access and land to be had, Council Grove was no longer a transitory junction on the road to New Mexico but a thriving small town where both commerce and agriculture held sway.

The town today: Council Grove, in Morris County, has 2,300 residents. Another 250, mostly retirees, live in a nearby lakeside community. The closest neighboring town is fifteen miles away, and its serving cities are forty miles away. Patients with medical emergencies are flown by helicopter to Topeka, the nearest city with a major medical facility. Most Council Grove residents are employed in the construction and agriculture industries, as well as in the emerging service industry.

Local institutions: As in many small towns, life in Council Grove centers around a few key institutions, most of which have a long history. Moreover, like many small towns, Council Grove has a Main Street where most of its stores are located.

A major institution and a means of information sharing in Council Grove is the *Council Grove Republican*, which has been in continuous operation since 1872 and under family ownership since 1947. The town newspaper, which is published daily, reports some national news, but the emphasis is on local news that ranges from welcoming newcomers to the visit of our research team. The Hays House restaurant, which boasts the honor of being the oldest restaurant still in operation west of the Mississippi, serves as the social hub for local residents and people from nearby towns.

As in many small towns, Council Grove has clubs and organizations that serve as venues for social gatherings and, occasionally, social care. These include the American Legion, Kiwanis Club, Rotary Club, and civic groups such as Community Arts, Friends of the Library, Friends of Kaw Heritage, and the Committee for the Bowers (civic) Center. There are also three investment clubs, which also include some residents of the Council Grove Lake.

Local customs and traditions are well preserved because Council Grove is a small town where everyone knows everyone else through work, church, leisure activities, and/or clubs and committees. This complex web of interactions strengthens and extends social networks and reinforces both formal and informal means of social control. People report to each other what they know, and behavior that is considered not normative is socially sanctioned. For example, a female minister who intended to marry a widower from the congregation was forced to take a leave of absence because the community felt that the marriage came too soon after the death of the wife. The feeling was that anyone who violated the town's norms of acceptable behavior, even a minister, should receive a sanction. Nevertheless, some members of the congregation supported her actions and left the church when she left her post. When her leave of absence ended, her denomination gave her a new pastorate, but not in town.

The Churches of Council Grove and Their Members

Council Grove has nine churches, seven of which we studied using all research instruments; two were studied separately for this chapter. These congregations were the Berean Baptist Church, Congregational Church, Council Grove Christian Church, Council Grove United Methodist Church, First Baptist Church, Lutheran Church, and United Pentecostal Church.[12] The only non-Protestant congregation in Council Grove is St. Rose of Lima, a Catholic church.

The Protestant congregations resembled one another with the exception of the United Pentecostal Church. This church, which serves mostly seasonal workers from all over the region and low-income families from the county, reported that it had no social ministry because its sole mission was to save souls. The part-time pastor, who also ran the local bakery, said he chose not to join any ministerial group because the other pastors became upset when he insisted that the only goal of clergy should be to help people find God.

Two churches in Council Grove have very small congregations. One, a Methodist church that meets in an abandoned one-room schoolhouse at the edge of town, has five active members. This church is located outside Council Grove, but its members are part of the town, and Council Grove is the center of their activities. The other, a Lutheran church on Main Street, has thirty-five active members. Despite the fact that neither has full-time clergy, the churches are determined to remain open. This resilience supports Rathge and Goreham's (1989) findings that rural congregations "show more tenacity in periods of residential loss than they show desire to expand in response to population growth" (p. 66). For the most part, the congregations in Council Grove have remained stable despite population changes over the past fifty years. In fact, even the number of residents remains stable: one of our interviewees informed us that when she grew up seventy-five years ago, there were 2,300 residents, the same as there are today. In her words: "only the people change. . . ."

Characteristics of the Council Grove congregations: Although we have discussed several characteristics of the Council Grove congregations in previous chapters, we wish to reiterate the characteristics of the seven congregations included in this particular study.

Each of the congregations was established before 1940. Active membership—those who attend at least monthly—ranged between sixty and 325 individuals per congregation (with the exception of the two small congregations). Five of the seven congregations (71.4 percent) reported an operating budget of less than $100,000; two congregations (28.6 percent) reported slightly higher budgets. In most cases, the cost of church maintenance was lower than that of congregations in big cities because members provided extensive volunteer and in-kind support and because salaries and goods are usually lower in rural areas. None of the congregations apply for grant support. With the exception of one congregation that benefits from a bequest, all income is from members' pledges and offerings. Most congregational members (89 percent) live within ten blocks or walking distance of the congregation. Only one church has two full-time ministers. Five have one full-time minister; one has a part-time minister.

Those who attend church and why: With few exceptions, Council Grove residents are white Christians. An African American church existed at one time but disbanded as the African American population in Council Grove decreased. One resident, raised as a Jew, described himself as nonreligious. He had moved to Council Grove to work for a company and eventually became the owner. His wife and children attend one of the mainline Protestant churches. This church does not require him to go through a formal conversion, and he attends the church on an infrequent basis and commits money and expertise when asked. To his way of thinking, church membership has more to do with being part of the community than with religious or spiritual goals. The community accepts him and the business he now owns.

One measure of the importance of congregational life in Council Grove is that every congregation in town, with the exception of the two small ones, has made extensive improvements within the past ten years. These improvements ranged from building new facilities to extensive remodeling of existing facilities. The congregations paid for the costs either by fundraising or by taking out a mortgage. Several congregations hired an architect and a construction company to perform the work; in others, the congregants did the work themselves.

Another measure of the importance of congregational life is church membership. Approximately half (1,305) of the town's residents are active members of local congregations. This number does not include residents of the local nursing home, who are ministered to separately by most of the local clergy on a rotating basis. On average, 1,140 people attend regular Sunday services. Many also meet regularly for Bible class before attending Sunday service. Attendance increases dramatically during Easter and Christmas services. It is interesting to note that 87.6 percent of Council Grove residents listed as active members attend church weekly, compared with only 68.9 percent in our urban sample. One possible explanation is that church attendance is indicative of expected behavior in this small town.

What is more important in a small town like Council Grove is the number of people who attend church regularly but are not official members of the congregation. These people show the real changes in the local religious ecology. Local people do not officially abandon their congregation; instead, they attend a different congregation that better meets their needs. The mainline Protestant churches reported an average of 140 nonmembers, or 10 percent of those who attend services at least once a week. Catholic and Pentecostal churches reported only four nonmembers who attend services at least once a week. Many of the town's pastors told us, with obvious pride, that local residents often switch churches because they are attracted by a new program or a new approach to Sunday services introduced by the pastor. Few, however, become official members. For example, when the female minister mentioned earlier left her position, she began to attend another church. She did this so that the new minister who replaced her would not feel pressured by her presence in the congregation. Although several members followed her to the other church, neither the former pastor nor her followers officially changed their religious affiliation. As such, she was still officially a Methodist but attended and supported another church.

Attending a church with which they are not formally affiliated does not imply that the people of Council Grove are not serious about their religious beliefs. On the contrary, most are sincerely concerned about leading good Christian lives. However, church life in Council Grove is an important part of the town's social fabric, and the people tend to attend the church in which they feel most at home, whose membership best reflects their own culture, and whose mission best represents their own values, rather than the church of their childhood (Eiesland, 1999).

Cooperation in Social Service Delivery

Ammerman (1997) studied many congregations in communities that have experienced demographic and or economic changes. She found that the congregation most likely to survive in a changing environment was the *niche congregation*. Ammerman noted that, "in the sense in which the term is used here, a niche congregation is one that successfully garners enough resources from a large institutional environment to be able to offer a distinctive array of services with little competitive overlap" (p. 384). In other words, a niche congregation does not isolate itself from its environment. Such a congregation studies the resources, needs, and opportunities of its environment and adapts itself to that environment. Ammerman's findings are important because it is often assumed that congregations develop their activities and social ministries in isolation from one another, either without knowledge or without regard for what other local congregations are doing. This was clearly not the case in Council Grove.

The congregations of Council Grove tend to be well-organized niche congregations. They know what the other local congregations are doing;

they plan their programs and activities in informal concert; and they avoid duplication of social services that are being provided by another congregation. For example, the staff of the Council Grove Christian Church reported that when their new pastor came to town, his first concern was religious preaching and teaching; his second was to determine what his church could do to attract new members. After reviewing the services provided by the other churches, he found that none of the extant services focused on the town's high school students. Consequently, the congregation committed itself to youth services. The congregation hired a youth minister, added a church wing with a huge hall that could serve as a venue for youth-related activities, and worked out an arrangement with the high school to work with the students during and after school time. The church has now became a hub for young people, and the pastor has gained access to the teen-age population of Council Grove.

Another niche congregation, the Berean Baptist Church, serves younger children. The congregation acquired a bus and transports young children to its location every Wednesday for a Kids Club. The club provides social activities, as well as "character building and religious teaching" activities. The program is open to children in kindergarten to sixth grade.

The Congregational Church has filled a niche through its social service provision. When the current pastor, a native of the region and the former pastor of an urban congregation, arrived, he found himself with a congregation whose members were, for the most part, age sixty-five years or over. To revitalize the church and to attract new members, the pastor and the congregation decided to provide a social service. In conducting a needs assessment of the community, they found that single mothers, eligible for the then-existing AFDC benefits, were running out of money three days before the end of each month, despite careful use of their benefits. The congregation identified these mothers and offered them cash support to make up for the shortfall. What is important here is not the program per se but the fact that the congregation actively sought a niche, identified it, and filled it. The church's unique social ministry revitalized the congregation and attracted local residents, previously unaffiliated with this congregation.

The Congregational Church, which had experienced dynamic growth under the leadership of its pastor, was devastated when he resigned for personal reasons. However, under the leadership of a new pastor, a former teacher in the town, the congregation began a collaboration with the local community center to provide drama classes and cultural activities for children and youth.

These examples show that congregations within the same geographic area, at least in a small town, do exchange information with one another, are aware of what others are doing, and are affected by one another's other activities. Although the Congregational Church would have liked direct access to the local youth in Council Grove, it recognized that provision of youth services would not only be competitive with the Christian Church but also unproductive, since it had neither a large assembly hall nor a youth minister and its members, for the most part, were elderly. Yet churches must attract young people if they are to survive. When direct service to youths is already being provided by another congregation, then congregations must seek access to this important population through other means, such as collaborative efforts with youth-serving groups such as the school or the community center. This was the approach taken by the Congregational Church, and it is indicative of the ways in which niche congregations adapt their programs to local needs and intercongregational dynamics.

In a small geographical area such as Council Grove, the town culture makes it very clear that it is not socially acceptable for congregations to compete with one another in service provision. Given the complex social web that connects the members of one congregation with the other residents of the town, the attitude seems to be that only an extremely worthy cause or an extremely charismatic pastor could ever justify taking over another congregation's service domain. Eiesland (1999), in her study of congregations in Dacula, Georgia, noted a similar attitude. She noted that "religious organizations often behave in ways that are more relational than autonomous—assisting with community projects, sharing information about distressed locals, or supporting anti-crime or pro-life campaigns" (p. 16).

Local Ministerial Coalitions

Historically, Council Grove was a stopping-off point for people headed west. From its earliest days, local people served traders and helped travelers in need. This tradition continues even today through a hospitality coalition composed of all the town's pastors, with the exception of the pastor of the Pentecostal Church, as previously noted. This coalition, "Care and Share," has a small budget earmarked for food, lodging, and, at times, travel costs for travelers in need and for new people. The pastors meet with them; determine their needs; offer ad hoc, short-term help; and, if necessary, contact relatives or friends who can provide additional help. For newcomers to Council Grove, "Care and Share" offers help with making a rent deposit, paying utilities, or getting a telephone connected. In addition, "Care and Share" asks each participating church to keep containers where people can see them and so are reminded of people's needs and where foodstuffs are collected. The local grocery owner, who is an active church member, also keeps a similar container in his store.

Modest as the hospitality coalition is, it is important for several reasons. First, it represents a collaborative effort by the town's clergy and the congregations that support the effort financially. Second, the coalition, which has been in operation for many years, is well known to the local police and business people, who alert the coalition when they encounter out-of-towners in need. Finally, this coalition has helped serve as the basis for other local ministerial coalitions in Council Grove.

Just as the hospitality coalition cares for out-of-towners in need, an informal mechanism is in place to help local residents in need. It is neighbor-to-neighbor help and not necessarily associated with church membership. People know and respond to the needs of others in their town. In some instances, a note will be left in the town's only grocery store. In others, news will be spread by word of mouth that a certain family or individual needs help. Goods, money, and needed services are often provided anonymously so that those in need may not be shamed. Only in extreme cases will people apply directly to the churches for assistance. No cash is provided, only goods and services.

The local thrift shop is sustained through a collaborative intercongregational effort. The shop, open twice a week, offers clothing and household items at very low prices and serves many needy families in the region. Two volunteers manage the store, and two congregations send volunteers each week to assist in sorting and stocking the items to be sold. Congregational support has been essential to the operation of the thrift shop and has enabled those in need to avoid the stigma that is often associated with direct handouts.

Another example of ministerial collaboration is the nursing home coalition. The coalition was initiated by the pastor of the First Baptist Church in response to a request from the local nursing home. He approached the other local pastors, who agreed to rotate responsibility for ministering to the spiritual and pastoral needs of the nursing home residents. Each Saturday, the designated pastor visits the nursing home, talks with the residents, and holds a worship service. The pastors are on call by the nursing home during the week prior to their scheduled visit should any of the residents require pastoral care. By banding together in this way, the local clergy have been able to serve this often neglected population without placing too heavy a burden on the individual pastors.

As noted previously, the Congregational minister and his congregation had considered ways in which they could improve the quality of life in Council Grove. To ensure greater civility in police work and to prevent police brutality, the pastor initiated a police pastoral coalition. As with the nursing home coalition, each of the participating pastors is on call for a week once every two months. These pastors meet with those who have been arrested and have requested pastoral counseling. They also ride with the police on patrol, which has helped reduce the incidence of violence and vulgarity among those on the force. In turn, the police have an opportunity to discuss their own needs and concerns with the clergy. The police pastoral coalition, like the other successful ministerial coalitions in the town, has helped to enhance the collaboration between the churches and civic and public bodies in Council Grove.

Ministerial coalitions in Council Grove provide convincing evidence that, although each church operates independently in term of its worship services and maintenance of its facilities, each pastor is well informed about what the others are doing. It is through the pastors that most of Council Grove hears and knows what is going in. Since all the pastors, whether full-time or part-time, live in the town, they are part of the local social network. What the pastors hear—when dining at the Hays House, shopping in the local stores, or talking with town and county officials—invariably makes its way to their pulpits. The voice of the local pastors is a strong one in Council Grove, and, despite the inevitable competition for new members, they willingly exchange ideas and opinions with one another, both in private and in public.

Shannon Jung and her colleagues (1998) have provided a typology of possible cooperative ministry structures. The model that is most applicable to Council Grove is that of *cluster group*: "a group of churches located in the same geographical area with a loosely knit organization which allows the congregations to engage in cooperative programs in varying degrees" (p. 188). According to the authors, ecumenical cooperative ministries are especially important in rural areas where formal authorities often fail to meet the unique needs of rural populations. Such cooperatives are most effective when they are initiated with the aid of the laity. Indeed, throughout our study we found that social programs that were initiated and owned by member congregants were the best protected and sustained.

Social Services Provided by Local Congregations

Earlier, we assessed the overall involvement of Council Grove congregations in social and community services provision. In this section, we recap several of these findings, while emphasizing the unique character of congregational social services provision in this small town. Specifically, social service provision is informally coordinated to meet as many needs as possible; each congregation has its own service niche; each congregation knows what the others are doing; and existing programs are taken into account before new programs are initiated.

As reported in Table 5-1, the fiscal value of the social and community programs provided by seven congregations in Council Grove is much less than that of programs provided by urban congregations ($1,066.46 versus $4,285.78). With the exception of cash contributions for social services, congregations in Council Grove give less in every category, including volunteer work, value of space, and in-kind support. On average, Council Grove congregations allotted 27.8 percent of their operating budget to social services, compared with the mean of 22.6 percent in our sample of 251 congregations.

Twenty-seven different programs were reported by seven congregations in Council Grove. On average, seventeen congregational members and fourteen nonmembers were involved in the provision of each program. On average, thirty-one congregational members and 182 nonmembers benefited from each program. The ratio of nonmembers to members was 5.9:1. The ratio for those served by urban congregations was 3.6:1.

The finding that beneficiaries of congregational programs in Council Grove were, for the most part, nonmembers indicates that the people of Council Grove know their neighbors and their needs. Moreover, every effort is made to spare recipients any public embarrassment. For example, a food parcel may be left at the door of a needy family with no indication of who provided or delivered the food. Family history and capability further determine specific courses of help. For example, one interviewee told of hiring the sons of a needy family to do some chores so that they could have a few dollars to spend like other kids their age. Furthermore, because the boys' parents had previously taken whatever money their sons made, the church opened an account for the boys and allowed them to charge purchases in two local stores and the "5-and-Dime." The church members' familiarity with the family and with the local merchants enabled them to tailor a specific response to a need. Small-town life enables people also to know who is "worthy" of help and who is not. People are judged on their past behavior and local reputation, and the churches do little to help those labeled "unworthy."

Self-sufficiency or the effort to become self-sufficient is a decisive factor in the willingness of people in Council Grove to help others. Should a person or family run into financial problems for what is viewed as a legitimate reason, such as job loss or disability, then help is generally available. However, should persons or families be perceived as not trying to help themselves, then little or no help is provided. For example, when we noticed a man who was most likely inebriated, we were told in no uncertain terms that his behavior was well known around town and that he would not be assisted by "our church," unless he were very ill. On the whole, the congregations in Council Grove do not appear to have strict eligibility rules for service provision. The decision-making algorithm is quite complex, and the amount of support offered to people with similar needs often differs according to their standing in the community and the congregation's perception of how well a particular person or family will use the resources provided.

Summary

Dudley and Johnson (1993) have categorized churches according to their involvement in the provision of social services. The *servant church* is defined as a congregation that "responds to individuals, whoever they are and whatever they need. Servants know people by name and reach out to help them one by one. In small towns this is a way of life" (p. 73). Over the years, servant churches tend to institutionalize their caring into more organized programs, yet still offer recipients care that is informal and personalized. This "servant church" spirit permeates not only the churches in Council Grove but also the entire town. This spirit is expressed in many ways: from the note in the local grocery store listing items needed by someone in need and the personalized response of congregations to requests for help to the efforts to improve quality of life for one's neighbors.

This spirit is also evident in the ways in which those who provide the help seek to assure the dignity of those being helped.

Servant churches tend, for the most part, to be politically conservative in their social attitudes. Our study of the congregations in Council Grove supported this finding. With the exception of the Methodist Church, the churches reported that most of their members were politically conservative. Those in the Methodist Church were reported to be politically moderate. We found the dominant ideology in Council Grove to be that of economic individualism (people are responsible for their own well-being and for that of their families), coupled with interpersonal loyalty that results in a preference for private, rather than public, support for those in need. With regard to theological orientation, the Pentecostal and the Baptist churches reported that most members were fundamentalists. The Catholic and the Methodist churches reported their members to be moderate in their beliefs. The remaining congregations reported their members to be liberal.

In their study of a small town, Dudley and Johnson (1993) reported that the poorer people did not attend the local United Methodist church but drove twenty miles to a Pentecostal church or to the Assembly of God church. Such self-selection based on socioeconomic status was also evident in Council Grove. The local Pentecostal church attracted only those whose annual income was less than $25,000. As mentioned, this church, the only one not involved in any form of social ministry, focused exclusively on theological teaching and worship. Its concept of a holistic ministry clearly did not include helping others but focused only on catering to people's spiritual needs. The Pentecostal pastor informed us that theologically he sees his role not in social ministry but rather in teaching people the ways of the Lord and in helping them become better Christians. In fact, he was quite annoyed with our interview schedule and preferred to focus our conversation on spiritual matters and on the level of religiosity that we possess.

Servant churches are more likely to form service coalitions with nearby churches of similar theological and socioeconomic backgrounds. In some cases, these are formal coalitions that have a board of directors, a separate budget, and organized procedures. In others, the coalitions are very informal and are based on a consensus reached by a group of local clergy or congregational representatives. However, "in general, servant churches form only a few partnerships, and they turn more to other churches than to agencies." Our findings support this view. We found that the churches of Council Grove had four such coalitions and one joint social ministry (a thrift shop). With the exception of the local school (a major ministry of one church) and the local nursing home, the churches were not involved in coalitions with local social service agencies.

David Roozen, William McKinney, and Jackson Carroll (1984), proposed a typology to characterize how congregations orient themselves vis-à-vis their communities. According to their typology, these congregational orientations may be classified as (1) civic; (2) activist; (3) sanctuary; or (4) evangelistic. Civic congregations strive to be good citizens of the community, provide assistance when possible, and do not significantly challenge the status quo. Civic congregations are the servant congregations described by Dudley and Johnson (1993), and their main emphasis is on helping the individual to do better in society. In contrast, activist congregations are involved in political lobbying, protests, and boycotts as a means of bringing about social change. Billingsley (1999) noted that many activist congregations tend to attack social problems and meet human needs independently, even when, "clearly, there are times when collaboration might be more timely and more effective" (p. 119). In our study, we found no activist congregation in Council Grove. The congregations were committed to helping those perceived as worthy of help but had no interest in initiating social change. Sanctuary congregations are those that seek to shield members from worldly temptations and prepare them for the world to come. None of the Council Grove congregations fit this classification. Evangelist congregations see themselves as agents for changing individual lives. The Pentecostal Church in Council Grove fit this classification because of its emphasis on personal religious transformation and salvation and its view of itself as a haven in a demanding and difficult world.

As noted previously, the only congregation in Council Grove that did not engage in any form of social service was the Pentecostal Church. There are two possible explanations for this decision: one is theological; the other, economic. Theologically, Pentecostals emphasize the gifts of the Holy Spirit (such as divine healing, speaking in tongues, and prophecy). They believe that God still speaks through prophets and that people must first be saved before they can change. Thus, most Pentecostal congregations focus on helping people find their way to God rather than on intervening in their worldly problems (Anderson, 1987). This was made evident during our study in Council Grove. The Pentecostal minister had no interest in assisting with our study and focused only on the issue of our personal salvation. He told us that the only role of the church should be bringing souls to Jesus, not engaging in social issues. His belief is so strong that he avoids meeting with the town's other pastors so as not to create tension.

Economics may also explain the nonparticipation of the Pentecostal Church in social service provision. Its pastor is part-time, and half of the families in the congregation have annual incomes of less than $25,000, and the remainder have incomes under $50,000. This means that the congregation has limited financial resources, and the pastor has limited time to devote to nonreligious issues. The literature suggests that monetary and staff resources are significant in explaining a congregation's level of involvement in social service provision. Compared with the other congregations in Council Grove, the Pentecostal Church had the fewest resources available for investing in social services and a pastoral leader with no personal interest in the matter.

What we learn from the study of congregations in one small town is that the network of congregations is viable and extensive. The clergy knew each other and civilly competed over members and status, while at the same time they cooperated and shared information. Each church dreams of being the strongest and largest and develops socially important projects that appeal to potential members. However, this does not detract from the many clergy coalitions they form and the support they give to any congregation in need. They cooperate mostly in not developing competing services, respecting each other's "turf," and supporting large-scale social projects. Thus, there is constant movement and constant changes in power, while, at the same time, there is a sense of stability among the old congregations: most have been in the town for more than fifty years. The congregational ecology of Council Grove is one of energy, exchange of information, and ongoing attempts to become more relevant and to attract new members.

9

Mediating Structures
The Greater New Orleans Federation of Churches

The Pluralistic Approach

Ideologies differ widely when it comes to the power relationship between a state and its citizens. Many people believe that the primary duty of government is to protect and serve citizens, including those in need, while others believe that the government should relegate the responsibility for service provision to others. The problem with these positions is that each views the relationship as a two-player game: government and citizens. What they fail to consider is that there is a third—and equally important—player: the many nonprofit and voluntary bodies that mediate the power relationship between government and citizens.

In contrast to those who take extreme ideological positions, some take a pluralistic approach that emphasizes the importance of competing interests in the political arena. This perspective, linked with the traditional American distrust of "Big Government," provides us with a more inclusive theory of social service provision. In simplest terms, it argues that the government cannot be all-protective and all-caring of all citizens and that a too-powerful government may override citizens' rights. Thus, mediating bodies are needed to moderate the state's power and protect the rights of all citizens, including the poorest ones. These mediating bodies are the many voluntary organizations that represent local residents or communities of shared interests.

Voluntary Organizations as Mediating Structures

Peter L. Berger and John Neuhaus, in their 1977 book *To Empower People: The Role of Mediating Structures in Public Policy*, characterized mediating voluntary associations as independent of the state and composed of citizens who are interested in protecting their shared interests vis-à-vis the power of the state. These associations, although not affiliated with the government, perform many essential public tasks. Ideally, the government should encourage the establishment of voluntary associations because these associations help the state to carry out its work. Thus, mediating associations share the public sphere with the government. Each respects the other's contributions, and each makes sure that the other will not become too powerful.

Our view is that the government has an important but limited role in helping people in need and that the government's role should be complemented by the work of mediating organizations. Although services such as income transfer (for example, social security) should be the primary responsibility of the government, other services can and should be delivered by local mediating structures. These organizations can better assess the unique needs of residents and develop ways to meet their many and constantly changing needs. One of the important local mediating organizations is the local religious congregation (Lugo, 1998).

In tandem with the pluralistic view of welfare, we need to examine the concept of *civic society*. We define civic society as a sphere of social interaction between economy and the state, composed above all of the intimate sphere (the family), the sphere of association (voluntary organizations), social movements, and forms of direct public communication (Cohen and Arato, 1994), which are the basis for the formation of social capital (Coleman, 1990). This term applies to a society in which intermediary organizations buffer the power of the state against its citizens. In fact, some people refer to nonprofit organizations as the "civic society sector." It is *civic* in the sense that concerned citizens organize themselves into groups that represent certain preferences or viewpoints; as a group, these citizens pressure politicians and other decision makers to support their agenda. These groups sometimes produce goods and services with the implicit or explicit approval of the state. Their existence helps to ensure that local viewpoints and preferences have a place at the decision-making table.

Congregations are authentic community mediating organizations. They exist in every part of every city and every town. People from all walks of life are members of congregations and are willing to contribute time and money for the benefit of others. Furthermore, clergy are authentic local leaders. The following story, which was highlighted in the public media, illustrates the role of clergy and churches as mediators between the state and local residents.

According to Berrien and Winship (1999), the continuing decline of juvenile homicide and delinquency in Boston, especially in the neighborhood of Dorchester-Roxbury, provides a model for the nation. Unlike other cities, in which the decline in these antisocial behaviors have resulted from massive arrests and excessive police force used against young, primarily African American, males, Boston has used minimal police force. This approach has won acceptance from an otherwise hostile and suspicious community.

Ten-Point Coalition: The Boston model began in 1992 when pastors from forty congregations and local leaders formed the Ten-Point Coalition. The key leaders were the Reverends Jerry Brown, Ray Hammond, and Eugene Rivers, three local ministers who were well known by neighborhood youths and their families.

Prior to the formation of Ten-Point, inner-city residents had refused to cooperate with the police, whom they felt were hostile to the community and who the community believed arrested young people without just cause. Once the coalition was in place, Ten-Point served as a buffer between the neighborhood and the police. To the community, the coalition leaders made the case for cooperation with legitimate police policies; to the police, they made the case for the community's need for respect and protection against police brutality. The ministers involved in Ten-Point are well recognized, respected, and trusted; the residents have followed their lead. Rates for juvenile crimes and homicide in Boston have continued to decline, with minimum cost to both sides. In the words of Berrien and Winship:

> Ten-Point has changed the way the police (and other elements of the criminal justice system) and Boston's inner city community relate to each other. They have done so by becoming an intermediary institution between the two parties. They have been able to create a balance between the community's desire for safe streets and its reluctance to see its children put in jail. In doing so, they have created what we term an "umbrella of legitimacy" for police to work under.

The success of the Ten-Point Coalition is due to several factors: the sense of crisis that permeated the community in the early and mid-1990s, the charisma of the key leaders, the tolerance and understanding of the police, and the residents' shared quest for solutions. Ten-Point is also unique in its intermediary pluralistic structure. As such, it shows the potential power of a local coalition to act on behalf of citizens in mediating the power of government.

The Ten-Point Coalition is a remarkable model. In particular, it demonstrates that clergy and congregations can become effective intermediary organizations when they form coalitions. Ammerman (1997) noted that:

> In other cases, congregations may belong to coalitions that help them to pool resources in meeting the needs of the community. Some of these coalitions may be explicitly religious, but others may include a variety of agencies and businesses and community organizations. In addition to these local alliances, congregations can extend their reach by participating with any of the hundreds of "parachurch" organizations, from Habitat for Humanity to the Christian Coalition. (p. 50)

The real power of faith-based coalitions, or coalitions that include congregations, is that it provides more representation and access to local residents than would otherwise be available. Few alternative organizations that resemble local religious congregations are to be found throughout the country, located close to where people live and attended regularly by at least half the adult population.

Jackson and his colleagues (1997) found that "belonging to a coalition increased the likelihood of offering programs in each of the eight categories [of service]. . . . Affiliation with a coalition made it more likely for a faith-based institution to offer a program, particularly in the areas of Emergency Services, Housing, Economic Development, and Health and Fitness" (p. 9). In other words, membership in a coalition is indicative of a congregation's willingness to serve others and to take part in the affairs of its neighborhood community.

The participation of congregations in religious coalitions can take many forms. These coalitions may be focused on a single issue or may encompass many issues. They can be limited to a group of denominational congregations, certain denominations (such as Protestant only), or ecumenical. They can be limited to congregations or open to all community organizations; be informal or well structured; impose dues or have no dues. A Community Development Corporation (CDC) is an example of an intermediary organization that often attracts congregations as members. In short, congregation-based coalitions differ widely in format and structure but share a common goal: to serve as a buffer between people's needs and the power of the state and powerful business interests.

Over the course of our study, we found that many congregations are involved in coalitions and that these coalitions are highly effective in mediating between the individual and the state. In the previous chapter, for example, we reported on four small coalitions in Council Grove whose efforts, individually and in combination, have improved the quality of life for many people in the town. In this chapter, we highlight several coalitions reported in the literature, and we present a detailed examination of the Greater New Orleans Federation of Churches, a coalition of Protestant churches. Our purpose is to show that religion-based coalitions are an important but little noted aspect of the overall contribution that congregations make to American society.

Examples of Religion-Based Coalitions

Perhaps the most successful example of community building is the social and economic development work undertaken by congregations in coalition with community organizations in 120 U.S. urban centers. These efforts are under the auspices of four national networks of urban community organizations made up, for the most part, of religious congregations. These national federations are the Industrial Areas Foundation (IAF), the Pacific Institute for Community Organization (PICO), Gamaliel, and DART (Direct Action & Research Training Center). Each local federation is composed of from ten to forty congregations or religious groups affiliated with and supported by the national organization (Wood, 1997). Organizers meet with individuals and small groups, usually representatives from local congregations, to identify problems and to discuss strategies for addressing them. Once a problem and a strategy are agreed upon, the group selects the target person or group to facilitate the change, such as City Hall, an individual politician, a utility company, transportation authority, or a private company. The fact that a federation of religious congregations can galvanize large numbers of people to advocate for an initiative is a compelling reason, in itself, for politicians and business owners to listen and to attempt to cooperate.

IAF and Religious Coalitions

The Industrial Areas Foundation (IAF) is the most prominent national organization committed to serving as a change agent at the local level. IAF, founded by Saul Alinsky in 1940, had its beginnings in Alinsky's "Back of the Yards" organization, a coalition between Catholic congregations and Labor and Communist party organizers that sought to enhance the quality of life in Chicago's neighborhoods through advocacy and lobbying. Its network of affiliates includes groups in California, Connecticut, Georgia, Illinois, New York, Tennessee, and Texas. IAF, which considers itself an "organization of organizations," provides professional organizers with expertise in the workings of metropolitan political economies, as well as in social movement dynamics. IAF does not determine political agendas at the local level but encourages the local coalitions, who pay fees to IAF as well as the salaries of lead organizers, to determine their courses of action.

Michael Byrd (1997) has described the work of IAF in Nashville, Tennessee. In 1993, a convention was held to form Tie Nashville Together (TNT). In the months that followed the founding convention, TNT visited schools, conducted public hearings regarding nursing homes, and held "Accountability Nights" for school board and local political candidates. Leaders also formulated an afterschool program for children in grades K–8 and a "strategy for labor force development and economic development," both of which were based on IAF initiatives in other communities. In addition, TNT members convinced the mayor's office to open and fund a Neighborhood Justice Center for mediating disputes without police intervention as a means of fostering a sense of community.

It was only TNT's large membership that enabled so much to be accomplished in so short a time. By 1995, TNT included forty-three congregations and associations representing approximately 5,000 people. Attendance at TNT meetings, actions, and assemblies has been remarkably high. At all TNT activities, members pray together and reaffirm that their raison d'etre is to fulfill their religious calling. This is only one of the more than 200 community-change projects supported by the Campaign for Human Development of the Catholic Church.

In New York, a coalition of East Brooklyn Churches (EBC) joined with the Industrial Area Foundations (IAF) to redevelop deteriorating neighborhoods that were experiencing financial instability, a growing number of abandoned properties, and outmigration of most working-class families. The first campaigns were well planned and well organized. First, street signs were replaced; food quality and sanitary conditions in local supermarkets were improved; long-abandoned buildings were demolished; smoke shops (places for selling illegal narcotics) were closed; and a voter registration campaign boasted an increase of 10,000 new voters in 1984.

The coalition then tackled a much larger problem: housing. EBC wanted to build 1,000 new homes in Brooklyn, and it was estimated that the cost would be $7.5 million. Support for the plan—the "Nehemiah Project"—came from the Missouri Synod Lutherans ($1 million), the Catholic Bishop of New York (who became an avid supporter of the coalition) ($2.5 million), and the Episcopalians of Long Island ($1 million). Pressured to support the Nehemiah Project, the City of New York donated the land, paid for landfill removal, and provided $10,000 in interest-free loans to new home owners.

This successful organizing effort was truly local, with each congregation represented by its clergy and three to four lay leaders. EBC has no president, and decisions are made by consensus. In a review of EBC, Gittings (1987) accounts for the success of this advocacy and housing coalition as follows: "In an area bereft of banks, civic clubs, industry, and professionals, the churches were the only organizations—apart from the rackets—that remained alive amid the wreckage of the community" (p. 10). Pastors of these churches were forced to become the entrepreneurs of the community because they were the only organized cohesive social organization remaining in the community. As such, they spearheaded the civic campaign to improve services and founded the Nehemiah Project.

Rogers and Ronsheim (1998) studied a coalition of churches in Pittsburgh in which the churches and two local organizations collaborated to provide health services and to increase health education. When these two organizations realized that they did not have the trust of the community and that the only community organizations trusted by residents were the churches, the organizations asked the churches for their help. However, such a coalition must be built slowly, and the leaders must deal with many issues that can cause contention and friction. The key issues are mutual trust among participants; control over resources, decision making, and representation; disparate values and perspectives; differing communication styles; the ecumenical/religious nature of the coalition; time commitment to the coalition by the partners; issues of racism and race relationships; and the art of involving everyone in the ongoing progress.

Wood (1997) has described the success of community organizing activities in Oakland, California, developed under auspices of a coalition of local churches. The residents wanted the city to pressure Montgomery Ward to take action on an abandoned store building in the community. As a means to that end, coalition leaders and community residents requested and were granted a meeting with a local councilman. The meeting opened with a prayer and a reading from the Bible. The leaders discussed the history of the building and the changes residents wanted. Another leader then asked the councilman—the target of the action—to take specific courses of action, namely to negotiate with Montgomery Ward for redevelopment or sale of the property; to include the coalition in the negotiation process; to submit a time line to community members showing what steps would be taken and when; and, last, to invoke the city's power of eminent domain if Montgomery Ward failed to take the necessary action. The coalition won agreement on its demands from the councilman with little or no conflict. The coalition was successful because it was able to attract many church members to the meeting and because the congregations were working in unison to achieve a common goal.

Not all faith-based coalitions are formed in the same manner. For example, the Clergy and Laity United for Economic Justice (CLUE) is a Los Angeles–based coalition of clergy whose congregants organized to support and assist the working poor. Their ongoing pressure was instrumental in the passage of the city's 1997 living-wage law. CLUE is currently collaborating with local labor unions to organize low-income workers in industries such as transportation and tourism. In 1999, CLUE held a parade on Los Angeles's famous Rodeo Drive, giving "biblical" gifts of milk and honey to hotels that had adopted the living wage—and bitter herbs to those who had not. Within a few weeks, the dissenting hotels had signed new working contracts that included living wages (Parker, 2000). In fact, the concept of the "living wage"—a salary that enables the earner to fully participate in social and communal life—was introduced in the end of the nineteenth century by Father John Ryan of the Roman Catholic Church.

Maynard and Jones (1998) described the Faith and Families program, a partnership between churches and local government in Mississippi that helps poor residents make the transition from welfare to work. The program, initiated by Don Taylor, director of the Department of Human Resources, and proposed by Mississippi Governor Kirk Fordice in 1994, matches welfare recipients with churches. Instead of assigning 200 to 300 clients to one social worker, welfare recipients are assigned to a congregation of 200 or more people. In 2000, the program had 850 participating congregations, which worked with more than 1,000 welfare recipients. These congregations provide practical assistance, such as day care, transportation, and ongoing support. In other words, the congregations act as a buffer between the state social service agencies and the individuals in need, while making the helping process more personal and less alienating.

The Direct Action and Research Training Center (DART) is also worth our attention. Its mission is to assist in the development of strong, congregation-based, grassroots community organizations committed to democratic principles and Judeo-Christian values of justice and fairness. DART's vision is strongly rooted in an understanding of religious congregations as having a prophetic role to play in holding society's political and economic systems accountable for acting fairly. Within this framework, the DART Network offers four services: building new congregation-based community organizations where there is an interest and potential for long-term, self-sustaining organizations; providing ongoing consulting and training for organizers and leaders in the DART Network; providing workshops on organizing skills for religious institutions and community groups; and recruiting and training organizers, particularly minorities and women.

One of the most interesting examples of congregational coalitions is the Greater New Orleans Federation of Churches. This coalition was originally established to provide Protestant congregations with a voice and an identity in a predominately Roman Catholic environment. Over time, however, the Federation became not only a major social and community services provider but also an important agent of social change and social justice.

The Greater New Orleans Federation of Churches

Historical background: Since its founding in 1718, New Orleans has had a strong Catholic influence. Since Protestantism has been the minority religion in the New Orleans area, it is interesting to assess the growth and development of the Greater New Orleans Federation of Churches, a local organization of some 250 Protestant churches

Prior to the purchase from France of Louisiana by the United States in 1803, it was unlawful for anyone to hold any worship service other than a Roman Catholic one in New Orleans. In 1780, for example, an African Baptist preacher, Joseph Willis, was prevented from preaching by the authorities. In 1795, an Episcopal minister, Adam Cloud, was brought to New Orleans in chains for conducting worship services on St. Catherine's Creek, near Natchez. Baron de Carondelet gave him a choice of leaving the Louisiana Territory forever or going to Spain as a prisoner.

With the introduction of U.S. laws and in response to disestablishment, prohibitions against Protestant worship were removed. On November 16, 1805, a small group of people gathered in the boarding house of Madame

Fourage, at 227 Bourbon Street, in New Orleans, to greet the Reverend Philander Chase, who had come from New York to be their leader. The group, which included Episcopalians, Presbyterians, and Methodists, became the first legally organized Protestant congregation in the Louisiana Territory. The next morning, Sunday, November 17, the ecumenical congregation, called the New Orleans Protestant Church, met at the Cabildo, an ancient building located in Jackson Square, the capital of the Louisiana Territory, for the eleven o'clock service and to hear the Reverend Chase read the Order of Morning Prayer of the Episcopal Church and preach the first Protestant sermon. This church later became the Episcopal Christ Church Cathedral.

The number of Protestant and evangelical congregants in New Orleans increased significantly over the years. By 1946, they represented a majority of the population in Greater New Orleans and wielded tremendous influence in all areas of the community. In 1947, twenty of these churches banded together to form the New Orleans Council of Churches. The churches believed that cooperating with one another on initiatives of mutual interest would increase their effectiveness and success. On January 27, 1947, an organizational meeting held at a local Methodist church created the New Orleans Council of Churches, later reorganized as the Greater New Orleans Federation of Churches.

The meeting organizers identified seven areas of likely interest to member churches: (1) evangelism; (2) scouting; (3) civic righteousness; (4) chaplaincy in hospitals; (5) chaplaincy in penal institutions; (6) weekday religious education on released time; and (7) broadcasting. It is noteworthy that, at this stage, social care and social justice were not mentioned as part of the fledgling coalition's agenda. For example, from the Federation minutes we learn that services provided to the churches and the city outpaced the Federation's income and that therefore appeals were made to churches to increase their contributions. Contributions were tax deductible. In 1954, approximately twenty church members, along with other interested individuals, contributed slightly more than $11,000 to the Federation. By 1964, 129 church members, with the support of individual gifts, supported a budget of $45,000. In 1974, the Federation budgeted $3,200 for its service ministries. By 1979–1980, that figure had increased to $169,000.

By 1954, when the Council was reorganized as the Federation, the membership included 130 congregations. In 1957, the Federation purchased "The Church House," at 330 St. Charles Avenue, where daily noontime worship services were held and the offices of the organization were located. In 1976, the building on St. Charles Avenue was sold, and the Federation moved one block to 322 Carondelet. The earlier location is now a hotel. In February 1980, the Federation moved again, this time to the top floor of the building at 301 Camp Street. This building, which had served as the headquarters of the Chamber of Commerce, had some of the finest meeting facilities in the central business district. In the 1990s, the Federation, in an effort to save in housing costs, moved its offices to 4640 South Carrollton Avenue.

By 1962, the Federation's staff included four full-time and three half-time workers, and outstanding clerical and lay leaders chaired many of its programs. Stanton Manor and Fink Home, facilities for the aging, for example, were operated by subsidiary boards under the general aegis of the Federation. In 1962, the Federation was recognized in the community as the instrument of member congregations in the field of civic affairs, evangelism, and education and as a voice for the Protestant, Evangelical, and Orthodox faiths. At that time, the Federation had a twofold mission: to combine and make use of the rich religious and historic heritage of all church groups and to meet the challenges and opportunities for service in the growing metropolis.

The Logic behind a Federation of Churches

The key reason for independent congregations to work in concert and to form formal coalitions or federations is that there are many issues that are of concern to them that no one congregation alone can master. From Federation minutes (1964):[13]

> A united Protestant, Evangelical and Orthodox voice gives strength and stability to every local church in New Orleans. No one church or denomination can speak for all. No local church or denominational office can serve as headquarters for the many services and demands met by a federation of Churches delegated and empowered to serve all the member churches.

The driving force behind the formation of the original New Orleans Council of Churches was the need to give Protestant churches a voice in a strongly Roman Catholic culture. By the early 1960s, however, the Federation recognized that the agenda of the original Council needed to be expanded to meet the changing needs of a changing city. As a result, the Federation began to broaden its role, becoming a catalyst for cooperative action among churches and a bridge linking churches and organizations. The Federation made it possible for congregations to recruit one another for specific causes and became a major force in shaping New Orleans's social policies. Equally important, the Federation made it possible for Protestant, Evangelical, and Orthodox churches to work together without compromising their traditional distinctiveness; and churches greatly increased their impact by working together rather than separately.

In a 1977 issue of *The Cables* (the Federation newsletter), the Federation likened its role to that of a bridge whose function is to connect the two shores, not to transform one shore into the other. It is a "bridge between liberals and conservatives, whites and blacks, the haves and the have-nots, the disadvantaged and the advantaged, the Protestants and non-Protestants, the powerful and the powerless, the ins and the outs, the suburban churches and the C.B.D., and it links the spiritually concerned and the socially concerned."

Structure and Organization

The Federation is an autonomous, independently controlled organization whose leaders are elected by the member churches that serve on the Board of Managers and on the Executive Committee of the Board. In 1964, the Federation required each member church to appoint one lay member, in addition to the minister, to serve on the Board of Managers as a means of expanding its leadership pool. As a result, the Federation moved from being a pastor-only organization to an organization that was more representative of local congregations and the many Protestants in Greater New Orleans. The inclusion of lay leaders also increased the circle of influence of the Federation and its contacts with potential donors and political contacts. (The practice of having a clerical-lay board, consisting of representatives from all member churches, continues today.) Thus, each member church had its own representatives, and each church paid dues. Each church was therefore free to carry out its programs and mission independently, but it could also suggest and persuade other churches to support its activities—and to have a powerful voice among the local civic institutions.

For many years, the Federation was "of the churches" of the Greater New Orleans area. Only duly constituted congregations could be members of the Federation. No individual, group of individuals, or associations outside the churches established by Christian people could be a member, except through regular church membership. The Federation was registered with the State of Louisiana as a nonprofit religious corporation, and the member congregations were the stockholders. The Federation was a voluntary association, organized by Protestant and evangelical congregations to carry out activities of mutual interest to its members. Consequently, all decisions and actions of the Federation reflected the service priorities of the member churches.

No church was required to surrender any tenet of faith, any method of operation, or any type of government when it associated itself with the Federation. Except for the requirement that a congregation be of a formally organized communion/denomination, the Federation had no theological standards as tests of fellowship.

In 1980, the Board of the Federation unanimously voted to open membership to Christian organizations and institutions other than churches. Criteria for membership required that such organizations and institutions be Christian in purpose/name; that they be locally controlled, that is, able to vote on local matters autonomously; and that they not be components or subsidiaries of members of the Federation.

At the time, the officers of the Federation included a president, vice presidents, a corporate secretary, a treasurer, an assistant treasurer, and a chancellor. The Board of Managers included a chair, a vice chair, a treasurer, and an executive committee with twenty-nine members. A paid executive director was in charge of operation.

When the Federation was first established, member churches were asked to contribute 1 percent of their annual operating budget, exclusive of building funds, as dues. This amount was later increased to 3 percent, although no congregation contributed at that level. Congregations that found it difficult to contribute even at the 1 percent level were not pressured to pay dues. Financial support by individuals and corporations helped the Federation remain financially viable.

Most Federation work is done by the board and the more than fifty program committees. Representative committees include those for crime prevention, leadership training, suburban church study, hospitality, police chaplaincy, prison chaplaincy, nursing homes, comfort ministry, and fundraising. In addition, the Federation has a Senior Adult Steering Committee, Rabbinical Council, Governor's Conference Committee, a Mayor's Prayer Breakfast Committee, and an Opera Committee. (The opera committee lasted only one year and staged one opera, with Jerome Hines as its star.) Final responsibility for these and all other Federation programs rests with the executive director and the board.

Over the years, the Federation has "stepped forward as advocates of public morality, Christian cooperation, and concerted Christian witness and service." The Federation has initiated programs to feed the hungry; teach literacy; and offer both counsel and practical help to the disadvantaged, the bereaved, senior adults, the jobless, prisoners, and victims of crime. It has established chapters to help reduce child abuse; operated a police chaplaincy; conducted areawide prayer breakfasts and Easter morning worship services; established a cable television channel for use by all congregations; established a network of churches to feed the poor; and represented the constituency of New Orleans to scores of outside groups. The Federation also organized the most comprehensive ministry ever offered in the United States, on the occasion of the 1984 Louisiana World Exposition.

Federation Service Programs: Overview

In the following sections, we highlight areas of social and community service that have been the focus of Federation initiatives. It should be noted that most of our material covers the years that the Reverend Dr. David Mason was at the helm of the federation. Upon his departure in the late 1980s, the scope of work and areas of involvement shrank significantly. Yet, the many years covered in this chapter illuminate the potential that exists in a coalition of congregations.

Education and training: The Federation sponsored workshops and seminars designed to meet a range of human needs. Some were held annually, others on an ad hoc or ongoing basis. Representative workshop and seminar topics have included stress management in the workplace, parent effectiveness training, dealing with violence in the family, suicide, depression, marriage and the home, church preparedness for disasters (with the local Red Cross), time management, income tax assistance for poor people (with the Internal Revenue Service), widows and the church, personal relationships, and communications skills. The Federation also had a marriage clinic for engaged and newly married couples and a divorce mediation clinic. The Federation's education and training programs were more social than religious in their orientation, since they were designed to meet people's needs.

Arts and culture: In 1978, with funding from the National Endowment for the Arts, the Federation sponsored a series of art workshops. Workshop topics included architecture, film making, poetry and writing for publication, doll making, play production, furniture design, commercial art, clay sculpture, silk screen printing, photography, mural painting, weaving, ceramic tile painting, and papermaking. The arts programs have continued through the years, and many grants and programs have been developed to maintain the churches' involvement in art education.

Senior citizens: In 1959, the Stanton Manor Corporation, a subsidiary of the Federation, purchased the Buena Vista hotel for use as a senior citizens' hotel. Known today as the Pratt-Stanton Manor, the facility enables elderly New Orleans people to live in dignified surrounding at nominal cost. From 1975 until the mid–1980s, the Federation had a full-time worker assisting member churches in setting up programs and services for senior citizens. In later years the Federation relinquished this program and gave it up to the social service agency.

The Federation also worked with the Louisiana Department of Transportation and Development in coordinating applications for vehicles to be used for the transportation of the elderly and individuals with disabilities. Applicants paid 22 percent of the purchase price and all operating expenses. The balance of the purchase price was underwritten by funding from the federal government.

Grief counseling: A staff person ran the Federation's Comfort Ministry. Through the program, widows and widowers were brought together and encouraged to support each other in their grief. Most communication was by phone, but personal contacts were also encouraged. In addition to helping widows through the grieving process, the program provides practical support, such as financial planning, and monthly socials that include dances, outings, tours, and lectures.

Advocacy: The most far-reaching and important of the Federation's outreach activities was its ability to link congregations with public authorities. For example, in 1967, the Federation's Department of Aging, in cooperation with the Louisiana Council of Churches and the Louisiana Commission, sponsored a conference entitled "The Church and Aging." The conference attracted 157 clergy and church leaders representing fifty churches and twelve denominations. Staff from several social service agencies also attended. Sessions covered topics such as the responsibility of the church for its senior citizens, community needs of senior citizens, youth involvement in senior citizen programs, psychological effects of retirement, and development of senior citizen programs. As a result of this conference, several churches set up their own senior citizen programs. The Federation, through its Department of Aging, began a public relations program and, in conjunction with the Louisiana Division of Employment Security, set up programs to provide aid and personal consultations to the elderly. The conference on the church and aging is representative of the Federation's power to act as an intermediary linking member congregations with public authorities and as a catalyst in initiating services for the elderly by member congregations, as well as by public authorities.

Adult literacy: In 1977, the Federation launched its adult literacy campaign, known as Operation Mainstream. The goal of the program was to train 1,000 tutors to teach 1,400 learners in thirty centers, while providing opportunities for face-to-face expressions of Christian compassion. The program was enormously successful in helping people, particularly those learning English as a second language, to enter mainstream American life and the American economy. The program was carried out in collaboration with, and eventually was turned over to, the local YMCA. The program is considered one of the most viable educational programs in the New Orleans area.

Food and shelter: By 1977, the Federation was sponsoring year-round regional food collections through churches in response to the "feast-or-famine" problem of local food banks, namely variable contributions that left the food banks with oversupplies during holiday times and near-empty shelves at other times. In 1982, the Federation became the Local Recipient Organization for the federal government's emergency food funds program. Within a few years, the Federation was coordinating the distribution of more than $200,000 in emergency funds for food and shelter annually through approximately sixty member churches. By 1999, the Federation was coordinating the use of $350,000 to provide food to the needy.

Services to children: The Federation has sponsored many child abuse awareness seminars. In 1982, the Federation launched a Parents Anonymous Program to help parents of abused and/or neglected children to rechannel their destructive behaviors and to learn good parenting skills.

Because the majority of day care centers in New Orleans were held in congregational facilities, the Federation assumed responsibility for helping them provide quality service and developed a set of standards for church-based child care. The program, ChildCare Network, was open to congregations from all denominations and was run by volunteers recruited by the Federation. Church-based day care personnel could obtain donated educational supplies at no charge from the ChildCare Network.

Prison ministry: Long before ministering to prisoners became popular, the Federation was already working in the local prison, paying the salary of a prison chaplain, and providing prisoners with clothing and personal items donated by member churches. In 1977, the Federation's Parish Prison program was accredited as only the second center of its kind for providing clinical pastoral education. Clergy who enter the program are prepared as prison chaplains.

Federation Social Change Programs: Overview

Community issues: The Federation is a voice for those ignored and forgotten by society. For example, the Federation, in conjunction with other agencies and organizations, sponsored an annual Mental Health Awareness Week. Throughout the week, the Federation cosponsored seminars that advised clergy on ways to assist mentally ill congregants and their families. This is but one example of how the Federation reached out to the religious and the secular communities on issues of social responsibility.

The Federation sought to heighten public awareness through issue-focused campaigns. Long opposed to legalized gambling, the Federation campaigned to educate people about the dangers of trying to solve economic problems through methods that were likely to adversely affect families and communities alike. In large part as a result of the Federation's efforts, the Louisiana House rejected a casino gambling bill in 1986. The victory, however, was short-lived; a few years later, the Louisiana House passed a legalized gambling bill. Still, that the Federation was successful, however briefly, against "big money" is an impressive demonstration of the Federation's ability to organize and lobby.

Racial integration: The Federation has been a leader in issues of civil rights and racial integration. Its efforts during the civil rights movement of the 1960s, for example, attracted national attention. In one case, the photo of a white pastor walking hand-in-hand with a black girl through a jeering white crowd that wanted to prevent her from attending an all-white school became a symbol of the civil rights struggle. In another case, *Life* magazine featured the story of clergy in New Orleans who opened their homes to blacks at a time when the community was openly racist. In both cases, the clergy were members of the Federation, which had lobbied for full integration long before it was fashionable.

Largely thanks to the efforts of the Federation, New Orleans proclaimed November 8, 1978, as Black Recognition Day. In honor of the occasion, the city held special events that celebrated the contributions of the black community to the welfare and advancement of New Orleans.

School breakfast program: One Federation social change project focused on the provision of school breakfasts. Members of the Federation were concerned about the number of poor school children who went without breakfast. Although federal money (through the Federal Emergency Management Agency, or FEMA) was available for a school breakfast program, only two schools in New Orleans had applied for these funds. The Federation forged a citywide coalition that included churches, community and civic groups, and government officials. The coalition pressured city and school officials, and soon other schools began to participate in the program. By the end of the second year, the Hot Breakfast Program, initiated by the Federation, was serving 10,500 children in forty-six schools in Orleans Parish.

In 1976, the Center for Science in the Public Interest recognized the Federation's breakfast program with a national award as one of the Terrific Ten Citizen Initiative Programs in the Nation.

Use of state tax monies: Although the Federation represented the local churches, the Federation opposed the use of public state tax monies to support private and parochial education. It argued that such support would undermine public education and do a disservice to nonpublic schools. As early as 1967, the Federation had adopted a statement recognizing the right of citizens to decide whether their children would attend public, private, or parochial schools. However, the statement also urged all citizens and public officials to oppose any diversion of state tax monies to nonpublic education. While the Federation's position can be viewed simply as opposition to state support for the Catholic school system, it nonetheless provides sacred support to the struggle to separate state and church.

Dual-Purpose Programs

While our focus in this chapter has been on social and community services provision by the Greater New Orleans Federation of Churches, it is
important to remember that the Federation's primary concern is with spiritual and religious matters. Thus, some Federation programs clearly have
a religious as well as a service purpose. For example, the regional vacation
Bible school program, begun in 1974, provided religious education as well
as recreational activities for city children and youth during the summer.

Public media: In 1978, the Federation initiated a television program called
"Forward Together," which was broadcast on the local ABC affiliate on Sunday mornings. It was an elaborate program that featured religious news, a
guest church every week, a feature about a local activity (with a call for fiscal or volunteer support), an interview with an outstanding Christian public figure, and an editorial called "Comment on Cooperation," by the Federation president, the Reverend David Mason. The purpose was religious and
social outreach to the wider New Orleans community.

In 1984, the Federation began a cable television ministry, REACH 47
(Religious Ecumenical Access Channel), which gave churches the opportunity to telecast religious and educational programs to viewers in the
greater New Orleans area. The Federation also sponsored training programs in television production. By 1998, the Federation no longer had its
own channel. However, the Federation still produces its own television
show, "Forward Together with the Greater New Orleans Federation of
Churches," which airs on a local public television station.

Louisiana World Exposition: In 1984, the Federation decided that it should
participate in the Louisiana World Exposition as a means of presenting the
Christian message to nonbelievers and to encourage believers to express
their faith through service to others. To this end, the Federation developed
and operated a pavilion as a major exhibitor at the Louisiana World Exposition; coordinated a chaplaincy program to assist with emergency situ-
ations and special problems of people in attendance; and helped establish
and enforce policies and guidelines for religious groups that wanted to
conduct worship services at the fair site. To carry out the work, the Federation recruited 750 volunteers representing 110 congregations and raised
$1 million to pay for the pavilion and related expenses. Most of funds
came from private and corporate donations. This project was more ecu-

menical than most activities of the Federation; Jewish and Catholic chaplains were included in the planning of the event and participated in each of the three shifts of the fair.

Chaplaincy programs: The Federation pays the salaries of full-time chaplains in a few key locations that would otherwise lack spiritual influence. These include the previously mentioned Parish Prison program, a Boy Scout camp, and the Fire and Police departments. In 1998, the Federation received a grant to train four chaplains in police ministry. The Federation also supports the Port Ministry Coordination. The eight chaplains in this program serve seamen and others on the waterfront (New Orleans's largest industry). The Port Ministry Coordination program handles the day-to-day operations of the waterfront ministries and provides a number of services to expand their effectiveness.

Workshops for clergy and lay leaders: The Federation conducts workshops specifically designed to address church-related issues. Representative workshop topics have included organizational skills; urban church development in New Orleans; stress and time management for clergy and church leaders; survival seminars for new ministers; team planning; faith planning; the church and political action; enlisting, training, and supervising volunteer leaders; interpersonal skills, and a Christian approach to race relations.

Reaching out to the Christians in New Orleans: One of the goals of the Federation was to reach out to Christians in the region. Every decade, the Federation mobilized various campaigns to reach all Christians in the area. For example, the Federation conducted a telephone survey, in 1964, of 300,000 households to assess their religious needs. In 1976, 400 churches actively participated in the "Christian Spirit of '76."

In addition to the programs mentioned, another measure of the Federation's success is the replication of its model elsewhere. Examples include the Baton Rouge Federation of Churches and Synagogues and the Lake Charles Federation of Churches.

Finally, the Federation's success is such that it can attract distinguished speakers who can, in turn, influence the city's leadership and the media. In 1984, Mother Teresa, of Calcutta, spoke at the Annual Mayor's Prayer Breakfast. Her presence on behalf of the Federation attracted national attention and gave the Federation a public platform from which to broadcast its views. Robert Schuller, the televangelist from Garden Grove, California, came several times to speak at these prayer breakfasts and drew a large crowd from a cross-section of churches.

Summary

Congregation-based coalitions are best suited to the role of mediating between government and citizens, as well as representing the needs and preferences of local residents. Many urban social networks are built around congregations, and it is much easier to develop a successful group or coalition when people know and trust one another because of shared experiences. A congregation-based coalition has an advantage in that it can draw upon all these networks in carrying out projects of mutual interest to member churches.

If urban congregations are to become effective mediating structures in our society, they must open their doors to all members of the community and use congregational property as community hubs. In other words, the congregation must be a place where people meet to discuss community affairs. The Reverend John Beyers, a pastor in Anchorage, Alaska, has said, "In city communities, church buildings need to be used full-time. It's a crime to see our church buildings locked most of the week, especially when you calculate how much money is spent on mortgages, upkeep and utilities. And then it's a greater crime when you look at an inner city community where meeting space is at a premium. God has taught me much about making Mountain View Baptist Church open to our entire community throughout the week" (1999, p. 7).

Wood (1997) has argued that the most effective community organizing of low-income inner-city residents takes place through church-based coalitions. These efforts have significantly—and positively—affected the residents' social, political, and economic environment. The organizing process is most effective when the organizers consider both long-term and short-term goals. To build a strong church-based coalition over the long term, it is best to have the church members do most of the organizing, from holding one-on-one meetings with community members, holding house meetings, and having pastors make announcements in church to encourage attendance at the events.

The Greater New Orleans Federation of Churches provides a compelling case study of a congregation-based coalition serving as a mediating structure. The Federation is recognized in the Greater New Orleans area as the instrument of its 250 member congregations in the fields of social and community services provision, social change, public education, and evangelism.

Leaders of the Federation's departments and program committees keep current with trends in the religious community to ensure that new directions are reflected in the work of the Federation. The Federation serves as a center for many types of religious functions, including daily noon worship services for all who wish to meditate. Counseling services for those who need help are available upon arrangement through the office of the Federation. Community problems are met in a unified manner, with all churches speaking as one voice for law enforcement. Many interfaith projects, including "Operation Understanding" (aimed at fostering understanding and cooperation between members of different faiths), are channeled through and represented by the Federation.

In describing itself as a bridge that "links the spiritually concerned and the socially concerned," the Federation underscores its function in connecting the religious, social, political, and economic communities of New Orleans in order to serve the needs of all in the city. Since its founding in 1947, the Federation has been an instrument for congregational cooperation, concerted witness, and service. The Federation has initiated programs to feed the hungry; teach literacy; and offer both counsel and practical help to the disadvantaged, the bereaved, senior citizens, the unemployed, prisoners, and victims of crime. It has established chapters to help reduce child abuse; operated a police chaplaincy; conducted areawide prayer breakfasts and worship services; established a cable television channel for use by all congregations; and represented the people of New Orleans to scores of outside groups. Perhaps the most telling measure of the Federation's success is that it is serving as a model for similar coalitions in other cities.

As we have argued in this chapter, some services can and should be delivered by local mediating structures, because these organizations can better assess the unique needs of residents and develop ways to meet these needs. In our opinion, congregation-based coalitions such as the Greater New Orleans Federation of Churches are ideally suited to the role of mediating structures in our society.

10

Social Ministry in the Community

The Case of St. Gabriel's Episcopal Church and Urban Bridges

[W]ith God nothing shall be impossible.

—Luke, 4:37

In the previous chapters, we have discussed social and community services delivery as an ancillary aspect of the work of religious congregations. We stress *ancillary* because, as we have made clear and reemphasize in chapter 14, the primary function of a congregation is to be a place of worship. People do not come to a religious congregation to provide social services. They come because they want to pray with others, worship with others, and find spiritual guidance. Although American religious congregations have become a hub of social and community care, the religious mission of the congregation takes precedence over its social mission. While this is true for most religious congregations, we found several exceptions.

Among the most interesting exceptions we encountered were several cases in which religion-based social services led to the formation of a new congregation or the revival of a dying one. According to McGavran and Winfield (1977), viability in congregations—that is, increased membership and sustained income—is linked with active involvement in social and community affairs. Nevertheless, we contend that, in some cases, viability is predicated on the existence of a social ministry that attracts people to come together and either form or revive a congregation. The case we describe in this chapter is one example of how a congregation was revitalized through social services provision.

Introduction

By any measure, Urban Bridges, at St. Gabriel's Episcopal Church, is a remarkably successful program. Begun in 1990 in the undercroft of a deteriorating Episcopal church in the decaying Olney-Feltonville section of Philadelphia, its goal was to provide safe refuge, as well as art education and homework help, for neighborhood children. In less than a decade, Urban Bridges has grown from a one-day-a-week program for just ten children to a vibrant, diversified, faith-based nonprofit community social service organization serving more than 1,000 neighborhood residents. Moreover, Urban Bridges is housed in a growing and active religious congregation. The programs include year-round art and academic enrichment programs for children, youth, and adults; a summer day camp; and literacy training and computer training programs for adults and youth. In 1999, Urban Bridges raised more than $400,000 in cash and in-kind support from more than sixty foundations, corporations, governmental agencies, churches, community organizations, and more than 350 individual donors. In addition, Urban Bridges had the assistance of a substantial cadre of volunteers. These included faculty members and students from five Philadelphia colleges and universities, as well as collaborators from the Philadelphia public school system and community organizations.

The ingredients for this success story are a neighborhood in need, a place to house programs, and a leader who knows how to convert vision into reality. Olney-Feltonville, one of the most stressed neighborhoods in the City of Philadelphia, is a bottomless pit of human needs. St. Gabriel's Episcopal Church offers a safe haven for programs that respond to these needs. As vicar and board chair of Urban Bridges, Mother Mary Laney brings energy, intelligence, singleness of purpose, self-confidence, and optimism to her roles, as well as a clear sense of Christian mission and limitless faith. Her faith is symbolized by a sixteen-foot-high mosaic that she has installed on the wall of her rectory for all the world to see. The mosaic, which portrays the Angel Gabriel, bears this inscription, in large letters: "With God all things are possible." Mother Mary believes this, and all who work with her come to share her belief. Of prime importance, Mother Mary fully understands that relationships with others are the key to success—a leader, no matter how determined, cannot "do it all." Urban Bridges works because the leadership knows how to bring together, motivate, and direct the talents and resources of many individuals.

Finally, because Urban Bridges is a creature of St. Gabriel's Episcopal

Church and because of the faith held by its leaders and those who serve it, Urban Bridges is inherently the product of faith-based values. These values permeate its outlook, goals and modus operandi and the relationships it establishes with all who come within its ambit. These faith-based values are not inconsistent with the commitments made by Urban Bridges when it incorporated as a Pennsylvania nonprofit corporation and obtained tax exempt status under Section 501(c)(3) of the Internal Revenue Code. Urban Bridges values and respects each person it encounters, regardless of creed, color, race, or any other characteristic. Its mission statement, which reflects its faith-based values, states:

> Urban Bridges . . . embraces a vision of hope, renewal, and revitalization for Olney-Feltonville and other urban neighborhoods. Our mission is to provide nurturing educational opportunities for people of all ages in literacy, technology and the creative arts; to inspire, strengthen and unite people through positive learning experiences otherwise unavailable; to encourage city neighborhoods to experience growth and transformation by building bridges of cooperation and mutual respect with other communities and organizations; and to develop effective learning models and programs that may prove useful to others in search of common social objectives.

The Historical Setting

St. Gabriel's history begins in 1915, when an Episcopal priest was assigned to visit and conduct services in the newly developing Olney-Feltonville area of Philadelphia. At first, services were held in a movie theater. A wooden frame church was built in the early 1920s, and the present stone church building was completed in 1928. In 1929, St. Gabriel's was constituted as a parish of the Episcopal Diocese of Pennsylvania. The neighboring population was white and middle class and included white-collar workers, blue-collar workers, and small business owners, of English, German, Irish, and other European stock. The Logan section, a short distance away, had a good-size Jewish population. Many residents worked in the nearby Heinz Foods factory and in a number of other manufacturing plants in the area. St. Gabriel's was located in a thriving part of the city.

In the 1950s and 1960s, the neighborhood began to change. Manufacturing facilities closed as companies moved to the suburbs or other cities.

Simultaneously, much of the white middle-class population moved away, some to the Greater Northeast, which was being developed at that time, some to new suburbs in Bucks and Montgomery counties and in New Jersey. Property values dropped. Families with lower incomes, many of whom were minorities, moved in to replace those who had moved out.

Although some middle-class white resident remain, the neighborhood in the vicinity of St. Gabriel's is now largely populated by the "working poor"—African Americans, Hispanics, and newer immigrants from Africa, the Caribbean, and Asia. (In fact, more than fifty different languages and dialects are spoken in the neighborhood around the church.) Housing in the area has become run down or abandoned. The income level of those who work is generally very low, and there is high unemployment and crime. Most of the businesses and local institutions, such as churches, that were in place in the 1950s have disappeared. Police protection, street cleaning, and trash collection are minimal. Playgrounds, recreation areas, and other public facilities are in disrepair. The once thriving neighborhood schools have been identified by Philadelphia's Superintendent of Schools as among the worst in the city. The businesses that remain, and the new ones that have started up, are small and struggling. Only recently did a supermarket open to replace the Acme supermarket that closed many years ago.

In the immediate post–World War II period, St. Gabriel's, with more than 150 members, was a solid middle-class parish in a solid middle-class neighborhood. In the mid-1950s, it built a new single-family house on the corner of its property to serve as a rectory. The new rector who arrived then stayed for nearly three decades. In the beginning of his term, the parish was in sound condition, but it began to lose members and strength as the neighborhood began to change. When the rector relinquished his post in the early 1980s, fewer than twenty parishioners remained, and the church building was in poor condition. Sadly, as changes unfolded and his parish declined, the rector became seriously depressed, argued with his parishioners, and stopped keeping records of births, baptisms, and marriages.

After his departure, no new priest was assigned to the church for more than six months. In order to keep the church open, the priest of a neighboring parish volunteered to conduct Sunday services in addition to the services he conducted at his own church. The bishop then assigned a newly ordained priest to St. Gabriel's on a part-time basis. She served in the post for approximately two years and succeeded in increasing membership slightly. This priest was succeeded by another part-time priest, who stayed for the next two years. By the time that priest moved on, the membership had fallen to ten parishioners. In 1986, a young priest was assigned to the church on a full-time basis. He remained for three years, during which time both he and his wife managed to complete their studies for graduate degrees. The church was open only for Sunday services. When this priest left, the church had fewer than two dozen parishioners. Upon his departure, the diocese, eager to keep the parish alive, promptly offered it on a six-month trial basis to Mother Mary Laney. She accepted and began her ministry at St. Gabriel's in October 1989. St. Gabriel's celebrated her tenth anniversary as vicar in October 1999.

A Leader with New Energy and a New Vision

Immediately upon her appointment as vicar, Mother Mary realized that St. Gabriel's was a gift, one that would enable her to transform lives in fulfillment of her calling to Christian ministry. Rather than perceive the parish and the community as liabilities, as many did, she perceived them as an opportunity. Mother Laney lost no time in seizing the opportunity. She had two objectives: to rebuild the congregation and to minister to the residents of the surrounding community, whatever their religious affiliation. Her preparation for ministry at St. Gabriel's had not been remarkable, and few would have predicted what she would accomplish.

Mother Mary is a trim tall woman in her mid-fifties with gray hair, a strong voice, and stronger convictions. Her goal is to live out her faith and to make a difference in the world. She asks the question "If I were on trial for being a Christian, what evidence would be presented and would I be convicted?" She wants the answer to be "Yes."

An only child, Mary Laney was born in Philadelphia and is a life-long Episcopalian. For most of her life, she has been deeply involved in the church and its work. At age nineteen, after graduation from Olney High School, a few blocks from St. Gabriel's, Mary married Earl Laney, who is now an executive for a newspaper publishing company. The Laneys have two daughters, both in their thirties, and a twelve-year-old granddaughter. They have lived in several Philadelphia neighborhoods and now live in a house on the edge of the city.

Shortly after the Laneys' marriage, a conflict developed between the priest and the lay members of the church they were attending. When the bishop sent a counselor to assist a parish committee in solving the problem, Mary was selected as a member of the committee. As a result of her work on

that committee, she was invited to enter a three-year training course to become a parish consultant. She completed the training in 1975 and began to
serve as a parish consultant. In addition, she took on a part-time job as a lay
administrator at an Episcopal church in South Philadelphia, a job in which
she was called upon to run various programs such as a day camp, a program
for college-age youth, and social outreach programs.

In 1976, after the first women priests had been ordained in the Episcopal Church, Mary began to consider the possibility of becoming an ordained priest and concluded that she had such a calling. Because she had
not attended college and needed a college degree in order to qualify for a
seminary, she decided to go to Temple University. She entered college the
same year her daughter started at Chestnut Hill College. Four years later,
each graduated. Mary earned a B.A. in history. She then entered General
Theological Seminary, in New York City. At that time, it was customary for
male students, including those who were married, to live on or near the
campus; Mary decided that she would do the same. She lived full-time in
New York for three years while her husband lived in Philadelphia. Mary
was the first married woman at the seminary to do that. She found her
years at General Theological Seminary very exciting. It was the first time
she had ever lived away from home on her own, and her field work at Trin-
ity Church, on Wall Street, was a challenging experience.

Upon graduation from General Theological Seminary in 1986, Mother
Mary asked the bishop for an urban ministry placement, but the bishop
prevailed upon her instead to make a three-year commitment to St.
Thomas, a prosperous suburban church. In 1989, at the conclusion of her
three-year term, Mother Mary again sought an urban ministry. She was interviewed at several inner-city parishes, which were not yet ready to accept
a woman priest as vicar. The parishioners at St. Gabriel's, however, were
willing to accept Mother Mary. (Mother Mary later learned that these
parishioners believed that no priest would have them.) Mother Mary
began her ministry with humility equal to that of her parishioners, bound-
less faith and energy, and preparation for hard work.

The Rebirth of St. Gabriel's

Upon Mother Mary's arrival at St. Gabriel's, in 1989, her congregation
consisted of seven Caucasians who had remained in the community as it
declined, five Puerto Ricans who had left the Catholic Church, one African

American, two Anglicans who had immigrated from the Caribbean, one Anglican immigrant from Nigeria, one Chinese Christian, and one Cambodian Buddhist who had been invited to the church by one of the other members. There are now approximately 135 regular members of the congregation, most of whom live in the immediate neighborhood of the church. Aside from the current members, there has been a constant flow of people through the church—some who stabilized their lives and moved on; others who have fallen back into addiction or crime and disappeared; and others who left the church and then returned, knowing that St. Gabriel's would be open to them.

Before Mother Mary arrived, as has been noted, the church was open only for Sunday morning services. There was an organist but no choir. There was no hot water and therefore no coffee hour. There was no Sunday School, no adult education program, no midweek services, and no Holy Week services. Today, St. Gabriel's is open seven days a week. There is one main service on Sunday mornings and a monthly healing service. There is a choir as well as an organist, and lay persons participate in the service as Bible readers and chalice bearers. Young people serve as acolytes. There is now hot water—and a coffee hour. Once a year, in the fall, the church celebrates St. Gabriel's Day with a festive service preceded by a procession through the neighborhood. There is music, a special sermon by an invited priest, and a luncheon for all following the service. There are Sunday School sessions for children, adult education sessions, and midweek Bible study at 12:15 P.M. and 7:00 P.M. on Wednesdays. The Stations of the Cross are celebrated during Lent, and four services are held during Holy Week.

Nevertheless, even with all these achievements, St. Gabriel's remains an assisted parish. This means that the diocese pays Mother Mary's salary, and has done so since her term began. When she first arrived, St. Gabriel's budget, exclusive of her salary, was approximately $15,000. The diocese paid a small amount of that, and her parishioners paid the rest. In 1999, the budget, exclusive of her salary, was approximately $45,000, all paid by parishioners. That is a creditable sum for a parish in a working-poor neighborhood with a membership of 135, including children. St. Gabriel's stewardship program, with forty-nine pledges, $900 each, has received recognition in the diocese.

At the start of her ministry, Mother Mary's only assistant was a theology student assigned to her as an advisee. Eventually, she was able to get volunteer help from church members and residents of the community. In September 1990, Judy Ray, a student at the Diaconate School who had requested an urban parish for her field work, was assigned to St. Gabriel's. During her first year, Judy was primarily an observer of the parish at work. In particular, she had the opportunity to observe the fledgling afterschool program, which was just starting up. The following year, for her senior project, Judy agreed to direct the afterschool program on a volunteer basis and expanded it to four days a week. When Judy was ordained, the bishop assigned her to St. Gabriel's as its deacon. The Reverend Judy Ray served in that position twenty hours a week. As an Episcopal deacon, Judy served without a stipend, taking Holy Communion to shutins and the sick, giving individual and spiritual counseling, and preaching on some Sundays. In addition, the Reverend Ray serves as vice chair of Urban Bridges's board and played a major role in its development. She has consistently devoted more than twenty hours per week to St. Gabriel's and Urban Bridges. The Reverend Judy Ray recently departed for an extended leave of absence.

In addition to the Reverend Judy Ray, Mother Mary has had some part-time help from seminarians and from an Episcopal priest who is in Philadelphia temporarily. In the first few years, Mother Mary had no secretarial and clerical help, except for occasional volunteers. More recently, the church hired a part-time secretary.

In 1989, the church building and the rectory were literally falling apart. The church building had no down spouts; the roof leaked, and the cover to the entrance was gone. Rain came through the roof and walls and into the undercroft, which was constantly wet. The heating system was in such bad condition that there was often no heat. As a consequence, the whole building usually felt damp and cold. There were no outside lights and no hot water. Many windows were broken or did not work. There was rubble everywhere, and the grounds were so overgrown that some windows were obscured. Weed trees had actually grown through some of the broken windows. The rectory was in better condition than the church, but its pipes and plumbing were in poor condition. The kitchen was in bad shape, and the building needed paint inside and out. The church and rectory have been restored to good condition, largely with donations of supplies and services and with volunteer help.

When St. Gabriel's celebrated Mother Mary's tenth anniversary, in 1999, both the congregation and its buildings were in good condition. The hopelessness that Mother Mary found upon her arrival had been replaced by optimism, self-confidence, and a realization that St. Gabriel's and its outreach programs could make a positive difference in the lives of members and neighbors.

Networking

As indicated, when Mother Mary began her ministry at St. Gabriel's, parish life had collapsed. There was little sense of community, and parishioners felt powerless. Mother Mary's first response was to meet with parishioners and members of the community in small groups to develop relationships. She also attempted to develop relationships with whatever community organizations she could find. One example is the collaboration with the Greater Olney Community Council, an organization that meets monthly to discuss community issues such as the Town Watch program, local parks, and local schools. In 1989, Mother Mary found these organizations to be remnants of the eroding white middle-class culture, small and ineffective. Nevertheless, the contacts that she established through the meetings proved helpful. Through her visits in the community, Mother Mary learned that new residents in the area tended to have low-paying jobs (if they had jobs at all), limited resources, minimal education, and little interest in participating in community organizations. Violence, shootings, drug abuse, physical abuse, and jail time were commonplace, and residents felt so devalued that they had little concern for community issues.

Mother Mary formed a network of relationships in the community. At the Greater Olney Community Council she met Niki and Ben, the former an elementary school teacher and the latter a middle-school teacher. Both were interested in working to improve the situation of neighborhood children and provided Mother Mary with crucial support. Through Niki, Ben, and another teacher, and with Feltonville United Neighbors, another community organization, Mother Mary became acquainted with the principals of the local elementary and middle schools. In connection with her work for St. Gabriel's afterschool program, she became acquainted with Constance Clayton, Philadelphia's Superintendent of Schools at the time. Later, in efforts to improve the quality of education at Olney High School, Mary worked with David Hornbeck, Constance Clayton's successor. Mary also met the city councilperson for her neighborhood and contacted the pastors of all local churches, as well as the local police. The captain of the thirty-fifth Police District, who was an Episcopalian, promptly invited Mother Mary to join his advisory council. When the Police Department established a minipolice station in a nearby store, Mother Mary became acquainted with the officers assigned there. She also contacted faculty members of the LaSalle University Urban Study Center, located near the church. The Episcopal church, with its hierarchical structure, proved to be an especially valuable asset. Through relationships established with other Episcopal parish churches, and at the deanery, diocesan, and national church levels, Mother Mary has been able to call on a wide range of individuals, church offices, and organizations for financial aid, volunteers, expertise, and personal support. Mother Mary's personal and leadership qualities have been recognized within the Diocese of Pennsylvania. She was elected to the highest-ranking committee of clergy and lay persons in the Diocese, the Standing Committee, which serves and advises the bishop.

Mother Mary has also made extensive contacts beyond the church and immediate community. These include administrators and board members of many philanthropic institutions. In addition, Mother Mary founded the Boulevard Gateway Coalition, a group of organizations interested in uniting communities divided by the local roadway. She is a founder of Philadelphia Interfaith Action (PIA), a coalition of forty churches and community organizations in Philadelphia that join forces and pool resources to address matters such as affordable housing, crime and public safety, education, jobs, and municipal finance. Mother Mary's work for PIA extended her relationships to churches of other denominations and community organizations throughout the entire Philadelphia area.

Mother Mary extended her relationships even beyond the Philadelphia area. For example, through contacts made at the national convention of the Episcopal Church in the summer of 1997, in Philadelphia, she was invited to Indiana, Mississippi, and five other states to tell the story of Urban Bridges. Urban Bridges applied for and received a grant from The Presiding Bishop's Fund, which is administered by the national church in New York, and, in the summer of 1999, Urban Bridges enjoyed the assistance of an intern from Yale University, in Connecticut.

Founding the After-School Program

The direction for Mother Mary's ministry in the community emerged from her discussions with neighbors who live closest to the church. They desperately wanted a safe place for their children. Around the corner from the church there was a drug dealer who "ran the block," and no child who did not work for him could play safely on the street. The children were in awe of the drug dealer, and their parents were afraid of him. Thus, for the first community project, Mother Mary decided to establish an afterschool program in the church for the neighborhood children. She took her idea to members, parents, and community members she had met who were interested in the welfare of children. She told them that, despite lack of funding, the church could provide room for an afterschool program. She brought together a small advisory group of eight people, including Niki and Ben, and obtained a grant of $5,000 from a nearby Methodist church to repair St. Gabriel's undercroft. The Methodist church supported St. Gabriel's as the site for the project because it had no space of its own to offer. In summer 1990, the group fixed up St. Gabriel's undercroft and in September began an ambitious five-day-a-week program called Focal Point for thirty children. "Focal" is an acronym for Feltonville-Olney Children's Art League.

The program's purpose was to establish a safe haven for children where the effects of violence and of drug and alcohol abuse might be alleviated. At the very beginning, the advisory group decided that art and academics would be integral parts of the program. Art, it was believed, could transcend the different ethnicities and languages found in the community. A local artist served as director, and several volunteers helped run the program. Despite its good intentions, Focal Point was unable to sustain itself beyond the first half of the school year. Mother Mary, determined to retain an afterschool program in some form, decided on a one-day-a-week program for ten children. Niki volunteered to serve as the teacher. Mother Mary vowed to reestablish a full afterschool program for the 1991–1992 school year and worked out the arrangement, described earlier in which Judy Ray took on the role of the executive director of the program as her senior project in the Diaconate School. Judy needed to raise the funds to put the program on a sound financial footing.

Plans were made to open in the fall of 1991 with an expanded four-day-a-week program for thirty children. The program was organized as an independent, voluntary nonprofit association, with its own officers and board of directors, a license from the State to operate as a child care provider, and a new name, "The After-School Program at St. Gabriel's" (ASP).

Mother Mary persuaded St. Thomas's, the church where she had previously served, to make a $5,000 grant as seed money to get the new program under way. By June 30, 1992, the end of the first fiscal year, ASP had raised $44,376 from thirteen foundations and corporations, nine churches and community organizations, and seventeen individuals. It also received $2,648 in tuition ($2.00 per child per week) and interest income.

With these funds and more than a dozen volunteers, ASP provided professional instruction in visual arts, music, and dance, as well as field trips and academic assistance. The facilities continued to improve, and equipment was purchased as necessary. Before the end of the first full year, ASP was able to set aside $20,819 to engage a professional executive director in 1992–1993.

In 1992–1993, Mary Kuhn became the new executive director. She was experienced both as a teacher and as a development officer for nonprofit schools. Under her leadership, ASP continued to grow and expanded to five afternoons per week. ASP initiated Saturday field trips in partnership with the Sierra Club's Inner City Outings group, held two evening talent shows for parents and friends and two exhibitions of the children's art work, one in a nearby branch bank and the other in the Philadelphia Protestant Home's Community Art Exhibit. The neighborhood's favorable response was demonstrated by ASP's waiting list, which grew to more than thirty within a year. (Admission to ASP is on a first-come, first-served basis.) ASP's 1992–1993 funding efforts raised $53,133, more than a 10 percent increase over the prior year's results. Only $8,000 of the $21,000 reserve that had been set aside at the end of the prior year was used to meet the $59,957 in program costs.

As ASP grew, so did the number of funders. Twenty-seven corporations, fourteen churches, and ninety-six individuals contributed to ASP. In January 1993, ASP formally incorporated as a Pennsylvania nonprofit corporation and received 501(c)(3) tax-exempt status as an educational institution. Over the next two years, the quality of ASP's educational programs improved as professional teachers were added and volunteer and funding support grew. The number of children participating grew to forty, the maximum St. Gabriel's undercroft could handle. By 1994–1995, ASP had $86,000 in funding, and the number of individual donors more than doubled to nearly 200.

For the 1995–1996 school year, Jeanette Liou, a Swarthmore College graduate, became executive director, replacing Mary Kuhn, who had moved from the area with her family. Jeanette brought little actual experience to the position but proved to have extraordinary qualities of leadership, creativity, good judgment, sensitivity, and tact. She was executive director for three years, through the 1997–1998 school year, at which time she left to enter graduate school. Under Jeanette's leadership, ASP was reorganized, and new programs were added that enabled ASP to reach beyond the walls of St. Gabriel's Church. The number of neighborhood children and others that ASP could serve multiplied. The original afterschool program, renamed the AAA Kids program (Arts and Academics for Kids), was given its own program director and continued to serve approximately forty children, while the waiting list grew to more than 100 over time.

The AAA Kids program continued to evolve. One innovation was community service projects, such as making large and colorful banners to beautify the Olney subway stop; planting marigolds in the median strip of a major road through the neighborhood; and forming the Watotos (*watoto* is Swahili for children), a traveling troop of children in grades five through eight. Under the tutelage of a professional music teacher, the Watotos play a wide variety of percussion instruments, specializing in African rhythms. The Watotos, who pledge to keep their grades up, give between eight and ten performances a year for community, church, and business organizations. Aside from their own fun, learning, and self-satisfaction, the Watotos have brought great enjoyment to those for whom they have performed and have drawn attention and credit to the After-School Program. In 1998, thanks to a benefactor who was impressed by one of their performances, the Watotos were able to make a CD, named *Positive Power*.

The new programs of ASP included the After-School Artists' Residencies with Children program (AAR) and a computer training program for children. In the AAR program for middle-school children, professional artists work with the children in planning community art projects, such as designing and creating a mosaic mural for a school or other community location. Once a project is planned and approved, the AAR group and the professional artist go to the location and work with children from the local school or community organization in executing the project. AAR's first project was a forty-three-foot indoor mural entitled *Olney and Me, Look Inside*, which combined oral history and personal images in an Olney neighborhood scene. Another imaginative project was the decoration of a large planter, approximately seventy-five feet long, located outside Olney High School. To augment the mural, the group grew seedlings to plant in the planter. The completed project, *Power Plant*, is a lovely sight for the entire neighborhood. In 1997–1998, 450 children from schools in Olney Cluster participated in AAR projects at their schools. AAR received a foundation grant in 1998–1999 for eighteen artist residencies projects in three local schools, to be implemented through 2002.

The computer training program was begun by ASP in 1995 to make use of three donated computers. For some time, inner-city children's lack of access to computer training had been identified as a serious problem, and the three donated computers offered a small way to begin addressing that issue. By 1997–1998, the number of donated computers had grown to twelve, and ASP offered basic computer training in afternoon, evening, and Saturday classes to more than fifty students. Adults, as well as children, participated in the training classes when staff realized that some of the parents wanted computer training so that they could get better jobs. The curriculum included introductory and intermediate courses, and students were encouraged to use their skills to compose articles for *LINK*, the afterschool program's quarterly newsletter, and *SPEAK*, a local newsletter for young people in Olney. By 1999, the multipurpose computer training had developed into one of Urban Bridges's most dynamic and fastest-growing programs.

By June 30, 1998, the After-School Program's expenses had grown to $179,000, and fund-raising produced $216,000, some of which was earmarked for the following year. The support of foundations and corporations accounted for $95,000; churches and community organizations for $52,000; individuals for $47,000; and government grants for $14,000. The balance came from miscellaneous sources. Individual contributors, including many who gave through the United Way, numbered more than 300. During the year, the After-School Program engaged forty-seven volunteers, including board members, regular volunteers, junior volunteers, and college volunteers. One group of college volunteers consisted of an entire social justice class from Villanova University.

The Emergence of "Urban Bridges": New Programs and New Horizons

Effective July 1, 1998, the After-School Program officially changed its name to "Urban Bridges at St. Gabriel's Episcopal Church" and expanded in important new directions. The board of directors agreed to accept full responsibility for two programs that the church had been incubating while ASP had been devoting its attention to the afterschool program. One new program was Vacation Ventures, a summer day camp for neighborhood children. The other was the Literacy Center, a literacy and English-as-a-second language educational program (ESL) for adults and some youth.

Vacation Ventures, founded by St. Gabriel's in the summer of 1996, had replaced two summer programs run by the church. One was the two-week vacation Bible school conducted weekday evenings for children of the parish. The other, known as Kirby Camp, was a four-day overnight camping experience for fifteen parish children. The latter was held at Kirby Center, a camping area outside the city that was owned by the diocese. Mother Mary realized that neighborhood children who sought refuge at ASP during the school year were just as much in need of a safe haven in the summer. Vacation Ventures attempts to provide that safe haven. With a paid camp director and assistant, several paid counselors, and a few volunteers, Vacation Ventures is open five days a week for eight weeks. It offers children supervised, constructive play and learning activities, including art, music, dance, physical activities, field trips, and academics. From an enrollment of approximately thirty children in summer 1996, its enrollment grew to forty children by 1999. One consequence of shifting Vacation Ventures from the church to Urban Bridges was the elimination of Bible study from the program, since the ASP board decided at the time of incorporation that religious doctrine would not be taught in its programs. This decision was made to facilitate funding by foundations and governmental agencies and to respect the religious traditions of all who attend ASP programs. Overall, ASP, and, later, Urban Bridges pledged not to discriminate against any person "on account of age, race, color, sex, sexual orientation, handicap, religious creed, ancestry or national origin" and to comply with all relevant statutes prohibiting discrimination against any student, staff, or volunteer.

The Literacy Center had its origins in 1991, when Mother Mary realized that some parishioners, as well as many parents of the children in the afterschool program, had trouble with English and reading. A parishioner told Mother Mary of the Mayor's Commission on Literacy, which provided training for volunteer tutors and assistance in setting up literacy programs. Mother Mary took immediate advantage of the opportunity. In 1992, St. Gabriel's established its Literacy Center as a community site of the Mayor's Commission on Literacy. In the first year, ten students met with tutors for one-on-one instruction one day a week. By 1993, additional volunteer tutors had become available, and LaSalle University, in partnership with St. Gabriel's, provided a faculty member who conducted ESL training two days a week. The number of students increased to thirty-one. The Literacy Center program increased incrementally through 1994–1995, with an enrollment of forty-six students and a waiting list of twenty. For the 1995–1996 academic year, there were 106 people in the Literacy Center.

By this time, volunteer tutors were working with more than one student. One reason was that students sometimes did not show up at the appointed time, leaving tutors feeling that their time had been wasted. The other reason was that some students were so embarrassed by their illiteracy that they were uncomfortable with one-on-one tutoring. The Literacy Center discovered that, by assigning several students to a tutor, the tutor would always have someone to work with, and students would not be embarrassed because they would be with others who shared their problem. The new arrangement solved the problems and improved the level of learning.

Beginning in 1996–1997, the number of students began to increase exponentially, because of the increased availability of new tutors. This increase was the result of a Partnering for Literacy program with local colleges and universities. In 1996–1997, Mother Mary met Dr. Suzanne Toton, a professor in the Department of Religious Studies at Villanova University, through her work with Philadelphia Interfaith Action. The professor wanted her students to have "hands-on" experience in community service. She agreed to bring one of her entire classes to the Literacy Center once a week to tutor. To cope with the problem of poor attendance, Villanova students were assigned only to those students who made a commitment to perfect attendance. As a result, students came to view having a Villanova student as a tutor as a very special opportunity. Dr. Toton was so pleased that she persuaded her husband, Dr. Jerry Zurek, of the Department of Communications and English of Cabrini College, to do the same thing with his students. Additional tutors were recruited through partnerships with community organizations, such as the National School and Community Corps and the Experience Corps.

The Literacy Center added a new dimension to its program in partnership with Olney High School. Six students, each failing ninth grade, were tutored through the summer at the Literary Center. As a result, all six students qualified for promotion to the tenth grade and kept up with their classes thereafter. As a consequence of that project, a tutoring and mentoring program for Olney High students was created in collaboration with Project Sunshine, a Villanova University volunteer student organization. Since then, the Literacy Center has formed additional tutoring partnerships with St. Joseph's University and with Swarthmore College.

In 1997–1998, the Literacy Center enlisted sixty-five tutors who helped 414 students. In 1998–1999, there were seventy-seven tutors and 522 students, and in the 1999–2000 academic year, more than 100 tutors were available and more than 400 students attended classes each week.

The Literacy Center offers adult beginning reader classes with basic reading instruction for nonreaders through the third grade level; pre-GED classes with basic English grammar and basic math for students at the fourth- to eighth-grade level; GED classes teaching specific math and English skills at the ninth- to twelfth-grade levels; and ESL classes for non-English speaking adults that teach conventional English grammar and writing skills. The classes, incidentally, offer exposure to American culture and traditions. Computers are used as instructional tools in these classes. In addition to its partnerships with local colleges and universities, the Literacy Center has formed partnerships with public elementary and middle schools to provide students in those schools with college tutors and mentors recruited through the college partnerships.

In 1998, at its national conference in Milwaukee, GATEWAY Paths to Adult Learning, honored the Literacy Center with its Life-Long Learning Award an annual award granted to an outstanding adult learning center. At the previous year's national conference, GATEWAY had honored the Literacy Center's program director, Mary Ann Borsuk, with awards for Outstanding Program Coordinator and Outstanding Program Coordination. GATEWAY also gave its national Adult Learner of the Year Award to one of the Literacy Center's students.

The Computer Center, which began in 1995 as part of the After-School Program, was consolidated into the Literacy Center. From its small start with three donated computers, it had evolved, by 1999, into the Urban Bridges Computer Center with fifteen networked personal computers, one of which had Internet access. Adult classes include training for Microsoft Windows 95 and 98 and Microsoft Word. The computers are also available for computer-assisted literacy training and interactive computer exercises for low-level readers and nonreaders. The Computer Center offers summer computer youth camp and an afterschool computer club one afternoon a week. One full-time staff member teaches all of the classes. Because of space and other constraints, the Computer Center can be used only thirty hours a week. A modest fee is charged, and the classes are largely filled.

Much of the credit for the extraordinary success of the Literacy Center, including the Computer Center, goes to Mary Ann Borsuk. Mary Ann is a prime example of Mother Mary's ability to recognize others' abilities and her willingness to give them a chance to develop. Mary Ann started at St. Gabriel's in 1992 by answering an ad in a community newspaper for a part-time tap dance instructor in the After-School Program. Subsequently, she took on the added duties of part-time church secretary. In 1994–1995,

Mother Mary assigned Mary Ann to work fulltime on developing and managing the Literacy Center. Mary Ann, who does not have a college degree and who had no prior experience in literacy training, has since won national acclaim and has more than justified Mother Mary's confidence in her.

Institutionalization

In June 1998, Urban Bridges reorganized, with expanded responsibilities for the executive director. The new executive director, who reported to Mother Mary, was responsible for supervising the five programs, overall administration, and fund-raising. Under the new structure, the five program directors reported to the executive director. One objective of the restructuring was to relieve Mother Mary of much of the day-to-day management, which had multiplied enormously as Urban Bridges grew. Mother Mary wanted to devote more time to parish duties and community activities.

The budget increased to $380,000, double the previous year's budget. The increase was to cover expected growth in the regular ASP programs, plus the acquisitions of the Literacy Center and Vacation Ventures. In addition, the budget included the new executive director's salary, as well as money for an administrative assistant. While St. Gabriel's had received some foundation and government agency funding, it was a relatively modest amount. Fortunately, Urban Bridges was able to begin the year with $120,000 in working capital, some of which had been raised in prior years, and had received certain foundation grants earmarked for 1998–1999. The fund-raising goal for 1998–1999 was nevertheless considered a major stretch when measured against the $250,000 that ASP and St. Gabriel's together had raised for 1997–1998. The goal was considered feasible because of Urban Bridges's reputation and its strong relationships in the community.

Financially, Urban Bridges came through the first year with its new structure with flying colors. Expenses came to $330,000 and revenues, nearly $350,000. There were, in addition, in-kind contributions of more than $60,000 (counting a value assigned to volunteer time). The $120,000 reserve was preserved and increased to nearly $150,000, so Urban Bridges could begin the 1999–2000 fiscal year on a sound footing. For 1998–1999, Urban Bridges raised $160,000 from twenty-nine foundations, corporations, and governmental agencies; $65,000 from thirty-seven churches;

196 of Social Ministry

$81,000 from 316 individuals; and $14,000 from forty-two United Way gifts. Urban Bridges also received $25,000 in fees, tuition, and interest. More than 140 people volunteered their time and talents.

Urban Bridges's transition year was not, however, without some rough spots. The new executive director was unfamiliar with Urban Bridges's programs and culture, and had a management style different from her predecessor's. The resulting difficulties were exacerbated when, at midyear, the executive director was diagnosed with a serious illness and left Urban Bridges. As of autumn 1999, the executive position had not been filled. To deal with this situation, Mother Mary found it necessary to devote more time than ever to the management of Urban Bridges, and staff members had to do double duty. Mother Mary and the board have acknowledged that a replacement had to be found, but, on the basis of their experience that year, they agreed that a careful assessment first had to be made of the functions and qualifications that would be required of a new senior staff member. Given Urban Bridges's special history, the conventional model of an executive director may not be the right fit.

There were other growing pains in 1998–1999. Restructuring and integrating the financial records of both the original ASP programs and the new programs at St. Gabriel's proved more difficult and complex than expected, as did readjusting personnel relationships and practices to accommodate the combining of staffs. These issues were worked out successfully, and the program directors executed Urban Bridges's programs magnificently.

For 1999–2000, Urban Bridges's tenth year, the expense budget was $413,000, along with appropriate fund-raising goals. It also budgeted in-kind gifts of $79,000. Further, the board approved the start of a capital campaign to raise $250,000 to be used to acquire, refurbish, and equip two nearby row houses as a technology center. The Urban Bridges board has focused on the enormous and increasing importance of computer skills in contemporary life and the difficulty many inner-city residents face in acquiring such skills. The new facility was named the Urban Bridges Technology Center.

In 2000, Urban Bridges reorganized the structure of its programs into two primary branches, each managed and administered by a director. Mary Ann Borsuk was named director of the Literacy and Computer Center, and Linda Alosi was appointed director of the Arts and Academic Enrichment Program. Linda, a local resident, began her Urban Bridges career as a volunteer parent in the After-School Program. At the time, she was working as a clerk in a local plant and garden supplies store. She later accepted a paying job as a program aide and worked her way up to the position of director. During her years at Urban Bridges, she has accepted many special assignments, including producing the Watotos's CD. Felice Simelaro was named director of development and assumed responsibility for planning and implementing Urban Bridges's fund-raising programs

As a result of this more efficient administrative structure, Urban Bridges was able to continue and expand its programs. In addition to their offerings in adult education and ESL, the Literacy and Computer Center added computer-assisted learning and computer training classes. The Arts and Academic Enrichment Program continued to offer afterschool art programs for children and the Artist Residency Project, as well as Vacation Ventures and the adult program at Olney High School.

Urban Bridges's accounting systems have gone through several phases. In the first phase, a volunteer treasurer handled the bookkeeping. In the next phase, a part-time professional accountant was employed to help those doing the bookkeeping in setting up accounts and preparing reports and to provide professional accounting expertise as needed, all under the overall direction of a volunteer treasurer. Over time, it has proved difficult to retain qualified part-time accountants and to cope with the transition when one accountant leaves and another is hired. At the same time, Urban Bridges had not reached a point where it required a full-time professional accountant or controller. Therefore, in 1999, Urban Bridges engaged an accounting firm specializing in computer-based accounting services for small, nonprofit organizations. Representatives of the firm, together with the Urban Bridges staff, established procedures, supplied both guidance and expertise, and provided the continuity that is not possible with a succession of part-time accountants.

Because of the lack of clerical assistance at Urban Bridges, the principal staff members must do most of their own clerical work. It is anticipated that, as Urban Bridges expands in scope and size, the volume of clerical work and the need to make efficient use of its operating staff will lead to the addition of clerical personnel to the staff.

The Underpinnings of Urban Bridges's Success

The best gauge of Urban Bridges's success is not its rapid growth or its funding success. The true measure of success is whether its programs are effective in teaching and transforming people. Until recently, Urban Bridges had not measured the effects of its programs, although it recognized the importance of such evaluation. In 1999, Urban Bridges recruited a group of college volunteers to contact former afterschool program students to ascertain their progress after leaving the program. One measure of progress is students' success in passing tests required by governmental agencies—the GED test, for example. The record of Urban Bridges's students on such tests has been outstanding. The awards granted to the Literacy Center by GATEWAY Paths to Adult Learning attest to this fact.

Despite sparse objective evidence, there is ample anecdotal evidence that Urban Bridges programs are successful. At the simplest level, teachers and volunteers in the afterschool program have uniformly observed genuine improvement in their students' artistic accomplishments, performance on homework, attention span, and general behavior at St. Gabriel's. With respect to the artist residencies conducted at local schools, the artworks have consistently been praised by community members, and children at the schools have expressed their appreciation for the opportunity to take part in the projects. Also testifying to Urban Bridges's success is the degree of acceptance it enjoys by school, colleges, and other community organizations. Organizations often seek out Urban Bridges to be a partner or collaborator. Long waiting lists provide strong evidence of community acceptance and appreciation and attest to the quality and value of Urban Bridges programs.

Urban Bridges has many individual success stories. Especially moving is the case of Michael, the thirty-year-old father of three who received the national GATEWAY Adult Learner of the Year Award. Michael went through the Philadelphia school system without learning how to read. Embarrassed, he hid his illiteracy from his young children. At his graduation from the Literacy Center, he was able to read aloud to the audience a paper he had written for the occasion. Could any gift have been more valuable? Another success story is Lydia, a married mother of two and an aspiring pediatrician. A student in the Literacy Center, Lydia passed her GED exam and was admitted to the Philadelphia Community College. At the time of our study, she was getting top grades and passionately pursuing her goal of entering medical school.

Miguel wanted to be a policeman. He passed the police examination but did not qualify because he had not completed high school. The Literacy Center helped him to pass the GED exam, and he is now a member of the Philadelphia Police Department. Forty-year-old Anthony, who had dropped out of high school, had a good job working for Pep Boys. When he discovered that his failure to finish high school was blocking his advancement into management, he applied to the Literacy Center, earned his GED, and was able to advance his career.

There are similar success stories among the children who have graduated from the afterschool program: Among them are Erneka, a high school honor student, and Vernon, one of the Watotos with aspirations for a career as a professional musician, who was accepted by Philadelphia's High School for the Performing Arts. Middle-school students who were failing but who took part in the summer tutoring program were able to enter high school the following fall with their classmates. Other indicators of success are the transformed volunteer college students who have come to the inner city as tutors and the volunteer board members who have made deep and enthusiastic commitments to Urban Bridges.

Urban Bridges's staff members have their own success stories. Mary Ann Borsuk and Linda Alosi have already been mentioned. Carmen Jimenez, a single mother with two children, grew up in Philadelphia in a Puerto Rican household, graduated from Olney High School, and spent two years at the Philadelphia Community College. Her goal was early childhood education, but she had to work and could not pursue her dream. Over the years, Carmen held a variety of retail and clerical jobs until she answered an advertisement in a neighborhood newspaper for a part-time homework coordinator at Urban Bridges. After a few months in that job, she was promoted to art instructor, then to leader of the afterschool art and academics program, and finally director of the Vacation Ventures Summer Camp. In addition, Carmen designed a Spanish language class, which she teaches every Friday afternoon.

What is the source of the success of Urban Bridges and its host and partner, St. Gabriel's Episcopal Church? Mother Mary, if asked, would say it is the Holy Spirit. While not challenging that belief, we suggest that there are practical factors to consider. First, and perhaps most important, was Mother Mary's initial response to her assignment at St. Gabriel's. She perceived it as a gift, an opportunity for urban ministry, rather than as a liability. Despite its seeming lack of resources, when the right person came to St. Gabriel's with a powerful vision and the requisite leadership qualities, St. Gabriel's provided the place for that vision to come to life. Every decaying inner-city parish offers the same potential opportunity.

A second important factor is that, while urban neighborhoods have extreme human needs, the larger community has abundance beyond measure. The task of urban ministry, whether faith based or secular, is to identify the human need and to marshal the abundant resources of society to answer that need. Urban Bridges and St. Gabriel's demonstrate one way in which it may be done. The key to success is the concept of *building relationships*. Urban Bridges's name is particularly apt, for the name signifies the relationships, or bridges, that have been critical to the programs' ongoing development and success. The critical role of relationships necessitates a closer examination of some of those relationships.

The first relationship to be considered is Mother Mary's relationship with the members of the parish and the immediate neighborhood, the foundation upon which Urban Bridges rests. As noted, Mother Mary's first step at St. Gabriel's was to go into the community, get to know the people, and make sure they knew she intended to be open to them and to minister to their needs, rather than impose preconceived "solutions." Although the process of getting to know one another and establish credibility was slow—and continues to this day—Mother Mary discovered at the outset that the prime concern of her neighbors was the safety and future of their children. Her response was immediate. She opened the After-School Program and a summer day camp. She also discovered the importance of literacy to those same neighbors. She responded by establishing St. Gabriel's Literacy Center. Mother Mary could pursue those initiatives with full confidence that they were answers to genuine needs and that, if she offered high-quality programs with high standards, the community would accept them, benefit from them, and appreciate them. Along the way, Mother Mary heard from her neighbors of promises made, by politicians and others, but never kept. She determined never to promise something she could not deliver and never to fail to deliver something she had promised. Over time, the neighborhood has learned that it can count on Mother Mary and that trust is the most crucial element of her ministry.

To the extent possible, Mother Mary has always included community members—parents, parishioners, local educators, local businessmen, and local community organization members—in the planning, initial execution, and continuing operations of whatever she has determined to do. This has ensured that the community understands its own stake in the projects Mother Mary devised. Also, the community cares about the success of the programs which provide some paying jobs for community members and which have begun, albeit slowly, to help community members to develop marketable leadership skills. Mary Ann Borsuk, Linda Alosi, and Carmen Jimenez are products of these programs, as are the youth who graduated from the After-School Program and returned as junior volunteers, and the parents of children in the afterschool program who have served as board members. Mother Mary also ensured that the community is aware of St. Gabriel's presence and programs through venues such community art projects, the newsletter for Olney youth, and the Watotos' performances. These efforts and others have forged a strong and mutually supportive relationship between Mother Mary, St. Gabriel's, and Urban Bridges on the one hand and the Olney-Feltonville community on the other. Again, it is the relationship that undergirds and gives power and credibility to every undertaking. It is the reason that a thousand community members have enrolled in Urban Bridges's programs, the reason that there are waiting lists, and the reason that community members, many of whom had never volunteered before, serve Urban Bridges as volunteers.

Mother Mary formed and cultivated bridges to the greater community as carefully as she formed relationships within the community. Every encounter she has with another person as she moves through the world is a potential building block for additional relationships. When Mother Mary establishes a relationship with a person and recruits this person for the Urban Bridges board, Urban Bridges can call on the prior relationships that that person has established. For purposes of raising funds and recruiting talents, for example, Urban Bridges has available to it not only the relationships Mother Mary has developed directly but also all of the existing relationships of its board members. This exponential leveraging of relationships has paid dividends for every aspect of Urban Bridges's endeavors. The result is that Urban Bridges has available to it a huge pool of talent and resources. The extent of this pool is evident in the qualifications and commitment of board members, donors, volunteers, staff members, supporters, and friends, which are drawn from a wide-ranging body of churches and church organizations, businesses, charitable foundations, educational institutions, governmental agencies, and community organizations.

The composition of Urban Bridges's board emphasizes this last point. In addition to Mother Mary, the board includes a banker, four parents and neighborhood representatives (two school teachers, one hospital registration clerk, and one retired business woman), two college professors (from Temple and St. Joseph's), three business executives, a consultant, two lawyers, and a suburban housewife. The board has seven men and nine women. Each is committed to Urban Bridges, and each devotes substantial time and energy to its mission. The Reverend Judy Ray, who recruited board members from the beginning, attempted to maintain a balance on the board between persons with diverse and necessary talents and people from both Olney-Feltonville and the larger community.

A balanced and diverse board is important, for board members set the organization's direction, resolve important problems, and provide a sounding board for Mother Mary and her staff. Board members are also available to lend their special expertise, identify prospective sources of funds, and provide conduits to both the local community and the community beyond. As Urban Bridges grew from its small beginnings to its present size, what it has needed from its board members has changed. At first, the primary task was to develop and fund an art and educational program for a relatively few young children, a task well within the special expertise of school teachers and parents. As of 2000, Urban Bridges requires board members to have knowledge and experience in education, community practice, finance, business management, and law.

Fund-raising has always been a matter for board members, but the nature of that task has changed as the budget has grown from $50,000 to more than $400,000. The proposed acquisition of real property adds a further dimension. Urban Bridges's ability to enlist qualified and committed board members is an example of Mother Mary's talent for relationship building.

Before leaving the matter of relationship building, it is appropriate to give examples of how relationships may be built. One relationship built by the Reverend Judy Ray was with a suburban Episcopal church. In response to an invitation from the rector, the Reverend Judy appeared at the church's coffee hour in 1994, described the After-School Program, and made it known that an outreach gift would be appreciated and that there were positions open for board members. The church's outreach committee decided to make a gift to ASP, and a committee member volunteered to be a board member. A lawyer, that board member provided professional legal assistance to Urban Bridges regarding employment, corporate, tax, and (unexpectedly) intellectual property law matters. In due course, others from the church volunteered to assist in programs. Children from ASP were invited to visit the church fair; the Watotos performed at church services; and Mother Mary has preached there twice. The church's outreach program is one of the largest donors among the churches that provide financial support for Urban Bridges. In addition, more than a dozen members of the church have contributed directly to Urban Bridges. A second member of the church, with substantial experience in the business world, has joined the board. This broad relationship between the suburban church and Urban Bridges will continue to strengthen and grow.

This case study has already detailed the important relationships developed through the Philadelphia Interfaith Action (PIA) and the contacts with professors from Villanova University, Cabrini St. Joseph University, and Swarthmore College, which substantially enlarged the volunteer tutor force available for the literacy program. Urban Bridges's remarkable growth is the product of just such relationship building.

There are other important explanations for Urban Bridges's success. Urban Bridges has been successful because, in addition to building relationships, its leaders have executed every aspect of its operations competently and responsibly. This high standard has been set by Mother Mary, who grasps the importance of quality work and insists on it in everything she does herself and everything that is done by those who work with her. Her energy level, capacity for hard work, attention to detail, and ability to keep her eye on the objective are beyond parallel. Because of her leadership and example, everyone who works at Urban Bridges strives to do his or her best at all times. This standard of excellence applies to mundane matters, as well as to more visible functions such as classroom work with children and projects to be presented to the public. Financial records are impeccable; correspondence is answered promptly; every gift is acknowledged. Budgeting and planning are viewed as important functions undertaken with great care.

The payoff from the high standards has been great. Urban Bridges's programs are uniformly good, and they are perceived as such by participants and their families. When the elementary-school-age children present their annual performance for parents and friends at the Olney High School auditorium, the quality of their performance matches comparable performances by their counterparts in affluent suburban schools. Parents and children alike appreciate their achievements; self-esteem and self-confidence soar. The second payoff is that those who work at Urban Bridges feel strongly about what they do. Staff delight in their work and devote effort and enthusiasm far beyond what might be reasonably expected. Each worker—paid or volunteer—knows that he or she is offering a priceless gift of time and talent and is grateful for that opportunity. A third payoff is Urban Bridges's reputation in the greater community. Foundations, corporate sponsors, churches and church organizations, individual donors, and other supporters have confidence that Urban Bridges will respond directly and effectively to human needs. Urban Bridges's credibility is a primary component in its success in attracting resources to Olney-Feltonville.

Two further attributes of Mother Mary's approach merit attention. First is her openness to new ideas and her willingness to take promising new directions. One example is her willingness to try out Jeanette's idea for resident artists to develop community art projects, staffed by ASP artist instructors and student participants, at host schools. The result was the artist residencies program, which enabled Urban Bridges to break out of its limited space, engage a much larger body of children, and enhance its community presence. Another example is the series of innovations that enabled the Literacy Center's programs to grow rapidly, such as the decisions to offer small group classes instead of one-on-one tutoring, to accept whole classes of college students and their faculty as tutors, and to experiment with a group of failing ninth graders. This flexibility has yielded great dividends.

Finally, it is often said that Mother Mary is a great risk taker. This perception grows out of her willingness to try new ideas and to plan for substantial growth without knowing where the funding will come from. Her motto, "With God nothing is impossible," sometimes lends an almost outrageous aura to her undertakings. On examination, however, the so-called risks she takes are not as great as some postulate. First, Mother Mary is not afraid of "failure" and readily states that if something does not work, she will regroup and try something else. Her first regrouping took place in 1990–1991, when Focal Point failed. The After-School Program, soundly based, arose in its place. Though some consider overly optimistic her belief that "nothing is impossible," Mother Mary has an exquisite sense of the possible. She well knows that needs exist in her community and that society has an abundance of resources with which to respond. As the anvil salesman says in *The Music Man,* "You gotta know the territory." Mother Mary knows her territory, can gauge what is possible, and, with reasonable certainty, knows that if she presents a convincing case for a proposal, those who control the resources will make them available to her.

The Significance of Urban Bridges for the Ministry of St. Gabriel's

Mother Mary asserts that Urban Bridges has greatly strengthened her parish, even though it is a separately organized nonprofit corporation. Indeed, Urban Bridges gives the members of the parish an important sense of visible participation in their community. Members perceive that, by extending the hospitality of their church to Urban Bridges and, through it, to the community, they are making a great gift—and serving as ministers—to human need as the Gospel teaches. Equally significant, many of the people touched by Urban Bridges have, as a result of the encounter, become active and important members of the parish. These include Niki and Ben, who were crucial to Urban Bridges's first steps and who still play important roles; Mary Ann Borsuk, Linda Alosi, and Carmen Jimenez, who hold top Urban Bridges staff positions; and Michael, who learned to read in the Literacy Center. St. Gabriel's also numbers among its members neighborhood residents who became acquainted through Urban Bridges, both as students and as parents. Finally, there are participants who have not become members of St. Gabriel's but who attend services from time to time. The parish rejoices in having them. In fact, a significant portion of the growth in St. Gabriel's membership in the past decade is directly attributable to the response of Olney-Feltonville to the social ministry of Urban Bridges.

A further question is how the faith-based nature of St. Gabriel's, as an Episcopal church, meshes with the secular status of Urban Bridges. For example, Urban Bridges may not teach the Bible to its participants, and existing Bible study programs had to be abandoned when Vacation Ventures was brought under the Urban Bridges umbrella. It is also a fact that, in 1992, when the After-School Program was organized as a secular institution, some churches declined to contribute further financial support. Nevertheless, Mother Mary is satisfied that the expanded dimension of ministry made possible by the adoption of the secular format fully justifies the decision to make the change. She sees her mission to minister to those in need as she finds them, or as they find her, no matter who they are or what their religious beliefs are. Mother Mary does not offer aid in exchange for a person's "acceptance" of Christ or church membership or becoming an Episcopalian. She has faith that Urban Bridges, by its work and by its example, will succeed in being true to its vision, "a welcoming community presence" bringing "hope, renewal, and revitalization for Olney-Feltonville and other urban neighborhoods." The Book of Micah (6:8) asks the question: "[W]hat does the Lord require of you but to do justice, and to love kindness, and to walk humbly with your God?" Mother Mary, together with Urban Bridges and St. Gabriel's, will continue to follow that course.

Summary

The story of St. Gabriel's Episcopal Church is very special, but it is not unique. In our study, we came across a few such cases. We were told, in several places, of congregations on the brink of extinction that managed to pull themselves out through a successful array of ministries/programs. Nancy Ammerman's (1997) study of congregations in communities that underwent drastic demographic and/or economic changes alludes to the same finding. She noted that "the congregations that have begun new programs have today, on average, far larger memberships and far bigger budgets than do the congregations that have maintained existing patterns" (p. 324). Indeed, this chapter could have been part of the Ammerman study; as St. Gabriel's community underwent a major decline, the church adapted to the changing ecology and learned how to be meaningful to the new residents and sensitive to their needs.

In this case, and in others of its kind, the traditional order is being reversed. While throughout this book we talk about congregations that are concerned primarily with religion and only secondarily with social ministry, in this chapter we describe a case where the social ministry was primary; through its success, the religious community was reborn. It took a devoted and charismatic clergy, backed by the denomination, to pull St. Gabriel's Episcopal Church back to viability. The means was the social ministry; the end was the revived religious community.

It is important to remember that social services provision, even the most successful, cannot guarantee a strong congregation. If a congregation is in decline, a renewed commitment to social care may be helpful, but it cannot guarantee a revived congregation. Milofsky (1997) provides an insightful account of a church in Central North Pennsylvania in which a new pastor aimed at rejuvenating the congregation by introducing new social ministries. However, other factors such as a generational gap, factions within the congregation, building-related problems, and cultural heritage all served as stumbling blocks to success. In other words, while new and enhanced social services can help a congregation lift itself from a state of entropy to vitality, many conditions, including innovative leadership and strong relationships, must be met before such a transformation can take place.

Another word of caution comes from Nancy Ammerman (1997). Not all social services provision is of relevance. Any clergy or lay leader contemplating social programs should make sure that the programs meet the needs of people in the community at that given time:

Believing that congregations should be good citizens and servants of the community only helps when a congregation has also understood the nature of—and is willing to welcome—the community in which it is located. Believing that the congregation should be about the business of saving souls is no more helpful in the process of adaptation, if the congregation does not understand and welcome the diversity those souls represent. Being oriented to activism in the community does seem to assist the congregation in adapting, and being oriented to sanctuary from this world does often seem to stand between congregations and change. (p. 342)

Overall, this chapter shows us the intricate connections between social programs and religious congregations. It is amazing that the two are perceived to operate so much in tandem. In fact, there is no real reason for the two to be so interwoven. Local religious congregations are in the business of catering to spiritual and religious needs that are not necessarily social in nature. Nevertheless, many congregations are involved in social care, and this chapter describes a congregation that stayed alive because of its extensive social services programs.

PART IV

Concluding Remarks

11

Volunteerism and Organized Religion

The United States may justly lay claim to two closely related titles. First, it is the most religious of all modern democracies. According to the World Value Survey, conducted from 1990 to 1993, more people in the United States (82 percent) defined themselves as religious than did those in any other country (*The Economist*, 1995). In a 1993 CNN/USA Today/Gallup poll, 71 percent of Americans reported membership in a church or synagogue, and 41 percent reported attendance at a church or synagogue in the seven days prior to the poll (McAneny & Saad, 1993). A more recent study, by the Pew Research Center for the People and the Press (2001), found that Americans show fairly high rates of observance. Six in ten said that they attend religious services, not including wedding and funerals, at least once a month, while 43 percent claimed to attend at least weekly. Overall, slightly less than half the those polled (46 percent) said that they had attended church in the previous seven days. As noted in chapter 8, the United States is notably more religious than its neighbor to the North, Canada. Second, the United States has the highest rate of volunteerism, defined by the Independent Sector as helping a person or a cause. According to recent studies (Hodgkinson & Weitzman, 1994), more than half of the adult population volunteers in a given year. On average, each volunteer provides 4.2 hours of service a week. One-sixth of the adult American population (13.6 percent) can be described as *committed volunteers*; that is, they average more than five hours of service per week. Formal and informal volunteering accounted for an estimated 20.5 billion hours of service in 1991. This volunteer service was equivalent to approximately 10 million paid full-time positions, with an estimated worth of $176 billion. Such high rates of volunteering are unparalleled in any other country (Ascoli & Cnaan, 1997; Stehle, 1995).

In this chapter, our purpose is to determine whether religion and volunteerism are connected, and, if so, whether the association is direct or indirect. The answers are critical, because they will provide important information regarding potential religion-based volunteerism in the United States. Furthermore, the strength of our civil society is predicated on individuals who extend themselves generously to provide time and resources for the betterment of others or the collective as a whole and who disregard the temptation to be "free riders."

It is our contention that volunteerism is strongly associated with membership in a religious congregation and that personal religious faith alone is a weaker explanation for the decision to volunteer. Three factors account for congregational membership as a strong motivator for volunteerism. First, congregations are not only religious settings but also social settings that enable people to fulfill their psychological need for meaning, self worth, and love. Second, congregations are small groups that, according to social psychologists, hold significant power over their members. Third, membership in an active group that holds many face-to-face meetings increases one's chances of being asked to participate in a volunteer activity. In this respect, we follow Ellison and George's (1994) ideas about positive association between church attendance and social resources, such as larger networks and telephone and in-person contacts, that can support volunteering. Thus, social group processes, coupled with religious culture and an emphasis on helping others, are powerful motivators for volunteerism among people formally affiliated with congregations.

Our hypothesis is supported by three independent sets of data. First, comparative studies of volunteers and nonvolunteers show that religious belief alone is not significantly associated with the decision to volunteer. Second, members of evangelical congregations are less likely or equally likely to engage in social volunteering than main line denominations because the group culture is more concerned with salvation and proselytization than with social service. Furthermore, being "more" religious is not associated with higher rates of volunteer activity. Finally, religious people in other countries are less involved in volunteerism than are those in the United States. In light of these findings, we see a nondirect association between volunteerism and organized religion. This association is mediated by participation in a congregation that acts as a small group and whose culture and social structure emphasizes social responsibility and encourages volunteerism.

The data presented in this chapter concern: (a) the scope and magnitude of social service volunteering within the context of local religious congregations, and (b) the relationships between volunteerism and religion. We then consider the theoretical underpinning of the motivation to volunteer under religious auspices, namely the psychological rewards of joining a congregation and the power of the congregation as a small group. Next, we address strategies congregations use to recruit volunteers, a recruitment that benefits society as a whole. Finally, we summarize our discussions and present recommendations for future research and theory development.

Scope of Volunteering in Local Congregations

Determining the impact of congregation-based volunteerism must necessarily begin with determining its scope and magnitude. According to the Independent Sector study (Hodgkinson, Weitzman, 1994), one-third of all those who volunteer, or 17.6 percent of the population, volunteer within, and for, religious organizations. The Census Bureau's study, which had numerous methodological weaknesses, reported that only 20.4 percent of those age sixteen years and over in the civilian noninstitutional population (those not in prisons, hospitals, and other institutions) had volunteered. However, 37.4 percent of these individuals reported volunteering within, and for, religious organizations (Hayghe, 1991). Peter Dobkin Hall (1990, p. 38) estimated that "churches and church-based institutions currently command approximately 66% of all contributions, 34% of all volunteer work, and 10% of all wages and salaries in the nonprofit sector." These studies, however, did not differentiate between volunteering to maintain the congregation and volunteering on behalf of the congregation to help others. The numbers given are impressive, but they can be misleading.

Volunteerism under the auspices of congregations is important because "without this (volunteer) work force, the education, outreach, and ministry programs of churches would be reduced to a token of their present size and significance" (McDonough, 1976, p. 9). Thus, religion-based volunteerism has a direct effect on the extent to which the social needs of the people in the community are met.

The Independent Sector's *From Belief to Commitment* (Hodgkinson, Weitzman, Kirsch, Noga, & Gorski, 1993) studied congregations across the nation and the extent of their community involvement. As seen in Table 5-1 (p. 98), paid employees and volunteers provide, on a monthly basis, more than 26 million hours for human services or welfare work. Of these, 12 million hours (46 percent) are provided by volunteers. If we add to this other volunteer activities, including those concerned with health, the arts, the environment, or international relief, the total number of hours per month rises to nearly 81 million hours, of which 41 million hours (50 percent) are provided by volunteers. These numbers do not include time allocated for religious ministry, maintaining and serving the congregation, and educational programs.

It is important to note that the Independent Sector study was based on mailed questionnaires to an audience not known for its enthusiasm in cooperating with researchers. Since nonresponse rates can significantly bias findings, the actual scope and magnitude of volunteerism under the auspices of local religious congregations have not been reliably examined. Our study, which involved interviews with representatives of 251 congregations (Appendix), contributes to filling this gap in the literature. We asked our respondents to list up to five programs that best exemplified their congregation's involvement in social and community service provision. Many congregations in our sample, however, had more than five such programs. Thus, our findings underreport the scope of volunteering for social services under congregational auspices. Furthermore, when respondents could not determine the number of hours that volunteers gave to a program, we assigned a value of zero hours to these programs. Our findings thus underreport the number of volunteer hours.

Our findings show that volunteers are an important resource to congregations in providing community service. Of the 1,005 social programs provided by congregations, 788 (78.4 percent) programs used volunteers. The number of volunteer hours per month per program ranged from twenty-five to 23,560 hours, with a mean of 151.5 hours, equivalent to three-quarters of one full-time employee per program.

Using the estimates for monetary value of volunteer work developed earlier in this book, and given that there are between 250,000 and 400,000 religious congregations in the United States, the overall monetary value of volunteer work generated via religious congregations can be estimated at between $21 billion and $37 billion annually.

As impressive as these figures are, they represent primarily urban congregations, rely on conservative estimates of the number of programs and volunteer hours, and provide a sample that is biased toward larger congregations. Nevertheless, these data strongly suggest that organized religion is the source of a very large and active pool of volunteers and that its most frequent and visible manifestation in each neighborhood is the local religious congregation.

Relationships between Volunteerism and Religion

The data suggest a strong association between organized religion and social responsibility that is actualized into volunteerism. Two competing hypotheses have been advanced to explain the relationship between religion and social concern (volunteering to help others). The *direct-link* theory holds that religious people, by theological education or personality, are more concerned with the welfare of others and therefore help the needy more than people who are not religious. The *club* theory holds that religious people are not more concerned with the welfare of others but that belonging to a congregation that helps others influences them to comply with the group's norms and culture and to utilize active personal networks to recruit coreligionists to join in volunteer work. Consequently, congregants exhibit high rates of volunteerism. Wuthnow (1991), for example, doubts that personal faith alone, without the impetus of congregational membership, would motivate people to help others. In this respect, the club theory focuses on the "common cost" that results from *economies of scope*. Given that congregations produce two key goods (a means of religious expression for members and social service to members and others), the costs of producing these goods jointly are less than the cost of producing them separately. In a congregation where people wish to appear "good" in front of others, explicit norms of participation reduce the level of free-riding. Once a congregation overcomes the free-riding problem by instituting norms of behavior and producing certain types of localized social capital, the congregation can produce other sorts of public goods as well at a much lower cost (Iannaccone, 1994).

In this section, we present empirical data and anecdotal material that support the exclusive club theory and contradict the primacy of the direct-link theory. We first show that the decision to volunteer is most often a response to the invitation of others. We provide an example of why a congregational volunteer program is more likely to be successful when members participate as a group. Next, we report findings that demonstrate that volunteering increases as church attendance increases. These data contradict the direct-link hypothesis, in that conservative and evangelical religious people are less likely to volunteer service to others, compared with moderate to liberal religious people. Findings from our previous study (Cnaan, Kasternakis, & Wineburg, 1993) provide additional support for the club theory, specifically that religious people do not volunteer more compared with nonreligious people, nor do they give more hours to volunteering compared with nonreligious volunteers. Finally, we show that religious people volunteer within the context of a congregation and that this context leads to increased external (communal) volunteerism. Thus, religious beliefs, in and of themselves, do not explain the link between religion and volunteerism.

The Independent Sector's biannual national survey on volunteering and giving (Hodgkinson & Weitzman, 1994), conducted by Gallup, found that religious communities are a major source of volunteers. The majority (56 percent) of these volunteers reported they had been recruited by friends who were already involved, either as staff or as volunteers, in the helping organization. Others reported being recruited by religious institutions (26.4 percent), family members or relatives (18.7 percent), persons at the workplace (10.9 percent), employers (6 percent), and others (13.8 percent). It is important to note that the choices presented to respondents were not exclusive, and they sometimes gave more than one response. Hodgkinson and her colleagues also found that the average hours of volunteering per week rose from 1.6 hours for those who do not attend worship services to 3.4 hours for those who attend weekly. The correlation between volunteering and the organized religious community suggests that people who worship together form a community and therefore are more likely to volunteer as a group or as representatives of the group.

A congregational volunteer program is more likely to succeed when it is a group activity. For example, in Council Grove, Kansas, the popular thrift shop, run entirely by volunteers from local congregations, has been in operation for more than twenty years. That the operation has been smooth and efficient over such a long period is a result of the fact that each congregation sends volunteers as a group. Working as a unit keeps members committed and accountable to one another, and this ongoing commitment has been the key to the program's success.

According to Wymer (1997), a crucial factor that distinguishes congregational volunteers from nonvolunteers is regular attendance at worship services. The findings that volunteers attend 6.7 services per month compared to 2.4 times for nonvolunteers suggest that the former feel more connected to the religious community and are more willing to volunteer their time and labor. Robert Wuthnow (1994a) noted that "religious organizations tell people of opportunities to serve, both within and beyond the congregation itself, and provide personal contacts, committees, phone numbers, meeting space, transportation, or whatever it may take to help turn good intentions into action" (pp. 242–243).

This argument should be qualified because, as Wilson and Janoski (1995) have found, members of conservative Protestant denominations are less likely to be involved in secular volunteering than are members of other Protestant denominations. Their focus is assumed to be more on the interior spiritual life than on the community at large; that is, they focus on "other-worldly" affairs, rather than on "this-worldly" affairs. In other words, these congregants use their community and social skills for evangelical purposes and not to advance social and secular causes. However, these authors also found that only 38 percent of the conservative Protestants who did not attend church regularly were volunteers for social causes, compared with 71 percent of the conservative Protestants who attended church regularly. Thus, attendance at services—being part of a religious congregation—is associated with willingness to help others in the community, rather than the liberal or conservative slant of one's perspective (see also Ladd, 1999). In fact, the fundamentalist/liberal polarity may explain the place of volunteering, the cause served, and the meaning it has for the individual, but not the amount of volunteering. For example, other researchers found higher rates of volunteering among evangelicals and fundamentalists compared to mainline and liberal Protestants and Catholics (Regnerus & Smith, 1998). Another key finding by Wilson and Janoski (1995) is that those who attend services are more likely to volunteer than those who do not. Attendance/nonattendance is more important than frequency of attendance. Of those attending worship at least a few times a year, 48 percent reported volunteering, while only 34 percent of nonattenders reported volunteering.

Wilson and Janoski (1995) attempted to find the connection that links church membership, church activism, and secular volunteerism. It is risky to generalize, because this connection depends, to a large degree, on the theological interpretation of volunteering and the significance attached to frequent church attendance. For example, Wilson and Janoski found that, among Catholics, the connection between religion and volunteering is forged at an early age. Those who are introduced to volunteering as children continue to volunteer throughout their lives. Among liberal Protestants, however, the connection between religion and volunteering generally starts in midlife. They often are not encouraged to volunteer as children but are introduced to it as adults. On the other hand, among conservative Protestants, the connection to volunteering is often not developed, and volunteering is mostly inward, for the purpose of sustaining the church.

The Pew Research Center for the People and the Press (2001) studied 2,041 adults early in 2001. Researchers measured involvement in non-church volunteer activities among the respondents. Such activities included working with the homeless, visiting the sick, helping in an arts/cultural organization, and volunteering in child/youth program. In virtually every area, those who are heavily involved in activities at their congregation are among the most likely to volunteer. In the words of the authors of the study, "The same can be said of those who are highly committed to their faith, though the differences are not as drastic" (Section IV, p. 4). For example, volunteering in community child/youth development programs was reported by 39 percent of those highly involved in religious activities, 24 percent of those who are modestly involved in religious activities, and only 18 percent of those with low involvement.

Volunteering is not as widespread in Canada as it in the United States (31 percent and 49 percent, respectively). Nevertheless, much can be learned from Canadian volunteerism about motivation to volunteer. According to the first Canadian national survey of giving and volunteering (Statistics Canada, 1998), those with a religious affiliation volunteered more than those with no religious affiliation (33 percent versus 28 percent). The difference increased dramatically when those who attended church weekly were compared with those who did not attend church weekly (46 percent versus 28 percent). This difference was larger still when very religious people were compared with those who described themselves as not very religious (44 percent versus 30 percent). The report also found that those with strong religious ties contributed more time to volunteering than did other volunteers. "Volunteers who attended church weekly gave, on average, 197 hours over a 12-month period; those who did not attend services weekly gave an average of 136 hours" (p. 32). Similar findings were found for those who described themselves as very religious.

Volunteerism through participation in organized religious group, rather than as a result of religious beliefs, was also found in Belgium. Frans Lammertyn and Lesley Hustinx studied 715 students in Katholic University, Leuven. They found that religion and religious beliefs did not significantly impact volunteering. However, church attendance was strongly and significantly associated with volunteering. Among those who reported volunteering, 23 percent attended church at least monthly, while among those who never volunteered, only 12 percent attended church at least monthly. In other words, patterns from these Belgian students indicated that volunteering was twice as prevalent among those who attended church regularly, while religion and beliefs in God were not significantly associated with volunteering.

Yonish and Campbell (1998), in their analysis of the Independent Sector's data on volunteering, concluded that those who attend worship services, regardless of religious tradition, are more likely to volunteer than those who do not and that "more frequent church attendance corresponds with a greater proportion of volunteers" (p. 8). They further noted that "church is a common path of recruitment for the other types of volunteering as well—for advocacy volunteering, for example, church (32.5 percent) ranks with both family (34.6 percent) and friends (36.3 percent)" (p. 9). The common thread to all these forms of recruitment is the presence of social ties, rather than an awakening from within (a religious call) or a response to an advertisement in mass media. Church members also tend to volunteer along with family members. According to these authors, there is no better evidence for the impact of church attendance on volunteering "than the fact that, *ceteris paribus, church attendance rivals education as a predictor of volunteering*" (p. 12) (emphasis in original). Given that the literature on volunteering is rife with claims and assertions that education is the primary explanation for volunteering, Yonish and Campbell's claim that church attendance is an even stronger factor is highly significant.

Finally, an interesting footnote to the data on the variable impact of religious beliefs and religious participation on social volunteering is the impact of religiosity and actual religions participation on the impact of drug treatment. Richard, Bell, and Carlson (2000) found beneficiaries who actually attended church had better outcomes than those who merely professed religious belief.

Motivation to volunteer: Findings regarding the association between religious motivation and volunteering are inconsistent. Abdennur (1987), for example, reviewed the literature on volunteerism and concluded that religious motivation for volunteering is seldom supported by research. Hunter and Linn (1980–1981) found no significant difference in the "degree of religious feeling" between elderly volunteers and nonvolunteers. Similarly, Wuthnow (1991) found only very weak relationships between religious motivation and volunteering.

Cnaan, Kasternakis, and Wineburg (1993), who compared a sample of 500 volunteers with 500 nonvolunteers, found that the two groups did not differ in their religious motivation. They also found that volunteers with high religious motivation did not spend more time volunteering than did those with less religious motivation. These findings were supported by later studies by Jackson, Bachmeier, Wood, and Craft (1995) and Wymer (1997).

Cnaan, Kasternakis, and Wineburg (1993), however, found that levels of religious motivation were higher among human service volunteers who worked in religious settings than among those who worked in secular settings. This is significant because it validates the importance of contextual variables: congregations have greater access to religiously motivated people than do other agencies. Had their congregations not been involved in providing human services, "it is quite possible that these people would not have volunteered at all or would have volunteered at other agencies" (p. 47). Brooks (1980), in a sample of volunteers in religious congregations, found that the more volunteers were involved with the church, the longer they tended to serve. Finally, Myrom (1976), in a study of synodical volunteers in New England, found that the two most important motives in the decision to volunteer were the desire to be part of the larger community and the desire to put one's faith into action in meaningful ways.

Jackson, Bachmeier, Wood, and Craft (1995) found that most secular volunteer work by religious people is performed by "congregants whose attendance is translated into ties to smaller groups within the church" (p. 75). In this respect, although people might, through congregational attendance, become aware of the needs of others, their decision to volunteer was actually motivated by their ties with a significant group of individuals within the congregation. Volunteering represents active participation, rather than passive attendance at a communal worship service. This notion of active participation in the congregation and the sense of belonging has seldom been addressed in the literature. In the next section, we discuss what needs are met by active participation in the congregation and why one needs the group to meet these needs. Once an individual joins the group, group peer pressure and norms motivate volunteerism.

Penny Edgell Becker (2000) found that among church members, those who volunteer consider other congregation members among their best friends more often than those who do not volunteer. Moreover, once friendship is considered, the salience of religion loses any predictive power. In addition, Becker found that the relevant group for attenders who volunteer is not neighbors but congregational friends. Becker also found that importance of religion to a congregant does not predict the likelihood of his or her volunteering within the church; however, sharing confidences with fellow congregational members does predict volunteerism among church members. Becker stressed that congregations compete with other civil society groups and not all congregations are doing a good job of motivating members to volunteer. Congregations that have large staffs and that see themselves as leaders in the community attract fewer volunteers, since members assume that the paid staff will work in the community on behalf of the congregation. However, for a congregation to recruit volunteers for its projects, it must not only offer unique programs but also make members feel connected to the group and its other members.

Hoge and his colleagues (1998), who studied the volunteer contributions of church members, found that approximately half the members volunteer to help their congregations and the congregation's social services. The researchers also sought to understand what differentiates church members who volunteer from those who do not. While they found that education and income explained increased volunteering, the key was something else:

> Church attendance is a much stronger predictor than anything else. Put simply, church attendance and participation in church programs are by far the strongest predictors of volunteering. People who participate tend to volunteer and vice versa, telling us that volunteering should be conceptualized as a close cousin to worship attendance and program participation. Probably the motivations behind attendance, participation, and volunteering are closely related, and the motivations include the gratification of spending time with fellow church members and doing meaningful tasks together with them.

Volunteerism in international perspective: Kenneth Newton (1997) compared volunteerism in West Germany and in the United States. In his view, the fact that Americans are more active as congregational members than are Germans accounts for their higher rates of volunteerism, which is a major contribution to society. "If one estimates that a volunteer hour is worth the average salary paid to an American worker, the extra level of religious behavior in the United States (as compared to West Germany) adds the equivalent of $70 billion a year to the American economy" (p. 590). Furthermore, Newton, who used Independent Sector data for 1992, concluded that 34 percent of volunteers had been motivated by their religious affiliations.

Peter Kaldor and his colleagues (1999) studied church participation in Australia. In a random sample of 8,500 individuals, the authors asked a series of questions on religious participation and community volunteering.

Questions about volunteering outside the congregation produced significant findings: "The Australian Community Survey found that 21 percent of church attenders are involved in care, welfare or support groups, compared to 7 percent of non-attenders" (p. 72). Kaldor and his colleagues noted that "former attenders, who were once regularly involved in a church as an adult but are no longer involved, are also more likely to be involved in such groups than people who never regularly attended church as an adult." As such, congregational membership may have prolonged long-term effects that are sustained after active membership ends.

Another argument in favor of the club theory is that religious people in other highly religious countries, such as Ireland and Poland, seldom volunteer to help others in the community. Thus, the link between volunteerism and religion goes through the congregation and is uniquely American. In other words, it is through the congregation that members learn about the need for volunteers, and this information may come from the institution itself (for example, congregational flyers, bulletin board postings, or requests by clergy for volunteers) or from another person (for example, another member). The implication is that the urge to volunteer comes not from within the person but from social influences. Most volunteer coordinators know that the best way to recruit volunteers is to approach them through people they know and trust. Volunteering is social, and therefore it is the participation in a congregation and the bonding with other congregants that foster volunteering among religious people. It is the social function of the congregation that actualizes the religious teaching of helping others.

Psychological Needs and Volunteering

The impressive magnitude and scope of volunteering under congregational auspices may lead to the assumption that religious people volunteer more than nonreligious people. After all, religious people are traditionally associated with congregations, and religious theology calls for social responsibility. We have already established, however, that the available empirical data support the club theory (belonging to a religious congregation motivates people to volunteer) but do not support the direct-link theory (being religious, in and of itself, motivates people to volunteer).

The study of human need and its impact on motivation flourished in the 1950s, especially as a result of the atrocities in World War II. One of the most notable studies of motivation was Abraham Maslow's (1954) classic hierarchy of needs. Maslow identified five needs, ranging from the physiological (the need to meet basic needs, such as food and shelter) to the psychological (the need to achieve a sense of self-actualization) and theorized that individuals are motivated to act in order to meet these needs. This hierarchy met with a storm of criticism. Some charged that social-class bias was evident in the ranking of needs, while others questioned the inclusiveness of his hierarchy. Despite objections to this particular hierarchy, the quest to satisfy needs is now generally accepted as a main source of human motivation.

Maslow's hierarchy-of-needs theory presumed a motivation process based on deficit cycles: periods in the life of an individual in which he or she is motivated to have his or her needs met. The deficit cycle, which encompasses need, goal, behavior, and satisfaction, repeats itself until a person's needs are met. McDonough (1976) argued that motivation should be a growth process, rather than a deficit cycle. The growth process proposed by McDonough (1976, p. 54) encompassed need, goal, behavior, and objective. Those whose motivation stems from this growth process are characterized by a sense of autonomy and altruism.

Volunteering meets several key psychological needs. First is what Victor Frankl (1963) defined as the *search for meaning*. Frankl, a Holocaust survivor, struggled with the question of why some survived the Holocaust and others did not, despite similar circumstances. He concluded that those who had found a meaning to life were better able to cope with hardships and to do more with what resources were available. In the mid-1960s, William Glasser, in his book *Reality Therapy* (1965), asserted that all human beings struggle to attain self-worth and love. He argued that prisoners who knew they were loved and valued by people (even if actual contact was denied) were likely to survive isolation and torture, while those who did not have this reassurance often perished. Although we may not consider the need for meaning, love, and self-worth to be a life-and-death matter, it remains the most powerful psychological force in our lives.

For many, organized religion is the means by which they find meaning for their lives. Joseph (1987) noted that "religion has a remarkable capacity to provide a sense of *identity* and *rootedness* for both the person and the group. Through its corporate belief system and community of faith, a deep sense of affiliation can develop. This is particularly significant for many who feel alienated at this time of social and cultural transition" (p. 17) (italics in original).

Andrew Greeley (1972) noted that people join congregations to satisfy their basic personal needs. He identified these needs as meaning (religious), belongingness (social), and comfort (psychological). "Belongingness" fulfills members' need for social recognition when they take on positions of responsibility and perform public duties. The appreciation of others tells these members that they are respected and accepted.

Few community-based organizations generate fellowship and moral support to the degree congregations do. Roof (1996) noted that, with the decline in the importance of and trust in traditional structures such as the family, neighborhood, fraternal/sororal organizations, the political system, and religious denominations, the flourishing of small, intentional, and narrowly focused groups represents "new forms of community . . . organized around personal concerns and feelings" (p. 157). We would add that the congregation is one of the few remaining locally based social institutions that provide people with a strong sense of belonging and trust, even though the membership may change over time and people may switch from one group to another. Roof considered changes in membership as indicative of "a movement of de-centralization and reshaping of structures to fit needs of individuals" (p. 157).

A search for meaning in one's life is not the only purpose served when one joins a religious congregation. Congregations are also social settings where people of similar backgrounds and interests come together to form small groups. This is true for many of the megachurches, and it is true for the popular movement known as "Promise Keepers" (PK).[14] PK's complex structure of "ambassadors" and "key men" is based on the idea of small groups networking into extremely large groups. The goal is recruitment: each recruit seeks out others who, in turn, seek out still others. Important links in this loose yet loyal structure are the "key men" in evangelical churches across the country who spread the word about PK. This activity fills stadiums with men and establishes churches. The technique parallels that used by early Christians to spread their religion.

Even in big new churches, people form small home-study prayer groups, much as the communists used to form small cells. Sometimes, these groups grow into separate churches. Two PK groups, known as the Calvary and the Vineyard groups, encourage this kind of decentralized, nonbureaucratic religious intimacy (Ross & Cokorinos, 1997). Baby boomers respond well to the entrepreneurial spirit of these groups. In the Chapel of Champions, for example, the pastor's goal is the creation of eighty small groups of five men each. The goal is to bring together men committed to the key values of PK: worship, discipleship, community, ministry, and evangelism.

Membership in a religious congregation or a small religious group means belonging to a social network (Ellison & George, 1994). Involvement in the social life of a congregation increases the likelihood that an individual will engage in activities shared by other members with whom he or she has face-to-face contacts. Given that many congregations are involved in carrying out social services, it is likely that congregants will come into personal contact with—and join with—others already engaged in volunteer work. People who join groups, especially religious congregations, are likely to internalize the norms and activities prevalent in these groups.

More than any other scholar of religion, Wuthnow (1988) has focused on the essence and power of small groups within the congregation (and society) and on their power to motivate people for action within an organized religious context. Wuthnow noted that:

At the local level, special-purpose groups are constantly coming into being and taking new directions as leadership, information, and other kinds of resources become available. At one local church, for example, three special-purpose groups emerged within the space of about 18 months: one was concerned with promoting greater equality for women in the church, another with providing care for needy people in the community, the third with revitalizing the church's worship services. All three came about when small informal groups of parishioners started to communicate with one another, discovered common concerns, and decided to advocate for changes in church policy. In each case, the church's leadership structure was sufficiently flexible to accommodate the inclusion of new members with new interests, to oversee the creation of new programs, and to form new committees so that the special purpose groups could be incorporated into the official activities of the church. As a result, people who were previously dissatisfied, and who might otherwise have left the church in search of greener pastures, stayed on and became active participants in the church. Indeed, the new special purpose groups that were established ran largely on this additional energy rather than draining resources from existing programs. (p. 123)

In his book *Sharing the Journey*, Wuthnow (1994b) asserted that Americans are transforming the way they contribute to the community and the public good through reliance on small groups, rather than on formal institutional arrangements. While many people continue to donate money to institutional arrangements, others need to feel that their personal actions are meaningful. For Wuthnow, "the small-group movement has emerged as a serious effort to combat the forces of fragmentation and anonymity in our society and to reunite spirituality with its roots in human community" (p. 40). Is this really a new social phenomenon, or simply one that has only recently been noticed? Perhaps other arrangements, such as fraternal and sororal organizations, formerly provided people with the small-group experience; with their disappearance (Hall, 1996), religious settings are becoming the primary providers of small-group experiences.

Wuthnow found that small groups play a vital role in institutional religious settings. According to his survey, 40 percent of the adult population in America claims involvement in "a small group that meets regularly and provides caring and support for those who participate in it" (p. 45). Of those who participate in small groups, 69 percent reported that their participation helped them serve people outside the group, and 43 percent reported volunteering in their community as a result of their small-group involvement. Wuthnow concluded that "the members of small groups are quite often prompted to become more active in their communities, to help others who may be in need, and to think more deeply about pressing social and political issues" (p. 346).

These findings strongly suggest that involvement in projects to benefit others is a result more of the culture of the small group within the congregation than of personal religious conviction. We suggest that, in America, people in the congregation, as well as those outside the congregation, accept it as natural that congregations will help people in need and that people in need are expected to approach congregations for help. This is so pervasive in our culture that it is a norm accepted by all members of society. Unlike those in many other parts of the world, American congregations are perceived as a source of social services and of community and political education and mobilization. For example, congregational involvement in political action is related to the congregation's religious life, which, in turn, reflects the local culture. On the basis of a study of thirteen congregations, Wood (1994) suggested that the most politically involved congregations are not those with the most politicized faith but, rather, those whose liturgy leads to a meaningful religious experience and those that interpret their religious symbols in "this-worldly" terms. In other words, members' political preferences are secondary to the congregational spirit and culture. Members join the congregation and become more or less politically and socially involved according the congregational spirit. Even passive people tend to increase their participation if the congregation is active, while more active and involved members will tame their activity if the group norm in the congregation is not to get too involved.

A Model of Congregational Volunteering

Findings from our interviews and the literature review support the view that volunteering is not the direct result of religious beliefs and teaching. These findings show that volunteering is mediated by congregational activity and social connections that channel religious beliefs and teaching into action. The importance of the congregation as the mediator between religion and volunteerism suggests the following model:

> Religious beliefs and religious meaning——>
> Congregational attendance——>
> Formation of face-to-face links——>
> Congregational involvement——>
> Acceptance of group norms for serving/volunteering——>
> Volunteering in the context of the congregation

This proposed model puts extra emphasis on the central links of the model, because they are the necessary catalysts that transform religious beliefs into action (club theory). In our model, if the congregation ceases to exist, people will remain faithful; what will decrease is the level of volunteering for social causes. Volunteerism is enhanced through conformity with group norms that call upon members to come together and help others in need.

Another important finding is that congregational social programs attract nonmember volunteers, many of whom are friends and relatives of member volunteers. While these individuals may not share the religious beliefs of the congregants, they are motivated to volunteer because of personal contact with members who adhere to the congregational norm of social responsibility and active social service. As was reported in chapter 5, for every 100 congregational volunteers there are an additional forty-five volunteers from the community.

Implications for Volunteer Management

Recognition of the congregation as the mediator between religion and volunteerism requires a new perspective on the recruiting, training, and retaining of volunteers who are members of religious congregations and their guests. Recruitment of a congregational volunteer can often yield a cluster of volunteers. For example, one congregation in Oakland, California, adopted the nearby nursing home. The decision was made by the congregation after a few meetings; a sizable portion of the congregation agreed to participate, with each congregant giving one afternoon a month to volunteer at the nursing home. Together, the congregants cover the whole nursing home twice a week for making friendly visits, reading, chatting, praying if asked for, accompanying residents on walks, if possible, shopping, or simply being there to cheer up the residents. We see from this example that it may be more productive to recruit a group of congregants than to recruit one individual at a time. Retaining congregational volunteers is likely to be more successful for two reasons: first, the volunteers will sustain one another; second, volunteers will be rewarded not only by the personal satisfaction that comes from doing good deeds but also by the sense of self-worth that comes from knowing that they are perceived by other congregants as being caring individuals and exemplary role models.

Group volunteering by congregants exemplifies what Sue Vineyard (1993) defined as "building community." Vineyard describes these "communities" as groups of people who are bonded in a common mission, network on many levels, and share a common identity; these characteristics are a key force in successful volunteerism. The power of the group, coupled with careful supervision by program organizers, ensures minimal absenteeism and more cost-effective service. Moreover, retention is higher because volunteer work, when done with friends, provides a basis for social interaction and gratification from significant people such as close friends, relatives, and religious counterparts. We are most likely to be influenced by what significant people think of us and to attempt to meet their expectations. A volunteer who works side by side with such people is more likely to obtain their approval—and thus remain on staff—than is one who works alone.

Thus, a congregation's decision to assist the needy is neither frivolous nor a response to external pressure. Social ministry requires that a need be identified and that someone, generally a leader of the congregation, advocate that the service be delivered. As is discussed in next chapter, the most influential actors in initiating congregational volunteer programs were the clergy (39.2 percent) and individual members/groups (35.6 percent), while congregational committees (9 percent) and staff members (11.2 percent) had considerably less clout. Few programs in our study were initiated in response to requests from those outside the congregation: other congregations (3.3 percent); diocese/judicatory (2.6 percent); neighborhood coalitions (1.9 percent); human service organizations (1.9 percent); and government agencies (1.4 percent). In hierarchical congregations, the clergy had the most influence in initiating social programs; in more democratic congregations, lay leaders and active members were of equal or greater influence.

As these data show, it is those directly affiliated with the congregation who influence the decision to embark upon a new social program. In other words, the impetus for a new program begins within the congregation. This does not mean that outside influences have no effect. A member or the clergy may be contacted by someone outside the congregation who has identified a problem or who is involved in caring for people with certain needs. The internal decision-making process, however, requires that a person or group affiliated with the congregation advocate for the cause and obtain approval, support, and commitment from the membership. Consequently, the program remains internal in its initiation, development, and implementation.

If a communal volunteer program is to be successful, then congregational leaders and staff must allow the volunteers to assume ownership, provide leadership, and shape the program to meet their vision and interest. When recruiting additional volunteers, members should explain what the need is, describe what is being done, and allow new volunteers to shape the service as they see fit and in a manner with which they feel comfortable. If new recruits are forced into a mold that is not their own, they will withdraw and avoid participating. While new volunteers must accept some boundaries, as well as the basic structure of the existing program, they should also be encouraged to make it "their" program and to feel that they have a voice in how the program is run. This balance is not always easy, but it is crucial to retaining new volunteers.

The task of volunteer recruitment should be shared jointly by member volunteers and the clergy. Recruitment by members is often helpful because it involves a personal factor. For example, people are more likely to respond positively to a member volunteer who knows them personally than to a pastor who may not even know them by name. In addition, volunteers tend to be more sensitive to the needs of newly recruited volunteers because of their own experience as volunteers.

Conversely, recruitment by clergy is important when the recruitment is part of a plan to enhance the mission or ministry of a congregation or the spiritual or personal development of its members. When the clergy call members to address a certain concern, many members tend to follow. Important as this "call to arms" may be, it is even more important that the congregation have a plan in place that includes the appropriate use of volunteers. The reason is that, once a problem has been identified, pastoral leaders and volunteers do not always agree on what should be done and how. The appropriate use of volunteers should be guided by, and sensitive to, the needs of the congregation.

Importance of Well-Run Programs

Volunteer work is not a casual pastime; it is a serious commitment. Congregational members give of their time because they want to serve others and to be appreciated by peers. Like all volunteers, they want to be involved in a well-run operation, particularly when it represents their congregation. Although their contribution is voluntary and their ties are informal, they want to be associated with a project of the highest quality. If volunteers find that the congregation's leaders or staff do not value their work or that the program is poorly run, then recruitment and attendance will fall off; the program's reputation will decline; and the quality of service will deteriorate.

Professionalism in the organization of the program is essential, even though recruitment and retention are spiritual, social, and personal in nature. Good organization is like the digestive system of the body. "You are utterly unaware of digestion as long as it is working, but when it ceases to function properly, you aren't aware of anything else. But that is indigestion, not digestion. Now when you become aware of it, it means it is malfunctioning. Good organization is just as unnoticeable as the digestive system of the body when it is functioning properly" (Sullivan, 1971, p. 42).

Harris (1998) emphasizes the importance of ongoing encouragement and support for congregational volunteers. Congregations often take volunteers for granted, overlooking the fact that volunteers expect some type of reward, usually in terms of recognition, in return for their investment of time and energy. This applies to the lay leaders who basically run the congregations, as well as to those who volunteer only on certain occasions. Lack of recognition may alienate the former, whose expertise is essential to the congregation, and cause the latter to feel less involved.

A job description is an indicator of good organization and important for volunteer recruitment and retention. Unfortunately, church volunteer coordinators often recruit members for a project, only to lose many of them a month later. One reason volunteers drop out is undefined and unrealistic expectations (Wolfe, 1991). At recruitment, people should be told about the importance of the task they are being asked to do, the expectations of the congregation regarding the task, and how much time will be required to accomplish the task. Volunteer recruiters should be aware of the motivations and expectations of volunteers, as well as of their skills and time limitations. These are important factors in determining how volunteers will be recruited, assigned tasks, and trained. Once recruited, volunteers should feel confident that they are truly being of service and that they are making a meaningful contribution of their time and skills.

Summary

In this chapter, we proposed that the connection between religion and volunteerism to help others in the United States is not directly linked to personal religious belief. People, regardless of their level of religiosity, are involved in volunteering to support various causes in our society. What is seldom, if ever, discussed is the association between congregational membership and volunteerism. People who join congregations do so to meet certain religious, psychological, and social needs. We make the distinction between those who attend worship services only and those who are actively involved in the congregation because they value the fellowship it represents. For the latter, these social interactions and ties encourage them to comply with the group norm of actively caring for those in the community who are in need. If the norm includes and fosters volunteerism, then the individual is likely to volunteer. If the norm is to seek out new members, then the individual will likely comply. If the norm is solely to worship and to provide mutual support, then the individual is likely to conform to that standard.

A competing hypothesis posits a direct association between religious beliefs and increased volunteerism. It argues that religious teaching, in and of itself, fosters social responsibility. We contend that this hypothesis fails empirically in three key tests. First, comparisons of religious and nonreligious people have found no significant differences in the level of volunteering. Furthermore, more religious people do not tend to volunteer more frequently than do less religious people. Second, people of very conservative or evangelical religious orientation, regardless of denomination, are said to volunteer less than people of moderate religious orientation. While these data are debatable, even among this group, attenders volunteer significantly more than nonattenders. Finally, religious people in other countries volunteer less than religious people in the United States. Thus, we support the hypothesis of a nondirect association between volunteerism and religion, one that is mediated by participation in a religious congregation that acts as a small group and that sustains and perpetuates the norms and expectations of social responsibility and volunteerism under the auspices of the congregation.

People join religious congregations to practice their faith and, in the process, to fulfill their psychological needs for meaning, self-worth, and love. Through the congregational group, people are motivated to comply with the group's norms and culture. If the group stresses volunteerism, then it is assumed that more members will volunteer. This assumption also explains variations in volunteering among religious groups. Joining a more evangelical group that stresses evangelism rather than social service is likely to result in decreased volunteerism, even though the level of religious beliefs may be very high. Conversely, joining a mainline Protestant church that stresses social service as a means of practicing faith is likely to result in increased volunteerism. Similarly, congregational members in other countries volunteer less frequently than do those in the United States because their religious groups and national norms do not sustain the expectations of volunteerism under religious auspices. In those countries, congregants' psychological needs are fulfilled merely by participating in the worship services and at times assisting in the performance of these worship services. In the United States, however, the culture of most religious communities is to serve others in needs. Therefore, those most likely to obtain full psychological benefits from congregational membership are those who volunteer.

The confusion regarding this issue of volunteerism and religion is understandable. Given that members of congregations are generally religious people, it has been increasingly difficult to separate the two issues. We have found, however, that congregational membership, whether formal or informal, includes a small group who are not interested in religion per se. This group includes, but is not limited to, spouses of members; neighbors who appreciate the congregation's ambiance and culture; friends of members; and others who seek social contacts. In many congregations, this group of people is easily identified, because its members are often self-proclaimed and are prohibited from participation in some religious practices. It is our hypothesis that rates of volunteerism for this group are similar to those of people who joined the congregation to express their faith.

As the literature shows, theological and cultural expectations for social volunteering vary among and within denominations. It will be of great interest to follow a few congregations and to qualitatively assess their culture and their theology as actualized in sermons and prayers, and to assess their relationship with volunteering. Such a study will enhance our understanding of the group culture and group expectations and their impact on actual levels of volunteering. This is a research challenge awaiting study. Similarly, the organizational or personal characteristics of congregations and their members that are conducive to enhance volunteerism for others is another topic awaiting study. What we have identified in this chapter is the overall trend: congregations are a community hub that enhance civil involvement for their members and friends.

12

Why and How Congregations Get Involved in Service Delivery

> Those who train many in the ways of justice will sparkle like the
> stars for all eternity. —Daniel 12:3

In previous chapters, and in the following chapter, we show that the extensive involvement of congregations in the provision of social and community services is the norm in the United States. We also analyze the social factors behind this impressive involvement. The question of *why* congregations get involved in service delivery still needs to be answered. In this chapter, we explore this important issue.

In the first section, we present the rationale for congregational involvement in social services. For clarity and for brevity's sake, we delineate the primary motives and present them as though they were distinct from one another, despite their obvious overlap. We also discuss how these motives, in tandem, contribute to congregation-based social service delivery. Our discussion is based on data from open-ended questions on our "Core Form" questionnaire (see Appendix). We asked respondents to explain why their congregations were involved in social or community services and why they permitted other community groups to use their facilities. Clergy and lay leaders from 251 congregations in eight localities responded. The motives for congregational involvement were broadly classified as: (a) pragmatic considerations that support and/or maintain the congregation; (b) theological directives that promote care, compassion, and social justice; and (c) spiritual practices that encourage moral and faith development. We conclude by discussing two issues: proselytization, which is often incorrectly presumed to be a motive for providing social services, and the social bonding that social service delivery provides the congregation, a motive that is rarely mentioned but that was reflected in most of the interviews.

In the second section of this chapter, we discuss the role of government retrenchment in social services as a rationale for congregational involvement in social services. We then report our findings on the person or group identified as the initiator of the congregation's social and community programs. The data for this discussion are based on closed-ended questions on the "Specific Program Form" (see Appendix). These results further distinguish the social and community involvement of congregations according to the internal and external cues for initiating services.

Why Congregations Get Involved in Service Delivery

Pragmatic Considerations

Pragmatic considerations in service delivery, for the most part, were based on tradition, the need to care for members and the community, or the survival needs of the congregation.

Tradition: Many congregations reported tradition as their rationale for providing social and community services. Of the 1,005 programs reported, 185 (18.4 percent) were long-standing programs and had become part of the congregation's identity. Responses that indicated tradition as a motive included:

"It is the tradition of congregations to fill needs."

"There is no point for us to stop this beautiful tradition that the previous generation started."

"We have a long-term church commitment to the arts because the arts are a means of liberating the spirit."

"We provide these programs because it is the right thing to do. We have a tradition of doing things for the community at large."

"Historically, this has been the mission of the church and, by tradition, we have a strong commitment to the community."

The tradition of service often began with the work of one person. For example, several programs reflected the influence of a former clerical or lay leader on the congregation. One respondent noted:

Reverend X started the food pantry in the Depression. He retired in the 1970s and died two years ago. In his memory and as part of our pride in our history, we continue feeding people and will keep doing so as long as we are in business.

Other congregation leaders reported that their parents had served others through the congregation, and they (the interviewees) wanted to continue this tradition in memory of their parents, as well as for themselves, their congregation, and their own children. This practice of helping others through the local religious congregation was seen as a legacy to be passed from one generation to the next, even if the next generation joined a different congregation

Care for members and the community: Often the people in need have a relationship with the congregation or are essential to the congregation. The community around the congregation is as important as the members of the congregation for its ongoing functioning. As such, it is caring for "our" extended membership when a congregation serves the needs of people in the community. Some responses that suggested support as a motive for service delivery were:

"We care for the people in the community."

"There is a need to be met."

"We see the needs of the people, and we want to help in some way."

The needs of others often moved a congregation to be generous and caring. Respondents noted many instances in which a social program began after a member or clergy had observed a need and described what he or she had seen on the streets or heard from others. A typical response was: "We were moved by his testimony and wanted to do something for those unfortunate people." In other instances, the incentive for a new service came from individual members or committees, "people who witnessed a need and felt compassion towards those who suffer" and who brought their concerns to the attention of the congregation.

We found that congregations often initiated programs to help a group of members with a particular need. This motive was reflected in the following responses:

"The program was a response to the need of many members whose economic situation suddenly changed for the worse."

"The pastor believes that members are a part of the community and addressing the issues in the community will improve the quality of their lives."

"We were concerned about the needs of congregants—domestic violence, the impact of drug and alcohol on families, the lack of family structure."

At times, the motives were mixed, as in the case of a congregation that reported: "The community needed day care so members of our congregation who needed work run the program." One pastor expressed a more balanced view: "The church's mission is to serve the members and community equally."

In many cases, the pattern of social service followed demographic changes in the congregation and/or the community. A congregation that does not keep step with its own demographic changes and those of its community may not survive (Ammerman, 1997). As such, many services address the needs of the predominant group in the membership. For example, when the average age increases or the economic level of members declines, the congregation may develop services to meet members' changing needs. These services are often extended to the community, as well. For example, when a congregation in Oakland developed a residential home for its elderly members and their relatives, they also opened the program to the elderly in their community. Thus, as services that initially address the needs of the congregation expand to include nonmembers, the congregation ceases to be a member-serving organization and becomes a social institution that benefits the community.

Survival needs of the congregation: As a social institution, congregations have temporal needs and responsibilities. While their primary function is religious, congregations have other concerns: membership growth, financial obligations, maintenance and protection of church property, and the relationship between the congregation and the community. All congregations must give some consideration to these issues in order to survive and grow. For many of the congregations in our survey, these practical considerations were a primary rationale for involvement in social services.

A significant concern for most congregations is financial survival. In some cases, the congregation generated the resources necessary for its survival by renting space and/or providing services. Whether it be a grant from a foundation or government agency, renovation of the building by a tenant such as a day care center, or fees for services such as a counseling or day-care program, many congregations must look for ways to supplement members' contributions if they are to cover their financial expenditures. One congregation said its reason for establishing a day care center was "the need for rental, but also a sympathetic response to need." Similarly, a congregation that rents space for concerts said, "We have space that is acoustically good for music, and the rental revenues help us. We have been doing this for many years." In this instance, the communal service was motivated by financial considerations, as well as by tradition. Another response demonstrates the complexity of such motives: "We did it for both reasons. The extra income and because we felt that, as we are a church, we should help them . . . as part of our outreach."

Several congregations became involved in service delivery as a means of gaining respect and acceptance in the community. This was often an important consideration in congregations where many members did not live in the neighborhood. Helping the community improve its quality of life, in turn, helped the congregation and its members feel more like "insiders." A member of a church in Mobile explained the church's community involvement as follows: "It is a way to raise the visibility of church. We have good location and can help them." A recurring theme among members and leaders of the congregation was the desire to be seen as an integral part of the community: "We want to be part of society and not alienate the community."

For many congregations, service delivery was a way to give something back to the community. Some congregations kept their doors open during the day, and others provided space for community meetings so that neighbors would feel free to use and enjoy their facilities. Congregation leaders said it was important for the community and the congregation to share a common interest and purpose rather than to feel alienated from and hostile toward each other. Responses that expressed this motive were as follows:

> "Social ministry lets the neighbors know that it isn't strange to be a church member—that it's just like them. We are trying together to make it in a world full of sin."

"More visibility; show people that we want to be involved; and that we are [an] extraverted, not an introverted, institution."

"A sense of mission. Survival for us and them. Need to be a part of neighborhood because this neighborhood is what and where we are even if we do not reside here."

"Open-door policy provides contact and image."

Another pragmatic motive for service provision was protection of property. For many urban congregations, the fear of vandalism is very real, and many of these congregations have members who live elsewhere and are therefore perceived as strangers in the community. (Although respondents gave high priority to security, they identified being a "good neighbor" as their primary motive in providing social services.)

The reasoning was as follows: if congregations want to be perceived as neighbors rather than as outsiders who simply drop by for worship, then the congregation must act like neighbors. If congregations help the community, then they will be treated as part of the community. At best, this will prevent vandalism and theft; at worst, community members will be more likely to call the police if someone is vandalizing church property. A response typical of this motive was: "We provide these services to be good neighbors to those in need, and we keep an open-door policy. We try to be friendly with the community so that they will be friendly with us and our church." For example, one large church in Indianapolis is located in a declining neighborhood, but all its members live in affluent urban and suburban neighborhoods. To protect itself, the congregation installed a sensitive alarm system. However, the congregation's most important security step was making itself a good neighbor by providing services and programs to local residents who, in turn, protect the church property.

Most congregations meet only on weekends and maybe once in between Monday and Friday for religious services and worship. Were it not for social services, the buildings would be deserted during the week. The frequent presence of congregation members and the increased traffic throughout the week serves as a deterrent to vandalism and theft. Responses that expressed this motivation were:

"Social service provision is self preservation—good public relations. This way we are not indifferent to the community."

"[Service delivery] builds friendships and helps make contact with others. We want to serve the community and be good neighbors."

"It is an issue that they [the assisted neighbors] are supportive of the congregation and responsible members of the community."

"We gain the trust of people and help them."

Again, motives for service delivery are a mixture of compassion and a desire for positive visibility in the community.

Many congregations have recognized that they must earn the right to be considered part of the community and that with this right comes the responsibility to give something back to the community. Other responses that express this motivation for service delivery were:

"The community gave us a lot, and we are now in debt to the community. We ought to serve the place that supported us."

"We owe the community. It is a privilege to be there free. Our responsibility is to give back."

Theological Directives

All major religions have a theology, a corresponding set of rules, and practices to encourage helping others in need (Cnaan, Boddie, & Wineburg, 1999; Queen, 1996). Thus, theological directives are the foremost motivation for congregational involvement in social services. The theologically based responses in our study were generally categorized as either "works-" or "grace-related." Many respondents indicated that they were involved in service provision because scripture instructed them to help others. Implicit in many of these answers was the notion that those who are truly religious obey religious doctrine and, through obedience, gain eternal salvation. Responses that suggested this motivation were as follows:

"We follow the spirit of God."

"Our theology is that we are engaged in the world. The job of the church is to bring it to light. God is bigger than the Bible. We try very hard to share in the community."

"We serve the visible needs of the people in the community. If the church doesn't do it, then who will? We believe in the social gospel. The gospel has to have feet, arms and legs. I have been groomed for this from the very beginning."

"It is the biblical mandate . . . our mission is to be part of community."

Others expressed their service as a response to God's grace and love. As stewards of God's abundance, they willingly share their bounty with others. Some said that God had blessed them materially and that they wanted to share the fruits of their success with others less fortunate. Responses that expressed this motivation were:

"We do what we do out of love. Just as God loves and protects us, we need to love and help others."

"We started our rummage sales because we had enough, and we could provide things people needed. It was a way to share with those who don't have much."

Although theologians continue to debate the distinction between faith and good works as a criterion for salvation, the issue seemed to pose no problem for respondents who cited both works and grace as motives for service delivery. The implication was that all religions require people to be faithful servants and compassionate neighbors. To do so under the aegis of the congregation is therefore religiously correct and a valid means of practicing one's faith. Responses that demonstrate this motivation were as follows:

"John Wesley says there is no religion other than social religion."

"It is a biblical mandate—the reason why the church exists. [Service] is modeled on the life of Christ expressing God's love in action. It is the great commandment given in Matthew 28."

Several respondents labeled their involvement as a holistic ministry: serving God through helping people. "We have a holistic view of ministry because we believe it is important to meet spiritual and physical needs as a way of evangelism."

The fact that faith-based volunteers engage in social ministry to extend their spiritual base is well documented. For example, Schneider (1999) reported that one Philadelphia Quaker Yearly Meeting was able "to create a sustained effort and provide opportunities for many other Friends to live out their concern for work in the world. Similarly, the volunteers engaged in the Burial Ground Project also saw this activity as a way to put faith into action.... On several occasions, volunteers have commented to me on the spiritual sustenance that they receive from participating in this project" (p. 283).

Issues of compassion were often cited as reasons for helping others in need. Many respondents noted that there are "many wonderful people" who "can't make it" and "we need to help them." Such sentiments moved the emphasis from religious duty to compassion for those in need. In fact, compassion was often the first motive cited. It was only later in the interview that respondents would elaborate on their religious commitment. This may have been due to their initial reluctance to express their personal religious feelings to the interviewer. If so, when they felt more comfortable with the interviewer and he or she probed for additional motives, they then expressed these religious motives.

Some respondents cited social justice issues as the motive for their involvement in service provision. Given the important role that many congregations, particularly those of black churches, had played in the civil rights movement of the 1960s, we had expected social justice to be a powerful motivation for social services involvement; yet, it played a relatively minor role for many of the congregations in our study and often only as part of the congregation's overall theology. Responses that indicate that social justice was a motivation were:

"Social justice is part of Jewish belief."

"We saw needs and felt we should provide for people's needs. It is the Christian thing to do."

"It is our calling: commitment to the arts and social justice."

"People have very specific interests in these areas. They see them as being expressions of our faith because these are faith and justice issues."

"We are called to be the voice for those who are voiceless."

Despite our probing, few congregations reported any involvement in social justice issues. Most preferred serving people in need to addressing social and political structural problems. Political involvement clearly was not a preferred mode of action. Many said the role of congregations is not to be political but to meet the spiritual needs of their members and to assist people in the community who are in need. Nevertheless, the few congregations that reported that they were motivated by social justice fought actively for the causes they embraced. Some defied the Immigration and Naturalization Services (INS) by helping illegal immigrants stay in the country, as in the sanctuary movement. Others lobbied against the 1996 Welfare Reform Act, and a few developed Community Development Corporations (CDCs) to improve the political and economic structure in their communities.

Gaining New Souls?

Proselytization played only a small role in motivating congregations to provide social and community services. Although most congregations said they would be pleased if recipients of their services become members, few provided services with this expectation. Furthermore, when asked whether the service provided had a religious component, most responded that they hoped so but that this was not always the case. Responses typical of those whose motivation was proselytization were:

"We engage in a social ministry out of evangelistic zeal. We want to reach out to the community with the gospel of Christ."

"We want to propagate the gospel. Teach. Help the community. Give love and help children. Give the community a sense of belonging."

Similar sentiments were voiced when David Apple (1999) asked volunteers at the Tenth Presbyterian Church in Philadelphia why they were involved in helping the needy. Apple reported: "A common sentiment was that because God transformed their lives, they wanted to help others, and because God used someone for their salvation, they wanted to bring saving faith to others" (p. 37).

Service provision by congregations, however, is seldom motivated by the desire to win souls. This was borne out by our finding that few or none of the service recipients became members of the congregation. Our personal observation of the programs supported this finding. We found that recipients were treated in a friendly manner but with little or no attempt to instill religion. Even in those instances where a meal blessing or a prayer was offered, there was no overt attempt to influence recipients. The most notable exceptions were the summer camps for children and youth. The main purpose of these summer camps was to introduce the faith tradition to children of members and not to recruit outside members. However, campers who were nonmembers were expected to participate in all religious activities. Yet, the majority of activities in these summer camps were recreational and educational and only marginally religious.

In this respect, it is interesting to view data from other parts of the country. Orr and his colleagues (1994) found that racism and a sense of powerlessness are the main issues that need to be addressed in South Central Los Angeles today. Churches are addressing these issues through social and community programs, much as they have in the past. "What has changed is that many, if not most, of these programs are directed toward the spiritual as well as the social and political transformation of individuals and neighborhoods" (p. 10). Congregations are now stressing "empowerment" to overcome psychological and structural barriers: helping African American men overcoming negative self-images, empowering families to take responsibility, and encouraging people to overcome poverty. Congregations are also being empowered to make changes in their neighborhoods in concrete ways, such as starting credit unions, community organizing, and helping people to start businesses.

Close examination of the data has shown that recruitment and evangelization are not major motives for congregational involvement in service provision. In fact, some clergy admitted that they were puzzled because so many were served, yet few, if any, became members. A few even asked us whether we had discovered the "secret" that would make members of service recipients. In those very few cases in which the congregation recruited new members from those who were served, the membership often changed as a result. In two cases, one in Philadelphia and one in Indianapolis, where the congregations have been largely professional, they now include more unemployed people, HIV patients, and poor and needy people, many of whom are drawn in through the congregation's feeding program and drug and alcohol rehabilitation. Such recruitment came at the expense of losing older members, who did not feel comfortable with the new members. Given that congregations meet many needs besides religious ones, older members sought a better fit in other congregations. In other words, admitting clients of social programs as members can threaten the current membership structure and can be detrimental to the congregation's survival.

In some cases, neither the congregation nor those who received the services wanted the membership to include more service recipients. Congregations are generally segregated in nature. Most are ethnically monolithic or have one dominant ethnic group. Others reflect certain vocations or specific social-economic levels. Even ethnically pluralistic congregations tend to be segregated along education levels and/or political orientations. This trend is not new. In the last days of the nineteenth century, W. E. B. Du Bois (1899) had already noted that each church in his sample was socially distinct. In his words:

> The various churches, too, represent social classes. At St. Thomas' one looks for the well-to-do Philadelphians, largely descendants of favorite mulatto house servants, and consequently well-bred and educated, but rather cold and reserve to strangers or newcomers; at Central Presbyterian one sees the older, simpler set of respectable Philadelphians with distinctly Quaker characteristics—pleasant but conservative; at Bethel may be seen the best of the great laboring class—steady, honest people, well dressed and well fed, with church and family traditions; at Wesley will be found the new arrivals, the sight-seers and the strangers to the city—hearty and easy-going people, who welcome all comers and ask few questions; at Union Baptist one may look for the Virginia servant girls and their young men; and so on throughout the city. Each church forms its own social circle, and not many stray beyond its bounds.

Those receiving the service often do not fit the demographic profile of the congregation. Just as service recipients would probably feel uncomfortable in joining some congregations, the congregations would probably feel equally uncomfortable having them as members. It is well known in church circles that diverse congregations tend to split. People feel most comfortable with those people who think and act like themselves. Bringing service recipients into the congregation as members is a recipe for social discomfort and future rifts and tension. Phillips (1999), for example, reported the case of the Church of the Latter Day Saints (LDS), in New Jersey, whose members had been encouraged to recruit new members. However, the converts came mostly from lower-income neighborhood and included those attracted to the church's substantial welfare programs. The increased diversity of the membership created constant tension. Dealing with the internal conflict also taxed the time and resources of the congregational leaders. Congregations are very cautious and tend to weigh the benefits and losses of providing social services as a means of evangelism. One pluralistic congregation reported by Warner (1993b) is the Roman Catholic church; St. Francis Borgia Church, in Chicago. Warner noted particularly that the membership of this congregation includes people from all ethnic groups, from various socioeconomic levels, native Americans as well as immigrant, and people from all walks of life. But this congregation, like many of its kind, is bonded by one common theme that is more powerful to its members than all other aspects of life—they are all deaf. They all use sign language to pray and communicate, and thus they constitute a segregated congregation.

The Power Within

A final pragmatic motive—one seldom articulated, yet a recurrent theme in the interviews—was the benefit that congregations, as a collective, accrue from a social ministry. The social ministry can act as the glue that holds the congregation together, beyond the spiritual aspect of worshiping together. As we articulated in the previous chapter, members find that involvement in a social ministry helps them to feel better about themselves and their fellow members. This, in turn, fosters a sense of belonging to a collective. Many clergy and lay leaders believe that the social ministry engenders a sense of purpose and commitment in the members involved. Moreover, the social services are often a means by which older members, by doing good, communicate their values and life perspectives to their children. Ammerman (1997) wrote in this respect that:

> congregations also engage in activities explicitly designed to strengthen the bonds of members, what many congregations call "fellowship." Both in shared tasks, where a sense of kinship is the by-product, and in small groups intentionally formed for fellowship, the congregation's members forge bonds of mutual identification and obligation. (p. 57)

Although this simple dynamic was rarely expressed directly by respondents, it was strongly implied. Several respondents noted instances in which congregations had been saved from extinction by establishing social ministries that attracted a loyal core membership. Responses that expressed this motivation included:

> "Our commitment to social services is based on meeting needs and survival. It is our conscious choice to serve the community. We need to be a tangible resource in community. Worship isn't enough. If we don't serve, we will disappear."

> "The purpose of our social ministry is to help our neighbors and keep our parish alive and healthy."

Similarly, Bartowski and Regis (1999), who interviewed clergy in Mississippi, reported that:

> aid provision should be a holistic endeavor that addresses the physical and material needs of the disadvantaged while simultaneously opening up avenues for moral development and spiritual substance. (p. 19)

How Congregations Get Involved in Service Delivery

Who Initiates the Programs?

A congregational decision to assist needy members and/or nonmembers is not a frivolous one. It requires that a need be identified and that someone (usually a leader of the congregation) advocate that a service be delivered. In most cases, someone thinks of the idea, marshals support for the idea, recruits others to the cause, and develops the program. As seen in Table 12-1, social programs provided by religious congregations have a wide range of initiators. Of the 1,005 programs reported in our study, those most influential in initiating these program were the clergy (39.2 percent) and individual members or groups (35.6 percent). One interviewee said that his congregation's social ministry resulted from "our Pastor's involvement in the missions department of his denomination. The church also supports community services." Another noted that "The pastor believes that members are a part of the community and addressing the issues in the community will improve the quality of their lives. It is the church's responsibility to address social issues. Christ changes people's lives." In other words, the pastor served as the driving force, and the congregation followed.

Table 12-1
Persons/Groups as Initiators of Programs by City*

Initiator	Chicago	Houston	Indianapolis	Mobile	New York	Philadelphia	S. Francisco	C.G.	Total
Clergy	41 (40.6%)	35 (37.6%)	46 (21.1%)	67 (45.6%)	33 (46.5%)	106 (44.0%)	56 (53.8%)	10 (33.3%)	394 (39.2%)
Staff member(s)	17 (16.8%)	5 (5.4%)	17 (7.8%)	14 (13.5%)	9 (12.7%)	40 (16.6%)	10 (15.3%)	0 (0%)	113 (11.2%)
Member(s)/ Groups	43 (42.6%)	24 (25.8%)	89 (40.8%)	48 (32.7%)	25 (35.2%)	84 (34.9%)	34 (32.7%)	11 (30.7%)	358 (35.6%)
Congregational committee	6 (5.9%)	0 (0%)	19 (8.7%)	7 (4.8%)	16 (22.5%)	27 (11.2%)	15 (14.4%)	0 (0%)	90 (9.0%)
Diocese/ Judicatory	4 (4.0%)	1 (1.1%)	5 (2.3%)	3 (2.0%)	3 (4.2%)	4 (1.7%)	4 (3.8%)	2 (6.7%)	26 (2.6%)
Other congregation	4 (4.0%)	0 (0%)	11 (5.0%)	1 (0.7%)	4 (5.6%)	4 (1.7%)	2 (1.9%)	7 (23.3%)	33 (3.3%)
Human Service Organization	1 (1.0%)	0 (0%)	3 (1.4%)	4 (3.4%)	3 (4.2%)	3 (1.2%)	4 (3.8%)	0 (0%)	19 (1.9%)
Neighborhood coalition	1 (1.0%)	0 (0%)	5 (2.3%)	3 (2.0%)	3 (4.2%)	2 (0.8%)	5 (4.8%)	0 (0%)	19 (1.9%)
Government agency	3 (3.0%)	0 (0%)	2 (0.9%)	1 (2.70%)	3 (4.2%)	1 (0.4%)	2 (1.9%)	0 (0%)	14 (1.4%)

* Totals for each city yield more than 100% as the answers to each question were not mutually exclusive. They can also yield less than 100% if respondents did not know/answer.

The role of members in initiating programs is also very important. A response typical of this role was: "People in the congregation have very specific interests in these (program) areas. They see them as being expressions of our faith because these are faith and justice issues." Jackson and his colleagues (1997), in their study of black congregations in Michigan also found "pastor's vision" and "laity's concern" as by far the most important reasons as to "how programs were originally initiated" (78 percent and 42 percent respectively). The next closest reason was "community request" with only 15 percent of programs reporting this as a reason for initiation. It should be noted that respondents were permitted to identify more than one initiator; hence, the total percentages exceed 100 percent.

While clergy and active members initiated most programs, staff members (usually those in large congregations) were reported to have initiated 11.2 percent of the programs and congregational committees initiated only 9.0 percent of the programs. While 18.4 percent of the programs had no initiator (usually those identified as "long-standing tradition") and 63.5 percent had only one initiator, some programs had two or more initiators. Eight initiators were reported for one program. Bartowski and Regis (1999) noted that many congregations based their social ministries on helping people who were known to a congregant or the clergy. One interviewee told them that "relief is offered when the congregation becomes aware of a 'problem' of need that, in their view, requires solution" (p. 45). Again, the congregational member or leader witnessed the need, shared it with others, and the collective or its representative (often the clergy) agreed on the help and its scope. Another of their interviewees said: "I think [government officials] need to be careful not to really allow the ministers to do everything, but allow the people [in the congregation] to get more involved...If you want any program to be in place, to work, and to have long-term effects, you are going to have the people [in the congregation] involved more. The people who are in the church [need to be involved because] they are going to be there for longer amounts of time" (p. 38). Bartowski and Regis concluded that "almost invariably, a critical mass of motivated members is required to transform the inertia that can accompany nebulous aid-giving visions into the momentum of collective action where newly sponsored church-based relief programs are concerned" (p. 39).

It is evident from these findings that social programs are initiated internally. It is unclear, however, the extent to which external bodies influence the formation of congregational programs. Few programs in our sample were initiated in response to requests from outside the congregation: responding to request from other congregations (3.3 percent); diocese/judicatory (2.6 percent); neighborhood and community coalitions (1.9 percent); human service organizations (1.9 percent); or government agencies (1.4 percent). These five external initiators accounted for only 9.3 percent of the programs. (The sum is lower than the five external sources combined as some programs were initiated in response to more than one external source). Thus, it is congregation leaders, members, and those affiliated with the congregation who largely influence the decision to embark upon a new social program.

We noted some geographical variation regarding those identified as program initiators. For example, the low frequency of clergy in initiating programs in Indianapolis (21.1 percent vs. a mean of 39.2 percent) was statistically significant.[13] Conversely, in San Francisco, clergy were most influential in initiating social programs (53.8 percent). Paid staff had no influence in Council Grove and ranked significantly low in Houston and Indianapolis (5.4 percent and 7.8 percent, respectively, vs. a mean of 11.2 percent). There were wide geographical variations regarding the role of the congregational committee. In Council Grove and Houston, no program was reported as having been initiated by a committee. In New York, 22.5 percent of the programs were initiated by congregational committees.

A surprising finding was that, of the 33 programs initiated due to the influence of other congregations, 7 were in Council Grove. Moreover, 23.3 percent of the programs reported by Council Grove were initiated by other congregations. In contrast, Houston reported no such programs. Differences among the cities in our study are reported in Table 12-1. With the exception of those noted above, we found no other significant differences.

These findings are of great importance for state and federal policy planners who hope to recruit local religious congregations as service providers in lieu of government programs, most notably charitable choice. It is essential to note that most of the programs we studied were not designed in response to a public call but rather followed an evolutionary process, beginning with the recognition of a need and governed by the internal group dynamics of the congregation. If congregations are to be enlisted in service provision, then the request must be made informally yet directly to the congregation—not as a political directive handed down by the state or federal government or even the denomination.

What Is the Impact of Social and Political Change on Congregational Involvement?

Since 1980, the budget for social services has constantly decreased at all levels of government, while the number of services contracted out to private providers has constantly increased. We therefore wanted to know to what extent public sector retrenchment of social service financing/provision, redlining, and/or community change had affected service provision by congregations. Despite this devolutionary trend, we found no significant relationship between government retrenchment and congregational involvement.

When respondents were asked why their congregation had initiated new programs, other than responding to an evident need, an interesting finding emerged. Of the 1,005 programs reported in our study, 215 (21.4 percent) had been initiated in response to a change in the community; 78 (7.8 percent) in response to cutbacks in local public funding; 69 (6.9 percent) in response to cutbacks in state funding; and 77 (7.7 percent) in response to cutbacks in federal funding (see Table 12-2). Overall, only 10 percent of the congregations reported that their programs were developed in response to funding cuts at any level of government. (It should be noted that some of the programs were initiated as a response to public cuts at more than one governmental level.) In addition, 21 programs (2.1 percent) were initiated in response to redlining of the community.

This finding that congregations do not develop social program directly as a response to government cutbacks is in line with our findings in the first parts of this chapter. Services are initiated internally as a response to witnessing a need in the community and as part of the congregation culture, theology, and pragmatic needs. While the need in the community may be the result of changing government policies, such as reduced investment in housing for the poor, the congregation is responding from within to the needs of identifiable people and ignores the policy picture.

The following geographical differences were significant and warrant special note. New York City and San Francisco respondents reported that three of every ten programs (31 percent and 29.8 percent, respectively) had been initiated in response to cutbacks in local public funding (see Table 12-2). Conversely, Philadelphia (6.2 percent), Indianapolis (2.8 percent), Mobile (1.4 percent), and Council Grove (1.1 percent) respondents reported initiating few, if any, programs as a direct result of cutbacks at any governmental level. Respondents in New York City and San Francisco

TABLE 12-2

Reasons for Initiating a Program by City

Reason*	Chicago	Houston	Indianapolis	Mobile	New York	Philadelphia	S. Francisco	C.G.	Total
Cuts in local public spending	19 (18.8%)	1 (1.1%)	4 (1.8%)	2 (1.4%)	22 (31.0%)	11 (4.6%)	19 (18.3%)	0 (0%)	78 (7.8%)
Cuts in state spending	15 (14.9%)	0 (0%)	4 (1.8%)	2 (1.4%)	20 (28.2%)	11 (4.6%)	16 (15.4%)	1 (3.3%)	69 (6.9%)
Cuts in federal spending	15 (14.9%)	0 (0%)	5 (2.3%)	2 (0.7%)	20 (28.2%)	12 (5.0%)	19 (18.3%)	4 (13.3%)	77 (7.7%)
Redlining	5 (5.5%)	0 (0%)	1 (0.5%)	1 (2.70%)	4 (5.6%)	6 (2.5%)	4 (3.8%)	0 (0%)	21 (2.1%)
Community change	53 (52.5%)	5 (5.4%)	22 (10.1%)	13 (8.8%)	26 (36.6%)	40 (16.6%)	42 (40.4%)	14 (46.7%)	215 (21.4%)

* In addition to responding to an evident need.

cited government retrenchment as the motivation for initiating programs significantly more often than did those in other cities. Findings regarding the initiation of programs in response to community change were similar. New York reported twenty-six programs (36.6 percent); Chicago, fifty-three programs (52.5 percent); and San Francisco, forty-two programs (40.4 percent). A similar trend was observed in Council Grove, which reported fourteen programs (46.7 percent). Houston and Mobile, the two southern cities, reported initiating significantly fewer programs in response to community change.

Summary

Our findings indicate that the congregations in our study did not perceive themselves as responding to external cues, such as government budget cuts or community changes. Neither government nor public sector financing was reported as a significant factor in motivating social service provision by congregations. This finding goes hand-in-hand with congregations' limited concern for social justice and social change. In general, the congregations responded to needs evident among their own members or in their community. They did not seek to discover the underlying causes of these needs. Their primary concern was to remedy the immediate situation by caring for the immediate need.

Most reported that their social services, whether soup kitchens or homeless shelters, were their response to a religious mandate to care for the poor and needy. There was, however, little or no consideration given to either the causes of homelessness or poverty or the consequences of government policies or budget cuts. While this macrostructural analysis was usually missing, what was found was genuine compassion and a desire to make a better society.

Impressive and extensive social and community services cannot exist if the congregations themselves do not reap benefits from their existence. As we have shown, the motives for providing these services are many and interrelated. In our view, the most important motives for service provision are the expression of faith and the bonding and solidarity that result from collective service. Such programs enable people to express their faith by improving the quality of life for others. These programs are attractive not only to members but also to nonmembers who assist congregants in delivering the service. A major reason is that people gravitate toward places where they can be with others like themselves and where they feel good about who they are and what they do.

Service provision strengthens the social fabric of the congregation, as well as its identity as a community institution. The social and community services enable the congregation to be anchored in the community and to gain the respect and support of local residents, even if congregation members are not from the local community. Service provision as a vehicle for evangelism offers minimal rewards and is ineffective as a means of recruiting new members.

Building a solid membership core is not an easy task for a congregation. Clergy and lay leaders must invest considerable energy and resources in maintaining a stable membership and community presence. An appealing social program can help attract and hold members of the congregation and make the congregation more visible in the community. Many congregational leaders believe that the vitality of the congregation and social programming go hand-in-hand. The decline of a community brings the decline of a congregation in its wake because of their close interrelationship.

Surprisingly, motives such as social change and fund-raising were seldom mentioned as reasons for service provision. Most congregations subsidized their social programs and did not expect to profit from such services. The exceptions were congregations that rented their facilities to cover building upkeep and staff expenses.

Finally, we find that, despite drastic changes in federal and state welfare policy at the end of the twentieth century, the orientation of congregations in the United States is less toward social change and more toward service provision. Congregations care for the needy, but they are not challenging the social structure or political institutions of our society. Their modus operandi appears to be one of seeking cooperation and complementing government and businesses rather than one of inciting conflict and challenging to the status quo.

13

The Congregational Norm of
Community Involvement

> Those, who liked one another so well as to join into Society, cannot
> but be supposed to have some Acquaintance and friendship to-
> gether, and some Trust one on another.
> —John Locke, *The Treatise on Government*

In 1995, Robert Putnam wrote a scholarly article on a fairly ob-
scure topic—the bowling habits of people—that managed to engage the
attention of the mainstream media, which generalized its findings into an
indictment of modern society. The same thesis appeared in various
venues, and a book-length treatment, *Bowling Alone: The Collapse and Revival of American Community*, was published in 2000. The essence of Putnam's argument was that although the number of people who bowl today
is greater than it was fifteen years ago, fewer do so in organized leagues.
Putnam used this finding as an example of a society where face-to-face
contacts are dwindling, in turn resulting in a decline in civic engagement.
He observed that "Without at first noticing, we have been pulled apart
from one another and from our communities over the last third of the
century" (Putnam, 2000, p. 27). His conclusion: "Every year over the last
decade or so, millions more have withdrawn from the affairs of their communities" (Putnam, 1995, p. 68).

Our book, by filling a gap in our knowledge regarding the generation
of human and social capital in America, refutes some of Putnam's assertions of declining civic engagement. *Civic engagement has not diminished;
its locus has merely shifted.* Today, congregations are key producers of social and human capital at the local level, and they provide the glue necessary to bind together a democratic society. Congregations fulfill these roles
by operating as sources of skill acquisition, social interactions, mutual

exchanges and obligations, and trust, all of which promote social activism and civic engagement. They do so in a variety of ways, the most important of which is through social and cultural norms that dictate that congregations become involved in enhancing the quality of life in their communities. The expectation that congregations should engage in community service makes them an alternative to many secular collectives, which traditionally have been sources of social and human capital. The result is the impressive social and community involvement of local religious congregations, a uniquely American social safety net.

In this chapter we illustrate how local religious congregations serve as a primary source of social and human capital in contemporary America. We begin by defining the terms *human capital* and *social capital*, with special attention to how they are used by James Coleman and Robert Putnam. We explain why the development of human and social capital is essential for civic engagement and a high quality of life at the local community level. We then review Putnam's key assertions as a basis for discussing the role of congregations in providing service to the community. We conclude with a discussion of the normative expectation that congregations will provide social services and enhance the quality of life for others less fortunate in their communities, and the rewards of such involvement.

Human and Social Capital

While these two concepts, *human capital* and *social capital*, have been discussed endlessly in the past ten years, they are often applied and defined loosely and unsystematically. To avoid confusion, we define them here.

Human capital comprises the skills, knowledge, experiences, and developed talents that individuals apply to solve problems and enhance their quality of life. Human capital can be increased by equipping people with skills and abilities or by trusting them with leadership and organizational responsibilities so that they can function more productively. Often, human skills learned in one context are later applied in other contexts; hence, they are transferable.

Social capital refers to the level of development of networks, both informal and formal, in a given community by its members or residents. It encompasses the ways and the extent to which people relate to and are engaged with others through informal social interactions; organized groups, such as associations or congregations; and professional relationships.

Coleman notes, "Social capital is defined by its function. It is not a single entity, but a variety of different entities having two characteristics in common: They all consist of some aspect of a social structure, and they facilitate certain actions of individuals who are within the structure" (Coleman, 1990, p. 302). This definition by function means that a given structure or behavior can be social capital in one instance but not in another. Thus, the distinguishing principle is whether or not a certain behavior facilitates interactions, exchanges, obligations, and the development of trust.

The concept of social capital lies in juxtaposition to rational choice theory, the foundation of modern economics. Social capital holds that a smooth and efficient society is not the sum of self-interests manifested and bargained simultaneously but rather the mutual exchanges and obligations that members of a given network share. As Coleman aptly writes, "Individuals do not act independently, goals are not independently arrived at, and interests are not wholly selfish" (Coleman, 1990, p. 301).

Social capital exists in the relations *between* and *among* individuals, rather than in the characteristics of specific individuals, which constitute their human capital. Social capital can be created by improving relations between people. It begins with interactions and progresses to exchanges, which may grow into obligations. Ideally, the end result is trust. Trust in this respect refers to people's beliefs that others, such as neighbors or elected officials, will act on their behalf and not against them. When all these elements exist, groups can be formed and civic associations may emerge.

Why Are Social and Human Capital So Important?

Why are so much time and ink devoted to human and social capital? The answer to this question is fundamental to our exploration of congregational contributions to civic engagement.

First, social and human capital are important because they enable people to achieve goals that would not be possible without them (Coleman, 1990). These goals fall into four categories: (1) overcoming social or political barriers, as exemplified by liberation theology practitioners; (2) attaining social prestige; (3) achieving safety, security, and freedom—when people are connected to each other, they tend to protect each other's property and children, rather than look the other way when something goes wrong; and (4) attaining economic success.

Clearly, achieving economic success and other individual goals are inextricably linked to one's human capital. It is obvious that people with greater human capital in the form of education are likely to earn more money in their lifetimes than their uneducated counterparts. There is also a direct connection between success and social capital. Just an individual's position in the exchange network can be an asset in its own right. A large and diverse network of exchanges is a source of valuable information, entrepreneurial contacts with people in a position to help, and a resource that can apply to one's work. However, the personal gains from being involved in extensive networks can be as simple as finding a reliable babysitter at the last minute, obtaining referrals to sources of support, and finding vendors who sell products at wholesale prices. Simply put, the more one is embedded in and trusted by members of a network of exchange, the more one can benefit from others' experience and information.

The second reason that social and human capital is important is that it is the foundation for creating *civic culture* (Potapchuk, Crocker, & Schechter, 1997). It is often too costly or too difficult for one individual— or even a small group of people—to even attempt to solve societal problems. However, when there is interaction among members of a community, as well as trust and norms of collective support, there is a higher chance that the collective will become organized and thereby offer a more successful and less costly solution to the problem. In Coleman's words, "Social organization constitutes social capital, facilitating the Social organization constitutes social capital, facilitating the achievement of goals that could not be achieved in its absence or could be achieved only at higher cost" (Coleman, 1990, p 304). Civic culture is based on the values and norms of cooperation and reciprocity. According to Potapchuk, Crocker, and Schechter (1997), informal *social interactions, social capital, community organization,* and *civic infrastructure* are the building blocks of civic culture, developing along a continuum called the *ladder of community building.*

Many research studies have confirmed a direct link between social capital and a community's economic health. Putnam et al.'s (1993) research in Italy—and, to some extent, in the United States—found that regions with a high degree of civic engagement and social capital had higher rates of economic growth, educational achievement, and efficient government. Midgley and Livermore (1998) note that, by enhancing human and social capital, it is possible to develop systems that will attract new businesses to the community and to persuade residents to buy in local stores rather than in the big suburban malls. Midgley and Livermore's example suggests that local social and economic development corporations and efforts go hand-in-hand, and one cannot be achieved without the other.

Finally, human capital is more likely to occur in systems with a high degree of social capital (Psacharopoulos, 1994). Coleman (1988, 1990) uses the example of sectarian schools (primarily Catholic ones) to show that the extent of associational activities among neighbors, teachers, and parents is directly related to higher educational attainments, it is lower in public schools that do not foster such associational activities. In this respect, when friends, parents, and teachers are coordinated and well connected to each other, the message to the child is a clear, singular one, and the child's opportunities to play one adult against the other are significantly reduced.

Bowling Alone

As described in the introduction to this chapter, Putnam's assertions of declining civic involvement have helped shape the debate on this issue, not only in academic circles but also among government, business, and community leaders. According to Putnam, the indicators of a decline in civic engagement include lower rates of voter turnout, smaller attendance at political rallies, smaller membership rolls of fraternal and civic groups, and a decline in the number of volunteers.

And just as Putnam notes that, while the number of bowlers has increased in recent years, the number who bowl in organized groups has actually decreased, so he sees a similar phenomenon in religious circles. Surprisingly, Putnam does not acknowledge that many of the teams of the past were workplace sponsored and initiated and that their decline therefore indicates changes in the work front and not in social capital. Although he acknowledges that Americans, particularly women, join church-related groups more than any other type of voluntary association, he concludes that the number who are involved in religious services and groups has declined by one-sixth since the 1960s as religion becomes less tied to institutions and more a matter of individual expression.

Putnam's treatment of the religious involvement of Americans deserves closer scrutiny. While he acknowledges that church-related groups and religious affiliation are by far the most common associational memberships among Americans, he also claims that, "broken down by type of group, the downward trend is most marked for church-related groups." (Putnam, 1995, p. 72). It is not clear where Putnam collected these statistics, since this major decline is only partially corroborated by other scholars, and some (Finke & Stark, 1992; Wuthnow, 1988) actually have found an increase—or at least no decline—in religious participation in the past twenty years. Finke and Stark's analysis reveals a tremendous growth in religiosity and congregational affiliation from 1776 onward; this phenomenon peaked in 1960, and levels have been stable since. Similarly, Roof (1996) suggests that the number of churchgoers has leveled off after declining in the 1960s. These findings are also supported by surveys carried out by the Gallup Organizations. Note that neither study found a decline in religious participation after 1960. In contrast, the General Social Survey shows a decline in church membership and related activities over the past twenty years, but only a slight one.

In addition to assigning the greatest decline in involvement to church-related groups, Putnam also dismisses congregations as being less socially relevant today than in the 1960s because people choose which congregation to attend not by family tradition but by what satisfies best their individual spiritual needs. Putnam uses this consumer orientation, which has also been noted by Warner (1993a) and Wuthnow (1988), as a means of downplaying the communal life of congregations. His position is that people who come for personal fulfillment are not likely to form strong associational ties of exchange. As we noted in chapter 11, we disagree. Those people who do not follow familial tradition tend to choose a congregation to a large extent on the basis of their sense of affinity with the other congregational members. In European congregations, one is likely to worship alongside the children of one's parents' friends. In America, one shops around for a congregation that meets one's religious needs as well as providing a community of co-congregants with whom one feels comfortable. We return to this issue later in the chapter.

Putnam does concede that Americans are still "joiners," but says that most are members of national organizations, such as the American Association of Retired Persons (AARP) or the Sierra Club, which are so large that members do not have social ties with one another. Indeed, such organizations do not produce social and human capital, though they do mediate between the individual and powerful authorities. Religious congregations, however, do provide social ties of exchange, obligations, and trust and in this way produce social and human capital.

Congregations as Sources of Human and Social Capital

Three elements are critical for social capital to be effective: face-to-face interactions, a high level of trust among members of the system, and a network of obligations held among them (Coleman, 1990). We now consider how these elements pertain to local religious congregations. People who attend congregations do so as a manifestation of a religious commitment. They choose the congregation because they trust its clergy and members. Many studies suggest that congregational affiliation is a matter of personal choice and that the decision is made carefully (Ammerman, 1997; Warner, 1993a; Wuthnow, 1988). Furthermore, through screening interviews, after-service coffee and cake, and informal discussions with other congregants, the new member becomes involved with others and shares resources with them. Often, he or she is the beneficiary of veteran members' experience and familiarity with the congregations and the community, which he or she later shares with other newer members.

Almost every one of the some 250 congregations that we visited in the past two years holds regular Bible (or religious) classes for adults and religious education for children ranging in age from toddlers to young adults. In the overwhelming majority of these congregations, such classes are conducted by congregational volunteers—members with or without prior teaching experience who were asked and agreed to serve as educators. This essential role sows the seeds of human and social capital as knowledge is disseminated and new skills are acquired in both adult education and the religious school. Some members learn to be teachers and group moderators, while others learn new ideas and information. Moreover, those who do not teach are in debt to the volunteers who take care of the education of others, and the infrastructure of the exchange of favors is institutionalized. For instance, when someone voluntarily teaches my child what I consider to be important, I am happy to reciprocate by helping that individual, as well as other members of the group, using the skills and abilities that I uniquely possess, whether by baking a cake or recommending a good mechanic. Now, multiply this network of reciprocation to include choir members, ushers, committee members, and other congregational volunteers, and the level of social embeddedness, exchanges, and trust becomes quite tangible. It is in the very nature of congregations that members come together. Some may give more than others and thus have more social credit for it (obligations); they will be supported in the future when they are in need.

Brady, Verba, and Schlozman (1995) define civic skills in terms of concrete activities such as letter writing, participation in decision-making meetings, planning and chairing meetings, and giving presentations or speeches in public forums. We can also call these skills human capital, since they are the same skills needed to achieve a higher degree of control over one's environment. In a national study, these authors found that religious communities were the most important places in which people reported acquiring these skills. Other places where people acquire these skills—at work and in nonpolitical organizations—attract and favor white middle- and upper-class members of society and as such perpetuate the power imbalance in society. It is only in religious organizations that women, people of color, and the poor are provided with the opportunities to enhance their human capital and to acquire political participation skills. The congregational member who learns to write letters in support of religious activities, collects money to pay for special holiday services, or organizes a weekly Bible class can use those skills to participate in political life at any level. Brady and his colleagues concluded that religion is the predominant institution working against the class bias of American civic engagement (the economically privileged control the greater portion of the resources needed for democratic participation). This role—the church as a place of empowerment—has particularly been the case for African American congregations. Brady and his colleagues found that churches attended by African Americans, regardless of denomination, were more likely to teach civic skills, promote political participation, and provide social services to the community than were those attended by white Americans.

Why Congregations Are So Successful in Building Social and Human Capital

Six factors in combination explain why local religious congregations are so effective in building social and human capital: (1) the emotional needs of congregants, fulfilled by joining other congregants in nonworship activities; (2) the historic disestablishment of religion, which necessitated an entrepreneurial spirit among congregations; (3) Americans' distrust of their government; (4) the homogeneity of congregations, a key factor in the willingness of congregants to give money and to volunteer alongside people like themselves, and the fact that congregations are the last normatively accepted segregated local institution; (5) religious teachings that emphasize social responsibility; and (6) the changing ecology of local associations, which has left the religious congregation as the primary local institution.

The Emotional Needs of Congregants: As discussed in chapter 11, people need to find meaning in their existence if they are to be fueled with the energy they need to cope with hardships and to be able to do more with seemingly limited resources. Moreover, all human beings are struggling to attain feelings of self-worth and love (Frankl, 1963; Glasser, 1965). Organized religion remains the primary source of meaning for many, if not all, people. Joseph noted, "Religion has a remarkable capacity to provide a sense of *identity* and *rootedness* for both the person and the group. Through its corporate belief system and community of faith, a deep sense of affiliation can develop. This is particularly significant for many who feel alienated at this time of social and cultural transition" (Joseph, 1987, p. 17). Thus, religious congregations provide friendship and a sense of purpose. Again, as discussed earlier, Andrew Greeley (1972) labeled people's basic needs as the need for meaning (religious), belongingness (social), and comfort (psychological). The need for belonging is satisfied by the social recognition gained through a public position of responsibility and the performance of public duties. Through the appreciation of others, people know that they are accepted and respected. Furthermore, as Ellison (1995) reminds us, there are many motivations for joining a congregation. Some people join because they seek a place to socialize their children in a belief system they view as moral, appropriate, and just. Others do so for the child care available to members or for opportunities to sing, find a suitable mate, or benefit from counseling services. Regardless of the reason, the best way to become involved in the life of the congregation is through small-group participation.

As noted, people join congregations to satisfy social as well as spiritual needs. People in the United States are not restricted to the religion of their birth. In fact, the practice of "religious switching" is increasing, as people choose their congregations for reasons other than family tradition. Moreover, as Donald E. Miller (1997) points out, many of today's congregations and denominations did not even exist twenty or thirty years ago. Miller studied the new "paradigm churches" and found that the church is the center of its members' lives. The church represents a refuge from the perceived violence and decay of secular society. Miller suggests that the dramatic success of these new churches is attributable to the fact that a sense of community is in short supply in America, and a congregation is an excellent source of a rich communal life.

The search for and the eventual choice of a church enables people to settle in a congregation where they feel similar to other members, or "at home." Congregations are also social settings where people of similar backgrounds and interests come together to form small groups. Some pastors seek to create numerous small groups, sometimes limited to as few as five people each. Even in the big new churches, people are encouraged to form small home-study prayer groups, and sometimes, these groups grow into churches of their own. Specifically, baby boomers respond well to the entrepreneurial spirit of the modern pulpit.

Being a member of a religious group means belonging to a network of social relations. Involvement in the social life of a congregation increases the likelihood of an individual's integration into the life of a community. Given that many congregations are involved in social services, individuals have multiple opportunities to meet and join with others already engaged in volunteer work. People who join groups—especially religious congregations—are likely to internalize the norms and activities prevalent in these groups.

As noted, Wuthnow (1988) has focused on small groups within the congregation (and society) and their power to motivate people for action within an organized religious context. Wuthnow (1994) asserts that Americans are transforming the way they contribute to community and the public good through reliance on small groups rather than formal institutional arrangements, and many of these groups are faith-based groups.

According to Wuthnow, small groups are playing a vital role in institutional religious settings: Some 40 percent of the adult population in America claims involvement in "a small group that meets regularly and provides caring and support for those who participate in it" (Wuthnow, 1994c, p. 45), with most attending regularly. Of those who participate in small groups, 69 percent reported that their participation helped them serve people outside the group, and 43 percent became involved in volunteer work in their community as a result of their small-group involvement. Wuthnow concludes, "The members of small groups are quite often prompted to become more active in their communities, to help others who may be in need, and to think more deeply about pressing social and political issues" (p. 346). The bonds formed between members foster consensual decision making and enhance members' loyalty and commitment to one another, as well as increasing their commitment to carry out the agreed-upon decisions (Peck, 1987). Also, in a study of what motivates people to volunteer, Crary and his colleagues found that actual voluntary helping is a positive response to an invitation that comes from someone personally known to the volunteering person and that the helping task is seen as a normal activity among members of their circle of friends or colleagues (Crary, Snyder, and Ridge, 1992).

In fact, most congregations *are* small groups: most are collectives of approximately 200 people who often know each other quite well. Larger congregations tend to break down into smaller groups. In such small groups, the problem of members taking a "free ride" is minimized, since the actions of each individual are noticeable and one's prestige and social position are dependent upon carrying one's load. Smith (1998) suggested that, in fact, congregations are "reference groups": a set of individuals with whom one meets face-to-face and according to whom one set standards of behavior, dress code, vocabulary, and social behavior.

One problem that faces many groups is how to motivate all members and avoid some members' inclination to rely on others to do the work and pay the money, a phenomenon mentioned earlier known as "free riding." In addition to the social pressure already mentioned, group deference to a charismatic or accepted leader can further minimize the "free ride" problem (Coleman, 1998). In this setting, it is natural for congregants to accept the religious authority of clergy and to extend that authority into the temporal aspects of life. "It appears, in fact, to be precisely the desire to bring into being the social capital needed to solve common problems that leads persons under certain circumstances to vest authority in a charismatic leader" (p. 311). This may explain why, in times of crises, we turn to religious leaders and await their guidance, both as individuals and as a nation.

The disestablishment of religion: In many European countries, including welfare states such as Sweden, the state supports and protects the church. Funds to provide salaries for clergy and to maintain religious properties come from general taxes or from a publicly collected church-designated tax. In France and Belgium, clergy are state employees. In Germany and Sweden, the state collects a church tax that is distributed among various religious groups (Monsma & Soper, 1997). This practice is referred to as "establishment." In this case, one religion or denomination (or a select few, as in the case of Germany and Switzerland) is designated as the state's religion and receives public support. Other recognized religious groups receive support, but at a lower level.

In European churches, because the salaries of the clergy are secured by the state, church leaders are not compelled to make special efforts to recruit new members, enliven their preaching, or manifest a dynamic leadership style. Clergy are not accountable to their congregants but rather serve as the local representatives of the higher being as understood by the state and its church. Furthermore, religious leaders are discouraged from speaking or acting against the state and its politicians for fear of losing monetary support. Such a system discourages clergy from developing social ministries, since they are difficult to organize and are unnecessary for the credibility and importance of the church in the community. In fact, in most European countries, the level of congregational involvement in local social welfare programs is minimal. European churches rely on the state to act on behalf of those in need (Chandler, 1997).

When the American colonies were founded, most had an "established" religion—the English Puritans in New England, the Dutch Reformed Church in New Amsterdam, the Anglicans in Virginia, and the Quakers in Pennsylvania (see chapter 2). Institutional or state churches in colonial America were supported by taxes similar to those collected in Europe. Clergymen were accountable only to their ecclesiastical superiors. In this respect, their role was to put forth the established religious doctrine, and they were not concerned with attracting new members. There were sufficient extrareligious incentives for joining the established church. Membership was often a formal prerequisite for holding public office, serving on a jury, or sharing in the distribution of common and undivided lands. People of other denominations or religions were viewed as lesser citizens and were often refused residency. In addition, the formation of dissenting congregations was often forbidden or strongly discouraged and the advocacy of unorthodox views punished. As such, the American church of the colonial period followed the European tradition.

A movement to "disestablish" churches emerged along with the quest for independence and gathered momentum in the decades that followed the Revolution. It was a slow process that began in 1776 when Virginia "disestablished" religion and ended in 1833 when Massachusetts foreswore Congregationalism as the state church. Today, disestablishment is most commonly known through the passage in the First Amendment that bars Congress from making any law "respecting an establishment of religion."

As was shown in chapter 2, the colonial church of the seventeenth and eighteenth century played only a minor role in social service provision, although it was an important social institution in all the colonies. The American church of colonial times, however, was not a benevolent institution per se; it focused on religious and moral matters and ignored other aspects of society. The civil authority was empowered to punish those who persisted in false beliefs, that is, anyone who disagreed with those of the established church. In their study of colonial America, Finke and Stark (1992) attributed the low rate of church membership—only 17 percent—to the fact that in each colony one religion had a stranglehold on the "market." It was disestablishment, which freed churches to innovate and to change to meet the needs of their members, that led to a growth in church attendance.

Only after the separation of church and state did churches begin to focus on the welfare of people in the community. Once congregants bore the cost of religious services, church leaders had to foster an environment in which members willingly provided the means to pay for the staff and maintain the building (Warner, 1993a). Thus, in America, the clergy were expected not only to bring the word of God but also to establish a community of members who would voluntarily support the congregation. This expectation created a new brand of clergy. American clergy are much more accountable to their congregants than are their European counterparts, because they are hired (and fired) by the congregation's executive committee, and they are expected to attract members sufficient to meet the congregation's financial needs. When prospective members have many options, agents of congregations are expected to be involved in attracting and retaining them as members. One way to enhance group loyalty, retain members, and improve the congregation's public image is to nurture a collective involvement in caring for needy people in the community. Members are attracted when they find their place of worship is the source of "good works," as well as a place where friends meet to do the "right thing." American clergy and lay leaders know that social and community involvement is essential not only to practice the word of the Lord but also for organizational survival and growth.

America is thus characterized by religious institutional competition. This means that, in an environment of religious pluralism, one must work to attract members. Competition, as we know from business, is related to market share. In order to increase market share, each religious group works to cater to members' needs when other religious groups are doing the same. Thus, American congregations tend to minister to people's needs at a level unheard of elsewhere in the world in order to recruit or retain members. This level of caring is epitomized by the "seekers" movement and by the increased popularity of megachurches. These churches provide singles meetings, diet workshops, coffee shops, and many other programs that members or residents may need but that are not otherwise available (Sargeant, 2000).

It should be noted, however, that we are not viewing clergy work and congregations simply as markets that operate in free competition. Congregations must be fiscally strong and attract members. The distinction is between profit for the sake of profit and fiscal solvency in the absence of public support. This notion of changing and enlarging the scope of religious practices and being active and dynamic in order to increase market share is not a new one. In fact, Max Weber noted that "Reinterpretations [of religious practices] adjust the revelations to the needs of the religious community. . . . Religious doctrines are adjusted to religious needs" (Weber, in Grath and Mills, 1958, p. 270).

Americans' distrust of government: Americans are known to distrust their government. Compared to most citizens of other modern democracies, Americans have less trust that their government has their interests in mind. The spirit of individualism and the desire to limit the power of government is quite powerful in the United States. The United States is the only country in the world where residents have proposed and passed referendums to limit governments' power to tax and thus to carry out the production of public goods. Along with the overall distrust in government, Americans also assume that government is ineffective in producing goods.

Government is perceived to be ineffective and uncaring in providing welfare and social services. It is assumed to be staffed by bureaucrats who focus on technical work and who do not care about the people they are supposed to help. Bureaucrats are considered unapproachable and uninterested in the individuals they serve. They are accused of doing their jobs "by the book" while ignoring the real-life circumstances of people. Moreover, government assistance is perceived as promoting an antiwork ethic among its beneficiaries. In other words, many Americans fear that people who are assisted by the public sector will become accustomed to receiving financial assistance without being asked to contribute anything and without being morally accountable. As such, the larger population often assumes that public welfare breeds dependency and instills values of sloth and irresponsibility.

Operating hand-in-hand with the principle of economic individualism (discussed later) is the belief that government should have as limited a role as possible, particularly in the economic realm, keeping taxes low and not regulating the market. This is the Lockean view of government as a bastion of inefficiency and suppression, which, by its very practice of catering to the needs of the majority, cannot hope to satisfy the demands of the diverse and competing groups that make up the United States (Weisbord, 1988).

This view persists in the United States and leaves much of the work of compassionate assistance to religious congregations, nonprofit organizations, and individual good people who help outside the realm of the public sector. The void in public involvement is filled by groups characterized by intensive face-to-face interaction and traditional concern for the needy.

Homogeneity within congregations: Quite a few factors combine to produce a weak public welfare system in the United States. One of them is the heterogeneous nature of American society. The United States is made up of diverse and distinct ethnic groups. Lacking a sense of a shared destiny and weak mutuality, citizens are not motivated to help one another through government. Helpers feel no intrinsic sense of attachment to those in need. In contrast, in a homogeneous society in which everyone hails from the same background and shares many characteristics, there is a sense of camaraderie and an incentive to help one another.

Another factor that contributes to a weak welfare system in the United States is the cultural belief in competition. One of the pillars of American capitalist culture is economic individualism, in which each family or individual is expected to earn enough to meet its needs without being dependent on the generosity of others. Furthermore, one's income level is seen as a key indicator of one's success in life and one's contribution to society; thus, disparity in income represents a continuum of success and failure in life. Kluegel and Smith (1986) conclude, "American culture contains a stable, widely held set of beliefs involving the availability of opportunity, individualistic explanations of achievement, and acceptance of unequal distribution of rewards" (p. 11).

It is a small step to the conclusion that the poor are unworthy. In fact, the Welfare Act of 1996 (the Personal Responsibility and Work Opportunity Reconciliation Act of 1996) embodies the norm of refusing to help the *unworthy poor*—especially those who are not members of one's ethnic, cultural, or social network. The belief that one is not responsible for another's welfare unless the other person is unable to care for his or herself, is a family member, or is related in some other way is a logical extension of the principle of economic individualism.

Considering the social and ethnic divisions that are present in the United States, along with the belief that inequality is just and the ingrained distrust of big government, it is unsurprising that among the industrialized nations of the world, the United States has the least developed public social service system. Nor is it surprising that, while some 3 million individuals a year find themselves homeless (Culhane et al., 1994), little is done to solve the problem. It is the accepted norm these days that one should be self-sufficient and that the public coffer should be used sparingly. Thus, a void has been created that congregations have attempted to fill. In the context of the congregation, people become more charitable and more willing to help the needy for the following reasons. First, the religious teaching is more amplified in the context of congregational social service than when the state is concerned. Second, the support is provided to people in the community who are screened by the congregation and deemed "worthy" of the support provided them. Finally, the helpers are also trusted as coreligionists rather than anonymous bureaucrats.

Congregations offer individuals a unique opportunity to assist others while working alongside people who share their ethnic, class, value system, and/or educational level. In fact, it is precisely because congregations are a collective of homogeneous people who get along well and share common values, in contrast to the wider society, that they become involved in welfare and advocacy for others.

Oscar Handlin (1951) emphasized the importance of the religious community to immigrant groups throughout American history. People who come to a new country with a different language, different norms and expectations, and few bonds of kinship tend to experience higher levels of anomie and to make less successful adaptations to the new country. Immigrants without a broad social network of assistance must find alternative support systems. For many, an ethnic congregation or religious community is the answer (Gelfand & Fandetti, 1986). For example, Chong (1988) found that, for Koreans of second-generation church membership, the church can play a dominant role in the group's quest for identity and a sense of belonging.

One reason that an ethnic congregation can be so supportive is that it is highly segregated and thus homogeneous. People are more likely to join efforts with and for people who are like themselves. Moberg (1984) noted, "The most segregated hour of the week may still be 11:00 A.M. Sunday, the customary Protestant worship hour, but most of it is by the minorities' choice" (p. 451). Ammerman (1997) noted in this respect that:

> It is in the nature of this focusing of social energy that congregations are relatively homogenous and particularistic. Warner argues, as we noted, that congregations are more often particularist than universalist in their orientation. He then adds Parsons's fifth pattern variable to note that congregations are also "collectively oriented." That is, they direct the participants' attention toward a group larger than themselves and their immediate kin in a way that avowedly asserts this group's difference from every other. In this combination of collective public commitment with particularistic belonging that gives U.S. congregations an important place in society. Drawing people to a public space beyond the household mobilizes collective sentiments. And in their very particularity, congregations allow the full range of U.S. pluralism to be expressed. (p. 355)

Most congregations evolve homogeneously because they serve as assimilation centers where members seek out the solidarity that they do without most of the week, whether in shared values, world view, ethnic identity, sense of familiarity, shared culture, or language. It is not surprising that church members' needs are supported by other congregants, since the help is given in a homogeneous environment. Furthermore, the homogeneous nature of congregations is culturally supported and accepted, whereas other social institutions, such as clubs or sport groups, that adopt similar practices are considered racist and undemocratic. Congregations are the last social institution where one can associate with people of the same religious, class, and ethnic background and feel good about it. In other words, they are the last remaining social institution where segregation, which is essential for collective action, is not merely sanctioned but actually encouraged.

Interestingly, the power of the congregation to be a unifying social institution is not at all new. Gough's (1995) study of the formation of Christ Church, in Philadelphia, showed that a bond was forged by using a form of worship common to all members, regardless of location. Gough noted:

Since all of these worship services were taken from the Book of Common Prayer, worshiping at Christ Church provided Anglicans with a sense of continuity with their religious and cultural life in England and an immediate bond with Anglicans who had emigrated from different parts of England. (p. 25)

The following example may demonstrate the power of homogeneity in congregations. Among Mormons, or Latter-Day Saints, the level of contributions to the church is the highest of any denomination—at 8.7 percent of the members' income it even approaches the biblical commandment of tithing. One explanation for this high rate of contribution is that Mormon congregations are among the most homogeneous of any in America and that the funds are used to supply social services to members in need.

Religious teachings: The desire to help others in need is not instinctive but is a norm acquired through socialization and observation (Keith-Lucas, 1972). All major religions have developed a theology, a corresponding set of rules, and mechanisms that support helping others in need (Cnaan, Wineburg, & Boddie, 1999; Queen, 1996). All emphasize collective responsibility for the welfare of others and for social justice.

Space here is too limited to describe the vast array of theological teachings on responsibility for and to others, so we give only a few examples. The Christian parable of the Good Samaritan tells of a man traveling to Jericho, who was attacked by thieves, stripped, robbed, wounded, and left for dead. A nobleman, a priest, and a Samaritan passed by, but only the Samaritan stopped to help. Jesus then said that he who showed mercy was the true neighbor and commanded his followers to do likewise. Wuthnow (1991) has found that most Christians who are engaged in helping others know this parable. A passage from the gospel of Matthew (25:31–46) is often cited as a direct command to feed the hungry, clothe the needy, help the stranger, and save the prisoner. In our interviews, when we asked people why they are involved in caring for others and acting as representatives of their community, they often replied that doing so is their religious calling, citing several religious texts as support for their motivation.

Similarly, an Independent Sector study (Hodgkinson et al., 1994) of more than 5,000 Americans, of whom 52 percent were involved in volunteer work, asked, "How did you first learn about the volunteer activities you have been involved in for the past twelve months?" Respondents were given the choice of answering that they had heard about the activity through their involvement in an organization or that someone had told them about the opportunity. Responses listed under "organizations" included participation in church, synagogue, or temple; options under "someone" included a church or synagogue member. Overall, 34 percent of respondents said that religion, in the form of an organization or personal involvement, was their motivation for volunteering. The largest proportion of volunteers—28 percent—did so for religious projects. Furthermore, the volunteers who were most strongly influenced by religion were those who volunteered for religious projects. In another national study, Cunningham (1995) found that two-thirds of those engaged in social movements, secular as well as religion-based ones, cited religious motivation as the reason for their involvement.

Three points regarding theological teachings on helping the needy and preserving social justice deserve emphasis. First, teachings of the major religions emphasize mutual responsibility, the need to assist strangers in need, and, most important, the legitimate claim of the weak and needy upon the community. Second, the major religions advocate social care and compassion for the needy, regardless of their location or economic condition. Third, religious teachings, even when they are not put into practice, remain part of the socialization process in the faith tradition and serve as instruction for desired behaviors of compassion and social care. If we assume that religion has a powerful and lasting effect on people's attitudes and behaviors, then religious teaching itself contributes to a more civil and caring society.

Religious tenets, regardless of specific faith tradition, are prosocial, if only in the sense that they foster a just and supportive community of believers. These tenets are taught to children and adults in formal religion classes such as Bible classes and through religious texts. We are not claiming that the teaching directly influences behavior, but, as a result of such teaching, social care, concern, and social activity have become crucial to public discourse. Religious teaching forms the moral foundation that makes congregational social action a legitimate cause and that allows congregants to organize around any common cause they deem relevant. Religious teachings foster the ideal of just relationships among people. Consequently, congregants are implicitly (by internalizing the teaching) and explicitly (through teaching and clergy sermons) encouraged to follow these theological instructions and apply them to everyday life.

The changing ecology of local institutions: The ecology of local institutions, which serve as mediating organizations between residents and powerful institutions (such as the state or big business), has changed greatly in recent years. As civic, political, cultural, and even sports organizations—recall Putnam's *Bowling Alone*—lose membership and clout, local religious congregations continue to grow and thrive. For example, in New Haven, Connecticut, from 1850 to 1990, while the number of local voluntary associations remained stable and the number of fraternal and sororal organizations decreased dramatically, the number of religious congregations increased greatly (Hall, 1996). Today, the local religious congregation is the most visible, stable, and trusted community institution.

Let us consider what John Orr (1998) discovered when he studied in depth the institutional ecology of four Los Angeles neighborhoods. He reported "an average of 35 religious congregations and 12.5 religiously-affiliated nonprofit corporations per square mile, far more than the number of gasoline stations, liquor stores, and supermarkets combined" (p. 3). Similarly, in our study of West Philadelphia, we found 433 places of worship in a territory thirteen square miles in size, approximately the same number of congregations per square mile that Orr found in Los Angeles.

In addition, religion-based organizations have become central to the operation of local human service networks, commanding 34 percent of all volunteer labor and 10 percent of all wages and salaries in the nonprofit sector (Hall, 1990, p. 38). Although this number does not represent only congregations, it is nevertheless an impressive statistic that shows the extent to which U.S. citizens support religious causes and campaigns. These findings provide further evidence that the one community institution still active and visible in most American communities is the local religious congregation.

In our study we focused on this local impact by asking congregations whether they planned to relocate in the near future. Almost all reported in the negative because of their continued commitment to the local neighborhood; this was true even of congregations in which much of the membership had moved away. In fact, with the exception of Jewish Orthodox synagogues, whose congregants must live within walking distance, most members live far enough from the congregation that they must drive to worship.

The congregations described meet the criteria for community institutions in that their location and activities provide a focal point for fostering a sense of community. Many people can also be recruited through local congregations to work on behalf of causes important to the community.

Norms of Social Capital

The impressive yet often ignored role of local religious congregations in building social capital, a key foundation for civic engagement, is more than a current social phenomenon; it is a long-standing social norm. The role of the local religious congregation in civic engagement exemplifies the norm that dictates the way in which people who come to worship together also become involved in community service.

One can be spiritually active (feel God), religiously active (pray daily, but alone), and live in accordance with one's beliefs without joining a congregation—in other words, "bowling alone." Joining a congregation and seeking out a community of worshipers involves accepting a set of norms that include participating in human and social capital building and civic affairs.

Norm is a frequently used term that is rarely defined. According to Coleman (1990), norms

> specify what actions are regarded by a set of persons as proper or correct, or improper or incorrect. They are purposively generated, in that those persons who initiated or help maintain a norm see themselves as benefitting from its being observed or harmed by its being violated. Norms are ordinarily enforced by sanctions, which are either rewards for carrying out those actions regarded as correct or punishments for carrying out those actions regarded as incorrect. (p. 242)

In other words, norms are dictated by others who have the power to provide rewards and punishments, but they reach full impact when they are internalized by the members of the group that is to carry them out.

The norm of social capital building and civic engagement embodied by local religious congregations yields numerous results—and very few negative ones. It saves the public sector money by its support for the provision of social services to people in need. The norms reinforce stability and social order in otherwise volatile environment. They also help newly relocated people become integrated into their new community.

Each member who conforms with the norms of active membership in a congregation strengthens group solidarity and its differentiation from others. In other words, the more members who become involved in supporting the collective norms of behavior, interacting with one another and being active in society, the more they feel part of a unique and special group. Clearly, the cost of participation should be sufficiently high so that outsiders will not be able to enter easily and insiders will not be tempted to throw away their investment and congregational membership.

The process by which norms are perpetuated and become internalized is complex. One essential component is the socialization and training of leaders to enable them to carry out their required tasks and to provide them with the needed skills. Most theological seminaries in America offer a course on social ministry or social action and often require seminarians to undertake projects that will prepare them to carry out such tasks in the future. Indeed, one of the distinguishing features of congregations that are involved in community affairs, as opposed to those that are not, is that their clergy have graduated from a theological seminary (Thomas, Quinn, Billingsley, & Caldwell, 1994). In other words, social and community involvement is not a natural inclination of all congregations but something learned and internalized by clergy who have been socialized to promote it while they were in training.

Ammerman (1997) summarized the spirit she found among congregants in her study in the following manner:

> Our culture sees helping the needy as a religious virtue and expects religious organizations to be engaged in service activities. The people in the congregations we studied were no exception. Eighty-eight percent said that helping the needy is very important or essential to living the Christian life, and 92 percent said that the service to the needy is very important or essential to the ministry of their congregation. Part of the cultural definition that surrounds religious institutions is that they will provide direct services to people who need their help. That same cultural definition makes it likely that people in need will seek out congregations as sources of help. (pp. 366–367)

Ammerman uses the term *cultural definition* to denote what we call norms. She acknowledges, however, that congregation members, people in need, and society at large expect religious congregations, as well as other religious groups, to care for the needy, even though they are not compensated for such help. There is no law requiring religious congregations to care for people in need, yet social norms in this respect are so profound that most people think this is how things should be everywhere in the United States.

Effective norms can constitute a powerful form of social capital. A norm of meeting and discussing shared problems can facilitate a local response to a communal threat. Similarly, the congregational norm of social and community involvement facilitates social capital building in an ongoing process in which members meet regularly, exchange favors, develop trust, and join together to practice their faith in a manner essential for civic engagement and civil society. As Coleman (1998, p. 312) notes, "Organizations brought into existence for one set of purposes can also aid others, thus constituting social capital that is available for use." Indeed, congregations originally designed to help people worship communally have become major actors in our communities and key sources for human and social capital generation, as well as normative protectors of civic engagement.

The extent to which helping others is a norm for American clergy is depicted by a study of African American church leaders in New York City. Tony Carnes and his colleagues found that "helping the poor here" and "helping the poor overseas," as well as "protecting the rights of minorities," were activities claimed by the overwhelming majority of respondents as the most important or very important for Christians to be involved (82 percent, 74 percent, and 73 percent respectively). In contrast, only 39 percent reported that "working for lower taxes" is the most important or very important for Christians to be involved (Carnes et al., 1998).

Rewards of Involvement in Congregations

While the rewards of congregational involvement for the individual member are many, the societal rewards to congregations as a whole are less noticeable. Congregations receive rewards from the larger society that reinforce and facilitate their efforts. Clearly, the tax-exempt status of congregations is an invaluable reward. Brown (1990, p. 1634) notes that Congress and the Supreme Court have held that the public benefits conferred by religious organizations outweigh the benefits accrued by congregations.

As mentioned, there are many psychological and emotional rewards of congregational individual involvement that at first glance may seem contrary to American culture. The freedom to do what one wants might be considered the most prized American ideal. This freedom is not only the right to choose a government; at the individual level, "it constitutes a basic right to individual autonomy. It means not having anyone tell us what to do, not having to listen if they do, not having to conform. It means having the capacity to make our own decisions, rather than simply living up to the expectations of the community or fulfilling obligations to someone else" (Wuthnow, 1991 p. 12).

Religious affiliation and volunteerism might be seen as antithetical to this freedom. After all, in religion one accepts subordination to a higher power and a doctrine of worship, and in volunteering one must adhere to the rules and guidelines of the program for which one volunteers. Wuthnow resolves this seeming contradiction by focusing on the rewards of volunteering and of joining a religious congregation. These rewards range from opportunities for individual choice through personal fulfillment to volunteer or congregant control over the length and magnitude of commitment. A person may always decide that he or she no longer wishes to volunteer or to participate with the group. Thus, compassion and care in United States are intertwined with personal freedom: individuals may choose to become involved in an activity, supporting whatever is dear to their hearts. The resulting social involvement sets the tone and forms the basis for a complex web of individualized commitments and a rich civic life.

Financial support for religious organizations and local religious congregations is not limited to affluent members of American society. In fact, contributing to congregations is a way for all people to assert themselves in support of those issues in which they believe. Nevertheless, there is no legal requirement to join a congregation, donate money, or engage in social ministry. People choose among many potential causes and organizations that they find appealing and worthy and participate accordingly. Even within a congregation, a member can donate to one cause and not to another. Thus, the norms of self-determination and individualism do not conflict but are easily compatible with religious congregations' civic engagement.

Clergy are distinguished by the duties they assume and reap both burdens and privileges from them. Local religious leaders are perceived favorably even in this modern age, and, thus, congregational members associated with them also enjoy the reward of that social approval. While we all know of religious leaders who are corrupt and morally bankrupt, most people also accept that the majority of clergy have answered a higher call and, by so doing, are earning far less than they could in other vocations. In most American cities, when a crisis occurs, the religious leaders are called upon to advise politicians, lend credibility to public action, or even to resolve the crisis (Orr et al., 1994). For example, when racial tension escalated in the Grays Ferry section of Philadelphia, the mayor recruited local religious leaders to assist in calming residents and to lead a campaign for tolerance and race harmony. The mayor chose this course of action because he recognized that religious leaders are revered and respected; residents trust the clergy more than they trust the politicians.

The public and the media agree that religious congregations are expected to serve their neighborhoods and are the community institutions most capable of coping with our social ills. *U.S. News & World Report* published an article entitled "The Faith Factor: Can Churches Cure America's Social Ills?" in which the authors, Shapiro and Wright (1996), summed up the issue as follows: "With President Clinton and Congress agreeing to end welfare as we know it, there is talk of a second welfare revolution: let churches and charities, not government, provide more of the safety net." When an expectation is so publicly explicit, the norm has been internalized not only by the actors expected to carry it out but also by the public at large.

14

The Broader Perspective
Congregations for Society and Beyond

This is the true joy in life—the being used for a purpose recognized
by yourself as a mighty one, the being a force of nature instead of a
feverish, selfish little clod of ailments and grievances, complaining
that the world will not devote itself to making you happy.
—George Bernard Shaw *Man and Superman, Epistolary Dedication*

I am of the opinion that my life belongs to whole community and
as long as I live, it is my privilege to do for it whatever I can. I want
to be thoroughly used up when I die, for the harder I work, the
more I live.   —George Bernard Shaw (quoted in Brighton, 1907)

The findings and ideas presented in this book represent one of
the first in-depth studies of the social and community involvement of
America's local religious congregations. The data bring to light the broad
scope and the previously unheralded role of local congregations in social
and community service provision.

American Local Religious Congregations as Our Social Safety Net

Findings from our own studies and from the literature provide compelling
evidence that religious congregations are a major force in today's society.
For many Americans, the local congregation makes the difference between
survival and destitution. For many others, the activities of the local congregation significantly enrich the quality of life in their community. The
reason, as we discussed in chapter 13, is that helping others has become
the norm for most local congregations, regardless of denomination. This
finding is corroborated by data from a national public opinion poll com-

missioned by the Pew Center for the People and the Press (1996). Eighty-seven percent of the churchgoing respondents cited the plight of the poor as the issue most frequently discussed by their clergy.

Societies have developed a wide range of social arrangements to help people in need after all else has failed. One such arrangement is based on the concept of a "safety net." The social safety net, which originated with the welfare state, guarantees certain public services to all citizens in times of need. The United States neither adopted nor practiced the concept of a welfare state and hence left the social safety net to the voluntary sector. As we pointed out in the preface, Americans believe in economic and social self-reliance, yet by age sixty-five, close to two-thirds of all Americans will have experienced at least one year of poverty (Rank & Hirschi, 1999). Because the U.S. government does not provide a safety net for those in extreme need, this responsibility has been delegated to local communities and, by default, also to local congregations. When someone is hungry and homeless, help is most likely to come from members of a local congregation. When children of working parents are left alone at home, the local congregation is most likely to offer an afterschool latchkey program. Similarly, when people are discharged from alcohol rehabilitation centers, it is most likely that they will turn for support to the AA group housed in the local congregation. In other words, in America, congregations are the "hidden" safety net.

As we have shown, the role played by local congregations in sustaining their communities is most impressive. In fact, the extent of social care provided is so great that, at times, we tend to forget that it is only the tertiary function of congregations. The primary function of a congregation is religious worship, with congregants coming together for the purpose of sharing their faith and worshiping together and remaining together as long as this purpose is met, and the secondary function is maintenance of the organization. Maintenance requires that members provide financial support and that positions of leadership and service be assumed. When a congregation has its own clergy, a mortgage-free property, and a measure of financial stability it is able to focus on "this-world" affairs such as social services. Another essential prerequisite for a social ministry is fellowship. A successful congregation generates a sense of belonging among members, which, in turn, creates a set of networks in which information, support, and "expressive" (personal) transactions are exchanged. This sense of fellowship is enhanced when members come together as a group to help others. This strong fellowship must already be in place if a congregation is to be successful in its tertiary function: the provision of social and community services.

The Tax-Exempt Status of Congregations and Its Merit

When a local or county authority is in a financial crisis, someone usually calls for a reexamination of the tax-exempt status granted religious congregations, as well as other nonprofit organizations. The argument is made that social services provided by religious congregations benefit only their own members or are used to attract new members and to convert those in need to their faith. Congregations are compared to social clubs in which members pay dues and are the primary or sole beneficiaries. However, as Brown (1990) has reminded us:

> The dominant rationale for exempting an organization from taxation is that the organization confers benefits on society as a whole. The organization's activities do not benefit only those who operate it or those to whom it provides services. . . . Hence, a government subsidy such as tax exemption is necessary to raise the level of an activity creating significant beneficial externalities.

> Congress grants section 501(c)(3) status to organizations that it believes convey these significant beneficial externalities. The government forgoes tax revenues to encourage production of the public benefits these organizations convey. The Supreme Court has held that the public benefits conferred by religious organizations are a "Beneficial and stabilizing influence in community life" and encouragement of diversified views and perspectives which contributes to a vigorous, pluralistic society.

Our findings in this study strongly support the Supreme Court's view of congregations as "a beneficial and stabilizing influence in community life." In fact, our findings provide an even broader perspective on social and community services provision by providing one of the first assessments of the dollar value of these services.

We found that the net value of congregational social and community services averaged $15,306.72 per month, or approximately $184,000 per congregation per year. This contribution is, for the most part, in the form of volunteer hours and other noncash support. The magnitude of this congregational contribution to social services provision can best be appreciated by comparing it to costs incurred by secular providers who must pay for the types of in-kind support that congregations voluntarily provide at no cash cost.

We believe these findings underscore the merit of the tax-exempt status of congregations. Although congregations can be viewed as being publicly subsidized because of their tax-exempt status, the value of their services to their communities exceeds the value of the public support provided in the form of tax exemption. There is also the value of services that cannot be measured in dollars such as informal help, pastoral counseling, value instruction, residents' representation, and community pride.

The economic value of the congregational contribution to the quality of life in America is staggering. As a key part of the nation's social safety net and the first to aid in time of local, national, and international emergencies, congregations allot a significant percentage of their budgets to helping others and are the major source for volunteer recruitment in urban America. In sum, the benefits provided to America's communities by congregations far outweigh the benefits afforded these same congregations by their tax-exempt status. In fact, one could say that our society is subsidized by congregations to a far greater extent than these same congregations are subsidized by the tax-exempt status granted by our society.

Given the extent of congregational involvement in service provision, it is not surprising to find a divergence of opinions about the appropriateness of this role. On the one hand, politicians from both major parties are calling for religious congregations to assume a greater responsibility in providing social services without losing their religious integrity (Cnaan, Wineburg, & Boddie, 1999). On the other hand, some observers prefer that congregations remain focused on worship and "other-worldly" matters. Jeavons (1994), for example, has warned that overemphasis on the provision of social services is likely to eclipse the religious mission of the congregation. A few of our interviewees agreed with this position, but the majority believe provision of social services to be an integral part of their religious mission and an expression of faith in action.

It is important to remember that, except for neighborhood schools, there is no other social institution as omnipresent in America's neighborhoods as the congregation. Other nonprofit organizations have only a minimal presence, since they are generally concentrated in selected urban locations. Because local congregations maintain a presence in the community, they are able to develop ties with the local residents even if those residents do not attend the congregations. In other words, the congregation is the one nonproprietary organization that is found in every neighborhood and within walking distance of every household.

In this respect, Ammerman (1997) noted, "The two institutions most likely to remain connected to the immediate neighborhoods they serve are elementary schools and congregations. But even that has changed. In many places, busing has strained the tie between school and community" (p. 35). In many places, this leaves the congregations as the final link between communities and their residents.

The Role of the Clergy

A recurrent theme in our fieldwork and in our review of the literature has been the role of the clergy. We have found that the clergy, who represent the apex of the congregational pyramid, exert enormous influence and leadership. This is particularly true in matters of service provision, since most congregational programs grow out of the visionary leadership of the clergy. In many instances, congregations continue to offer programs initiated by beloved religious leaders, long after the leaders' death or departure, in commemoration and acknowledgment of their legacy of service to others.

Above all, the clergy are the gatekeepers of the congregation and also its bridge to the wider society and its many institutions. When public authorities, health planners, political and community organizers, or business interests want access to people in the community, they often must go first to the clergy and ask their support. Clerical opposition can effectively deter any attempt to approach the congregation or gain its cooperation. Similarly, when residents wish to approach larger institution such as hospitals, city halls, transportation authorities, sheriffs, housing officials, and local businesses, they turn to the clergy as those most likely to be heard and accepted as the leaders of their communities.

It is not easy to be a member of the clergy at the beginning of the twenty-first century. Congregation members have three expectations of their religious leaders: first, that they can preach convincingly on spiritual and religious matters; second, that they can serve as role models whose lives reflect the highest moral and personal standards; and, finally, that they are able to counsel congregants on personal and social issues ranging from parenting to domestic abuse.

It is only after the clergy have met the congregations's expectations for religious leadership (preaching, role modeling, and counseling) that they can turn their attention to the maintenance of the congregation. Financial and brick-and-mortar issues determine whether a congregation survives, and it is the clergy, either alone or with the help of lay leaders, who must deal with these issues, be it leaking roofs or faulty heating systems. In addition to maintaining the physical plant, someone—often the clergy—must balance the books, file reports to the denomination, plan for the future of the congregation, and manage the day-to-day affairs of the congregation. In these instances, the clergy serve as both building engineers and chief executive officers.

There is another role of the clergy: that of social service visionary and leader. It is the role we have focused on in this book, although it represents only a fraction of the clerical work load. Nevertheless, American clergy are highly involved in social services provision; people in need expect help from congregations, and members expect their clergy to lead them in helping the poor and indigent.

In conducting our study, we met numerous clergy. Regardless of their monumental tasks and congregants' expectations, they are human beings like the rest of us. They differ from one another in their perspectives, capacities for service, age, and temperament. What sets them apart is their calling to serve God and their willingness to lead people in their spiritual and religious development. Most clergy have attended theological seminaries, studied religious doctrine, and taken courses in the interpretations of old texts, foreign languages, and even management and leadership courses. Nevertheless, no course of instruction can truly prepare a person for the multiple roles and expectations demanded of clergy today. To be a pastor in the United States at the beginning of the twenty-first century is challenging and rewarding, but also extremely demanding.

Our study of congregations over the past few years has given us a new respect for and appreciation of the clergy and what they do. They are the mediators between people in the neighborhood and all other powerful social institutions. They are the community leaders who best represent local residents. They are the conduits through which key information is disseminated to the community so that social change can be effected.

Local clergy, however, also require assistance (Jeavons & Cnaan, 1997). Clergy rarely get a break from the ever-increasing demands on their time. To ensure the continued effectiveness of their work, clergy should be given study leaves and sabbaticals. Many clergy also told us of their need for professional and technical support. A number of small and inexperienced congregations, for example, reported that they needed a professional accountant, rather than volunteers, to handle their finances but that they could not afford the service. We suggest that a central group of accountants, supported by a denomination or a foundation, be created to assist congregations in handling their finances and to reduce the level of stress among clergy and key lay leaders. To carry out their duties in the electronic age, the clergy need up-to-date computer equipment, as well as training in its use. Most clergy are not technologically savvy and need support in this department. This can be addressed through curricular modifications in the seminaries, through ongoing training and support by the denominations, and by pastoral-technical education and on-site support from the foundations (Mason, 1995).

Few clergy in our study have applied for grants, yet this is a proven way to secure program funds. We suggest that workshops on grant writing, supported by a denomination or a foundation, would benefit the clergy and congregations. The technical support made possible through grants is most needed by poor and minority congregations, which are generally least able to afford it.

The Role of Lay Leaders

We observed four tiers of membership within congregations. The first tier consists of those who come solely for the purpose of worship, attend infrequently, and seldom associate with other members. These people, though not central to the congregation's social life, are on the mailing list and generally are the reason for the overflow crowds at major holiday services.

The second tier consists of active members, those who attend services at least once a month and are personally known to other members. Active members have a sense of belonging to the congregation and volunteer, usually "ad hoc," when asked to carry out routine tasks.

The third tier consists of informal leaders; those who wield great influence because of their years of membership, special skills or occupation, or contributions to the congregation. These people have an interest in the congregation but also view the congregation as an extension of themselves. They are often informal historians of the congregations and are frequently defenders of congregational traditions. At times, they use their status and influence to prevent changes and attempts to modernize the congregations. They may previously have served in formal leadership roles but currently use their personal influence to get involved in decision making. The informal leaders are often asked to run or support new projects, and their opinion can influence planning and decision making by the congregation.

The fourth tier consists of formal lay leaders, those who shape the agenda of the congregation and serve, together with the clergy, as the gatekeepers of the congregation. Because they are well informed, willing to serve the congregation, and trusted by the members, they generally serve as committee chairs and members of the executive committee.

It is the formal and informal lay leadership of the congregation who have the inside information on every detail of the congregation functions. These are the people who know the due dates for bills, the names and telephone numbers of the plumber and the AA coordinator, the location of the fuse box and the holiday decorations, and how to run the coffee machine.

During our study, we found that each congregation tended to have a core of dedicated members who committed time, and often resources, to keep the congregation afloat. Small congregations generally had five such members, and we labeled this group the "core five," although the number can be higher in larger congregations. Most congregations owe their continued existence and vitality to the commitment of the "core five."

It is the "core five" who, in addition to the clergy, propose and initiate social services. Having witnessed a need, they come to the congregation and persuade the clergy and members to help. As leaders of the new social program, they then recruit volunteers from among the active membership. As one respondent from a congregation in the Midwest told us: "We have plenty of beehive members. We need good queens to lead us into new social ministries. If you come up with a good project and are willing to lead, we will have enough volunteers to support it." The role of this group in initiating programs adds an important democratic dimension to the congregation in that members have a voice in making major decisions.

Charitable Choice and the Congregational Spirit

The option of charitable choice makes it possible for public monies to be directed to religious congregations and organizations. This raises several issues. First, is the government using funding to coerce change in religious organizations (as it has done with universities)? Government has its own way of doing business. While the government may now contract directly with congregations for service, it may also impose additional requirements. This is true even for services that are funded with private money raised in-house by congregants. For example, church day care centers must be inspected and approved by government authorities to ensure that they comply with regulations. As congregations become contractors of services, they must adapt to government practices, and congregations may be forced to change the way they operate. For example, we found that, in one case in Philadelphia, the government's practice of delaying payments by a few months put unexpected pressures on the congregation and necessitated changes in its financial practices and in its relationship with banks and members. In other cases, day care regulations directly affected hiring practices by congregations; new employees need not represent the beliefs and doctrines of the congregation but must possess an academic degree.

It is important to remember that the congregations in our study own their social programs. Members and clergy alike perceive these programs not as responses to a public request for service provision but as responses to a need identified by the congregation. The service program developed in response to this need belongs to the congregation. Those who deliver the service may not be professionals, but they are committed volunteers willing to work on behalf of those in need.

Public expectations of congregations as service providers may well stamp out the voluntary spirit that distinguishes American congregations. As we have shown, members of congregations make possible the vast network of social and community services. Hundreds of thousands of volunteers serve without remuneration in order to serve others. Once public funds are targeted for congregations, however, and paid professional staff begin running programs, we risk the loss of these highly motivated volunteers, as congregational social services change from an expression of faith to yet another professional agency. Thus, while the provision of government funding to support congregational social services will be an important issue for decision makers in the twenty-first century, there are certain negative aspects that must be not be overlooked. As Franklin (1997) has noted: "For churches, the relationship is the system. Through relationships, the work of the church is accomplished. Churches do not need to become bureaucratized to fulfill their mission" (p. 109).

Religion in America

The secularization theory suggests that religion in modern societies—and especially in America—will continue to weaken and that society will become more secular with the advance of knowledge (Chaves, 1993). The secularization theory also holds that cities are inimical to religion and that continuing urbanization will diminish the impact and reduce the number of followers of religions. Proponents of this theory believe that religion is a marginal force in modern society and that it need not be included in our policy, social services, and research agenda (Berger, 1969). Our study does not support this. While the members of the majority of congregations neither identified religion as the sole issue in their lives nor sought an apocalyptic ending to society (a version of religion, prevalent in cults, whose adherents believe that God will soon end the world and that individuals should therefore focus their attention on religion to the exclusion of all other aspects of life), they did say that their religious beliefs had led them to service on behalf of those less fortunate. They viewed the United States as a society in which they were free to express their beliefs but not to force their beliefs on others. They also considered it their duty to care for others and to help foster a kinder and more civil society. In other words, religion is important to them, and the congregation provides the social space in which they can express their values and beliefs through serving others. They perceive religion as a compassionate framework that calls for connecting with others around them. This view is not unique to liberal congregations. We found that members of all congregations are engaged in helping others. The difference, however, is in the personal and theological interpretation of this act of compassion.

The freedom of the American congregation is also expressed in its separation from the state. Congregations in the United States have operated autonomously, without the regulation or support of a public authority. They have been more malleable and adaptable in form, structure, and alignment than have other social institutions (Warner, 1993a). Thus, congregations have been responsive to the changes in the society, particularly to the demands of those who choose a congregation to suit their lifestyle and needs. By incorporating social and community services into congregational life, congregations have been able to reinvent themselves as communities that are responsive to the changing needs of both current and potential members.

290 | *The Broader Perspective*

While the clergy and congregational members would be delighted if those they serve were to become coreligionists, this is not the driving force for most volunteers. Most of our interviewees saw service to others as a way to practice their faith, do what God asked of them, help those in need, and experience the satisfaction that comes from doing good for others. Despite the predictions of secularization, organized religion remains a major force in today's society and a powerful impetus for promoting civility and compassion. In America, we need the local religious congregations much more than they need us, and we need to help them be what they are.

Our findings strongly suggest that religion in America, the world's most technologically advanced country, is neither marginal nor privatized (i.e., organized so that one prays alone and focuses on personal spirituality, as opposed to worshiping together and forming a collective through the expression of religion—to the point of invisibility). People in the United States are more religious and are more willing to support religious activity than are citizens even of our neighbor to the north, Canada. Religion, according to our findings, is also central to the social welfare system and a norm among congregations in the United States. These findings suggest that the secularization theory failed to predict the prominence of religion at the end of the twentieth century and at the beginning of the new century. The increase in religion, and congregations in particular, is a result in large part of the unique experience of disestablishment and "the rise of an open market for religion" that distinguishes the United States from European countries (Warner, 1993, p. 1050). Since there is no established state religion in the United States, American congregations exist in a competitive environment that requires adjustment to a changing and pluralistic society.

Congregations as America's New Welfare Agent

John J. DiIulio, Jr., has told of a conversation with a local drug dealer. When asked why drug dealers win over kids, the reply was:

> I'm there; you're not. When the kids go to school, I'm there; you're not. When the boy goes for a loaf of bread or wants a pair of sneakers or just somebody older to talk to or feel safe and strong around. I'm there; you're not. I'm there, you're not. I win, you lose." (1997, p. 28)

In other words, drug dealers win because some communities have so few positive forces to counteract their influence. The middle class, businesses, and employers have fled; the once safe haven of the local schools has become an armed fortress with security guards and metal detectors. One major positive influence remains in every American neighborhood, however—the local religious congregation, which represents the community and which modestly invests in improving the quality of life, as well as providing moral and religious teaching.

The congregational approach to service differs from that of professional care in that it is holistic: contact with those being served does not end when the problem disappears. As Roberts and Thorsheim (1991) remind us, to be disempowered is to feel that one is neither seen as being worthwhile nor valued by significant people in one's life, that neither is one a contributing member of a group, whether a family, the community, or a congregation. On the other hand, to be empowered is to feel worthwhile, capable, and valued. The transition from disempowerment to empowerment occurs when the person being helped is given the opportunity to help others. It is through this reciprocity of help and personal contact that one gains a sense of worth and self-esteem. The congregational approach not only assists members with their own needs but also enables them to help others as volunteers in the congregation's social ministry. The opportunity to work side-by-side with those who are helping others gives those in need a sense of pride and provides meaning to their lives (Roberts & Thorsheim, 1991).

The United States increasingly looks to local congregations as the great hope for revitalizing its communities. Our study has shown that congregations are already heavily involved in meeting people's needs. From a public policy standpoint, this raises two questions: first, is the use of religious congregations as a formal rather than a "hidden" safety net and as a major element in our welfare system both practical and warranted? Second, are congregations capable of fulfilling the responsibility thrust upon them by society?

The American congregation is neither a panacea for all of society's problems nor a substitute for public sector support. Congregations, from one end of the United States to the other, do wonders in helping people in need. Nevertheless, the relationship between congregations and the public sector in the formal social services network is quite complex. As Joe Loconte (1998) reported, the Indianapolis-based Front Porch Alliance, which aims to encourage congregations to help needy people in their communities, has had several concerns regarding this relationship. First, the Alliance advised public authorities that they should support local congregations but not tell them what to do; nor should they dictate how the congregations carry out their programs. Second, the Alliance cautioned that building trust between the public sector and congregations is a slow process and requires patience from both parties. Finally, it pointed out a critical potential stumbling block: "government often makes the mistake of trying to 'scale up' small, successful initiatives. But these grass-roots initiatives work because they are small. They have no bureaucracy and little overhead. Most importantly, they wield unique assets for the specific challenges of the local neighborhood" (p. 32).

There is one important difference between a welfare service provided by public agency and the same service provided by a religious congregation. The former provides the service under a professional umbrella and the receiving client does not feel obliged to the serving agency. The scholars of gift giving remind us that:

> In general it is true that around the field of consumption we have a spontaneous, operative boundary between two kinds of services: professional, paid with money and to be classed with commerce, and personal, recompensed in kind and in no other way. Within the field of personal services, freely given and returned, moral judgement of the worth of people and things is exercised. (Douglas & Isherwood, 1996, p. 58)

Research teaches us that when people receive help from individuals they recognize and who are under no legal obligation to help, those who receive the help are expected to reciprocate in one way or another, and that taking on certain attitudes and behaviors is a critical form of this reciprocity. Georg Simmel (Simmel and Wolff, 1964) noted that, when a gift is given, gratitude appears as a complement, and the bond of reciprocity—the two-way traffic of service and return service—is established, even where no external force guarantees it. The French sociologist Marcel Mauss (1990) documented gift relationships among tribes and found that all gifts are binding. Gifts are not given in abstract or by a government; they are given by people to people. In the context of congregational help, the reciprocity is implied, even if not specifically required; the person helped is not expected to join the congregation, but is expected to attempt to do well and to acquire social skills and prosocial attitudes. Congregations send the implicit message to clients that "you are not required to join, but, to show gratitude and reciprocity, please reform your ways and demonstrate values and attitudes that are in line with social responsibility." This is the secret power of congregational help and this is why a publicly funded professional service is unlikely to match the quality of congregational services.

Nevertheless, we must not lose sight of the fact that congregations are not welfare agencies. Religious congregations cannot reasonably be expected to cure all of the nation's social problems. They cannot eradicate poverty, prevent substance abuse, or end crime. This is primarily the responsibility of government. Furthermore, given the enormous variety in size and religious orientation among congregations, there is no single religious community that could form the foundation for future welfare plans. It is unrealistic to ask any religious community to shoulder the burden of social service in the hope of doing away with public welfare. The nation's congregations are too small and too loosely structured to deal with the myriad problems in today's society.

How, then, do we put the involvement of congregations in service provision into a realistic perspective? One way is to ask what life in America would be like if there were no religious congregations. The nation would lose a substantial part of its social safety net and what the Supreme Court has called "a beneficial and stabilizing influence in community life." For those in need, the local religious congregation is a lifeline; for those seeking spiritual direction, it is a moral compass. Without these congregations, our society would be poorer in body, mind, and spirit. As one of the most impressive sources of neighborhood solidarity, pride, and service, the local congregation, now more than ever, deserves recognition and support by both the religious and the secular community. Congregations have the capacity to do more, but they do not have the capacity to substitute for the public sector.

Congregations as Mediating Structures

According to the pluralistic view, the most democratic state-citizen relationship is one in which people's interests are protected and goods and services are produced and delivered in a manner appropriate for the local conditions. Mediating structures are a key factor in ensuring that citizens are served in a just and equitable manner.

As we have shown, congregations are important intermediary structures that act as a buffer between local residents and powerful public and corporate interests. At a time when mobility and personal isolation are increasing, mistrust of government and big business is on the upswing, and traditional ethnic and fraternity organizations are in decline, it is becoming increasingly difficult for local residents to find an organization (or to organize one) that they trust to represent their shared interests. Such an institution must be able to organize a collective, shape a strong social identity, and create a bond of trust between members and the wider community. The local congregation meets these criteria, and, for this reason, congregations and coalitions of congregations rank among the nation's most important and trusted intermediary organizations.

Local congregations have an important advantage as mediating structures in that they are already communities. In the past, immigrants used the structure of religious congregations to form ethnic sanctuaries to help them maintain their ties with their homelands. Similarly, today, those who wish to be with others who share their religious beliefs (and other cherished characteristics) form their own congregations. This makes the congregation one of the most important organizations in a community, because it has a clear identity and because its members have chosen to join.

Congregations have another advantage in that they and their members are interconnected with other organizations. These organizations include those in which congregants are members; those to which relatives, friends, colleagues, and residents belong; and those with which the congregation itself interacts. These organizations represent potential collaborators that can provide both resources and influence for the community causes.

Thus, the institution best positioned and best qualified to serve as a mediating structure between government and citizen is the local religious congregation. In this respect, we cite Ammerman (1997), who noted:

> Connections not only prevent congregational isolation, they also are the web of relationships out of which community structure is created and maintained. Congregations are a significant part of that web. The social order is made up of both informal ties and formalized organizations, of norms and practices that make the production of goods and the delivery of services possible. While congregations are rarely in the business of producing material goods, they are central to the structures that deliver services, facilitate informal ties, and inculcate norms of sociability. In short, congregations are key institutions in local social structures and beyond. (p. 362)

Congregational Norms

A crucial finding in our study concerns the congregational norm that a congregation is obliged or expected to assist people in need. Almost every clergy we interviewed and every congregant we met shared their congregation's commitment to a social ministry and a better society, though the visions of the better society varied; it can be more religious or more socially just, but it is most often related to the congregation's social ministry/programs. As we discussed in chapter 13, the prevalent understanding is that American local religious congregations are responsible for the provision of social services.

Nine of every ten congregations in our study reported that they provided at least one human service. Virtually all congregations reported support for cultural activities, from choral groups to theater productions, and training in organizing skills, as well as instruction in moral and social responsibility for youth and adults. Congregations' involvement in the provision of social services and in the enhancement of the quality of life in their communities and beyond is so prevalent that it must be considered the norm, that is, a pattern taken to be typical in the behavior of a social group. From affordable housing to homeless shelters, from soup kitchens to refugee resettlements, from places for AA groups to meet to crime watch groups, congregations are at work in making their communities better places in which to live, firmly convinced that it is their obligation to do so.

It is important to keep in mind that none of the variables we considered explain which congregations are most likely to get involved in social services provision. Theology, for example, did not prove to be significant, because liberal and fundamentalist congregations alike are engaged in social services provision. This finding supports Mock's (1992) assertion that the assumptions about polarity between liberals and fundamentalists are incorrect. The failure of any one variable to explain congregational involvement in service provision leads to an extremely important conclusion, namely that congregational involvement is an American norm, rather than the outcome of specific preconditions.

The norm of congregational involvement in social provision did not develop in a vacuum. Such a norm develops only when a government neglects responsibility for the social needs of its citizens. This has been the case in the United States, the modern society in which public authorities are least concerned for the welfare and the rights of the poor. When the public sector fails to assume responsibility for the care of the indigent, then the responsibility falls on others. In the case of the United States, this responsibility has been taken on by the nation's congregations and religious organizations. When no single social entity takes responsibility for helping the disadvantaged, those whose faith calls for compassion and caring for the needy stranger find meaningful ways to put their faith into practice.

The congregational norm of service is powerful. The clergy preach it, and theological seminaries teach it. Lay leaders initiate programs in response to what they have witnessed, and congregants carry them out. Those in need approach congregations in the expectation of help, while politicians shower praise and press congregations to do even more. It is remarkable that we did not encounter any group that challenged the norm of congregational service or even expressed doubts about its importance. Yet, one should not consider congregations an appropriate substitute for the government. They should be viewed as fixing the holes in the public hall of welfare. Unfortunately, the welfare hall in the United States is crumbling.

The Uniqueness of American Congregations

A major premise of our book is that American congregations differ from congregations in other advanced modern societies. Their uniqueness grows out of three crucial factors in their historical development. First, beginning in the colonial era, church leaders, who had only intermittent contact with their superiors in Europe, particularly London, had to make decisions unilaterally. These decisions resulted in doctrines that are uniquely American. Second, after the American Revolution, individual states and, later, the federal government moved to disestablish churches. The separation of church and state meant that all religions were free to practice and that no religion was to be publicly supported. Over the years, disestablishment gave rise to an entrepreneurial clergy adept at providing relevant and timely religious services. These clergy, who were much more attuned to people's preferences than were their predecessors, were able to develop communities of believers who willingly supported the congregation with money and volunteer work. The third factor in American congregational development has been religious experimentation, that is, the development of independent churches, megachurches, new denominations, and even new religions. This development reflects the lack of a single dominant religion in the United States, the lack of government control over religious activities, and the lack of public sanctions against new modes of religion.

Just as American congregations differ from those in other developed countries, American congregations differ from one another, even from those that belong to the same denomination. This is a result of the fact that people form congregations that best fit their own preferences. When membership changes and tensions begin to develop among members, conflicts erupt, and the result is often a split in which a distinct group of members forms its own congregation. At other times, individual members may decide to switch to another congregation or denomination that can better meet their religious and social needs. Changes in religious affiliation are common in the United States, where religion is a choice and not dictated by birth: approximately one-third of American congregants do not belong to their parent's denomination.

An important outcome of the right of religious choice and the availability of alternatives is that the American religious congregation is a dynamic social institution that continually reinvents itself to remain relevant and responsive to people's needs and preferences. The common understanding is that no one religious congregation fits all people, and thus people form or select the congregation that best fits them. In other words, people seeking to worship in common also choose those with whom they will worship. This process often results in the formation of a homogeneous congregation in which people share ethnic and sociodemographic backgrounds. Within each religion and denomination, one can find congregations composed primarily of members of one ethnic and socioeconomic group. In areas where there are too few people to form such a congregation, the congregation will be more diverse, but where there is a choice, most people will choose to worship with others like themselves.

One might think that the homogeneous nature of congregations is divisive and antisocial. Yet people who freely come together to worship in common also form strong social bonds. In addition to being places of worship, congregations are places where members meet for fellowship. The impressive involvement of American congregations in social and community services provision can be understood only in the contexts of free religious choices, entrepreneurial ministry, group formation around the congregation, and the social norm of congregations as service providers.

We have shown that congregations in Ontario, Canada, which has freedom of religion but also enjoys a much higher level of government-provided social services, are less involved in service provision than are congregations in the United States. Furthermore, because fewer Canadians are religious, the impact of congregational social services is also limited, and such services cannot be a meaningful substitute for public services provision. If congregations could recruit all their members to provide social services, in the United States almost two-fifths of the population would be involved, whereas in Canada less than one-fifth of the population would be expected to help; in addition, Canadians have less income available for congregational support because they pay higher taxes. The differences are even more pronounced when American religious congregations are compared with their European counterparts. In most European countries, congregations are financially secure because they are supported directly by the state or by state-imposed taxes. While the state assists them, they do not assist the state. Unlike congregations in the United States, European congregations limit their involvement to religious issues and rarely become involved in efforts to better the quality of life in their communities.

While state-run social service is the preferred method of social care, this is currently not the American reality. Given the general antipathy toward the poor and the emphasis on economic self-reliance in the United States, it is unlikely that the government will mount a major antipoverty program in the near future. Meanwhile, a unique American institution—the local religious congregation—is serving as the nation's social safety net for those most in need of food, shelter, counseling, and emotional support. Congregational involvement in social services provision is as American as apple pie, though far less recognized and celebrated.

Appendix
Methodological Notes

Background and Sampling

Data collection took place during the years 1996–99. The study originated in late 1995, when Partners for Sacred Places envisioned the first study of the amount and value of social service provision of congregations housed in historic properties. The term *historic properties* is used in this context to mean properties built prior to 1940 that were designed as congregations and are still used as places of worship. It should be noted that, in some cases, the current congregation has no affiliation with the original denomination. For example, a few synagogues moved to the suburbs and sold their old properties to new and growing Baptist churches.

The study was a detailed survey of local religious congregations in six urban areas: Chicago, Indianapolis, Mobile, New York City, Philadelphia, and the San Francisco Bay area (including Oakland). We obtained a list of all congregations housed in historic properties for each city (provided by a local historic preservation association or assistance organization). From these lists, we generated a random list of congregations housed in historic properties. We also generated secondary and tertiary lists for cases in which the congregation refused to participate.

The total sample comprised 111 local religious congregations in six areas: sixteen congregations in Chicago, twenty-five congregations in Indianapolis, fifteen congregations in Mobile, 15 congregations in New York City, twenty-four congregations in Philadelphia, and sixteen congregations in the San Francisco Bay area. It should be noted that the Mobile sample included Bowdin County, which is partly rural. The Indianapolis sample included all of Marion County, which is urban. The Philadelphia sample included congregations in Camden, New Jersey, and the Chicago sample included one rural congregation. The New York City sample included congregations in all five boroughs. The San Francisco Bay area sample included equal number of congregations from Oakland and from San Francisco. Sampling in Indianapolis was supported by the Lilly Endowment. Sampling in the Philadelphia area was supported, in part, by the Historic Religious Properties Program of the Philadelphia Historic Preservation Corporation.

In 1997, in an attempt to increase the representativeness of our sample, we expanded the study to include newer congregations. We studied additional congregations in each of our original cities, with the exception of New York City. The final sample comprised twenty-one congregations in Chicago, fifty-four congregations in Indianapolis, forty congregations in Mobile, fifteen congregations in New York City, sixty-three congregations in Philadelphia, and twenty-seven congregations in the San Francisco Bay area. In addition, we studied Houston (twenty-four congregations) and one small town: Council Grove, Kansas (seven congregations). Thus, this study included 251 American congregations. In order to assess the uniqueness of the American congregations, we studied forty-six congregations in Ontario, Canada (fifteen in Kingston, fifteen in London, and sixteen in Toronto).

For each of the cities in this phase of the study, we obtained a list of all congregations listed in the Yellow Pages and in the White Pages and a list provided by the local Council of Churches or the equivalent local organization. In all cases, the rate of refusal was below 10 percent and in most cities was far below 5 percent. That said, we often decided to interview replacement congregations when access to congregations in our first list proved too difficult. Additional congregations were added in San Francisco and Indianapolis when we exhausted our three alternatives for inclusion in the study. In other words, if congregation number X on the list was inaccessible or refused to participate, we went to congregation number X on the second list and then, if necessary, to number X on the third list. In the few cases that a congregation on the third list was also inaccessible (refusing or no longer operating as a congregation), we did not choose other congregations on the second list or third lists but randomly assigned new alternatives in place of those that had refused to participate or were inaccessible.

Procedures

The authors or the research assistants contacted the congregations on the lists to solicit their participation. We informed the interviewers about the essential purposes of the study before they called to solicit participation. When approval was granted, the interviewer went to the relevant congregation and interviewed the clergy (face-to-face). The interviews averaged at least three hours and were usually limited to the first two instruments and, occasionally, the third (see discussion later in this appendix). If the clergy was unavailable, we interviewed the president, manager, or a leader of the congregation. Sometimes the interview included a group of people from the congregation, such as the clergy, lay leaders, and an administrator. For the first phase of the study, the same questions were asked of the clergy and then of at least one lay leader to triangulate (check the reliability of) the data obtained from the clergy or other primary interviewee. If a discrepancy was detected, the interviewer interviewed a third member of the congregation. As it turned out, there was never any need for a third interview, and the lay leader almost always confirmed the data obtained from the clergy. In one case, the interviewer mistakenly collected the same data from five people in the congregations, yet, when we reviewed the data, we found minimal discrepancies. We therefore dropped the second interview in the second phase and interviewed only a member of the clergy or a group of people for data related to the first two research instruments.

When the first two instruments were completed, the interviewee was asked to identify the five most representative social programs (social ministries in churches) supported by the congregation. We instructed the interviewees to start with large programs (those with staff and/or a designated budget) and those of which the congregation was most proud. For each selected program, up to a total of five, we asked a set of specific questions. This part of the interview was conducted with the clergy or key interviewee and then was triangulated with the person in charge of the social program (even if this person was not a member of the congregation). This part sometimes took weeks—even months—to complete. As with previous instruments, we found that one knowledgeable interviewee was sufficient for our purposes. Thus, in the second phase we asked the clergy if he or she knew enough about the program to answer our questions; if the answer was positive, we interviewed the clergy; if the answer was negative, we interviewed the person the clergy recommended.

We also had a building instrument in the first phase of the study. This required a full tour of the congregational property, listing all rooms and parts of the building and assessing their use and physical condition. We measured the room size and checked for cracks, leakage, exposed electrical wires, unpainted walls, and so forth. Given that this part of the study was supported by Partners for Sacred Places, such data were crucial. As we moved into the portion of the study concerned solely with social issues, we omitted this part of the research instrument.

Data for the chapter on Urban Bridges and St. Gabriel's Episcopal Church (chapter 10) were gathered through a series of participatory observations and written as part of a course assignment. Data collection included participation in board meetings, review of minutes and program reports, and interviews with program staff and the pastor of the church. Members of the congregations reviewed the chapter and gave us invaluable suggestions for additions and changes.

The data for the chapter about the New Orleans coalition of churches were based on the official publication of the organization, *The Cables*. We obtained the full set of issues from Dr. Rev. David Mason and analyzed them thoroughly. We spent many hours analyzing topics and trends, as well as the time and people involved. Dr. Mason and both current and past members of the coalition provided excellent feedback.

The research assistants were brought to Philadelphia for three days of training. At a later stage, the primary author trained research assistants where they worked. The training included a full day spent learning the logic behind the study, how to contact congregations, and the use of the various research instruments and their purpose. Since many questions were written for experienced interviewers, all interviews were conducted face-to-face in the congregational setting. No telephone or written responses were accepted. After the first day of training, the research assistants observed the primary author conducting an interview and then spent the afternoon discussing the interview and how data were elicited and recorded. The next day, each research assistant conducted an interview, followed by a lengthy process of feedback from the primary author or an experienced interviewer. In the Ontario study, graduate students at York University were recruited to serve as research assistants, and training took place on York campus.

Instrumentation

In conducting this study, we used a comprehensive range of research instruments. As noted, we used four instruments in the first phase of the study; in later phases, we dropped the fourth instrument (the building form) and used only the first three.

The first instrument is the *Core Questionnaire*. The Core Questionnaire is a ten-page instrument designed to elicit information regarding the history and background of the congregation. The essential areas covered in this instrument are:

the congregation's religious affiliation and theological and political orientation
history
membership
financial affairs and budget
governance
future plans
physical layout
relationships with the local community and other institutions active in the area

The second part of the interview involved completion of the *Inventory of Programs*, which was compiled after reviewing numerous reports and interviewing experts in congregational social services. The instrument asks for information about the congregation's areas of social services involvement (that is, nonreligious services to society). The interviewer covered 215 areas of possible social and community involvement. These 215 areas were grouped under thirteen key subgroups: counseling and programs for families; programs for seniors; programs for children and youth; services for homeless and poor people; programs for other people in need; health programs; educational opportunities; arts and culture programs; community security; community organizing; community economic development; social issues; and permanent housing. For each possible area of social service involvement, we used the following scale:

0 = No
1 = Upon request or when needed
2 = Formal program run on the congregation's property
3 = A program run by the congregation elsewhere
4 = A program run by someone else on the congregation's property
5 = Support for program carried out elsewhere

The interview focused on the previous year (the previous twelve months) in order to include summer camps and winter programs and to ensure similar coverage for all congregations regardless of the season in which the interview was conducted. This list of social programs helped interviewees list all of the congregation's programs. Previous studies have shown that people tend to forget many items when they are asked to recall them from memory. For example, individuals have difficulty remembering all the films they have seen in the past twelve months. Viewing the list of all film released in the past year and then marking those a person recognizes is a better way to ensure inclusion of relevant titles. Similarly, the list enabled the interviewees to identify most, if not all, their social programs.

The third part of the interview uses the *Specific Program* Form. This instrument was used to gather information about the most important social service programs provided by the congregation, up to a maximum of five programs. With regard to these five programs, the interviewee was asked detailed questions about the program's history—who initiated it, its legal status, staffing, who benefited from it, how many times a week/month/year it was offered—and about the seven items that composed the basis for calculating the replacement value (value of space used for the program, clergy hours, staff hours, and volunteer hours, cash support, in–kind support, and utilities costs). Because of the length of interviewing time, congregations with more than five social programs were asked to choose only the five "most representative of their work" and to give brief descriptions of other services or programs they provided. This method limited the reported contribution of very active congregations, but, since the basic interview taxed the patience of our interviewees, asking for more information seemed rude.

Notes

1. Many people assume that the Free Library is the brain child of Benjamin Franklin. He probably got the idea from Christ Church where the practice was applied before he started his Free Library.

2. Scholars have questioned whether the Church's decision compromised the quality of Church of England religious life in the colonies, as well as colonists' ability to be simultaneously true to the English doctrine and independent.

3. SD, or standard deviation, is a measure of the extent to which observations are close to or far from their mean. For example, if nine people earn 10K and a tenth person earns 110K, on average they each earn 20K, but the SD is very high. The smaller the SD, the more representative is the mean.

4. Some of these studies include Hill, Robert B. (1998). *Report on Study of Church-Based Human Services.* Baltimore: Associated Black Charities; Hodgkinson, Virginia A., and Murray S. Weitzman (1993). *From Belief to Commitment: The Community Service Activities and Finances of Religious Congregations in the United States, 1993 Edition.* Washington, DC: Independent Sector; Printz, Tobi Jennifer (1998), *Faith-Based Service Providers in the Nation's Capital: Can They Do More?*, Policy Brief No. 2 in *Charting Civil Society*, Center on Nonprofits and Philanthropy, Washington, DC: The Urban Institute; Silverman, Carol (2000). *Faith-Based Communities and Welfare Reform: California Religious Community Capacity Study.* San Francisco: Institute for Nonprofit Organization Management, University of San Francisco; Jackson, Maxie C., Jr., et al., (1997). *Faith-Based Institutions' Community and Economic Development Programs Serving Black Communities in Michigan.* Kalamazoo: Michigan State University; and Grettenberger, Susan, & Hovmand, Peter (1997, December). "The Role of Churches in Human Services: United Methodist Churches in Michigan." Paper presented at the twenty-sixth annual meeting of the Association for Research on Nonprofit Organizations and Voluntary Action, Indianapolis, IN.

5. A key question in science and social science is the extent to which one variable can explain a change or variability in another (e.g., to what extent can weight explain blood pressure?). The relationship and its strength are assessed by various statistical methods; when both variables are numerical, we use the Pearson correlation, denoted as "r." The stronger the correlation, the closer "r" is to +1 (a

perfect positive correlation) or -1 (a perfect negative correlation). A weak correlation is denoted by a zero or a value close to zero.

6. Statistical analyses in this chapter are based on a one-way analysis of variance and post hoc Scheffe tests at the .01 level.

7. When we have more than one variable that accounts for the changes in certain variables, we apply a more complex text, such as a regression analysis, which is denoted by R. For example, when we study weight, salt in food, and daily exercise in relation to their ability to account for high blood pressure, we are interested in each variable alone as well as all possible interactions between them that may impact on blood pressure. "Beta" denotes the individual contribution of a given variable in a regression analysis.

The letter "p" denotes whether or not the results obtained can be viewed as correct or significant if we accept a certain possible level of error. The accepted levels of error used in the social sciences are: one tenth of 1 percent (.001), 1 percent (.01), and 5 percent (.05). Any finding above that level is not considered significant.

8. Places of worship do not include convents, monasteries, religious foundations and trusts, missionary organizations, or corporations. They are classified under "religion" and account for 7.3 percent of registered charities (Hall & McPherson, 1997).

9. Chi Square is the simplest test to assess association between two variables. It is used when the two variables are nominal or ordinal—that is, they are not numerical. For example, money value is numerical; cities are nominal. All statistical tests in this chapter are based on Chi Square tests of associations and are at least at the .01 level of significance.

10. A detailed discussion on the city-based variation can be found in chapter 3 of this book for the U.S. sample and for the Ontario sample in Handy, Femida, & Cnaan, Ram A. (1999), *Religious Nonprofits: Social Service Provision by Congregations in Ontario*. Montreal: McGill-Queen's University Press.

11. A t-test is another set test that measures the association between two variables. It is usually used when comparing means of two groups.

12. The data regarding the Lutheran Church and Berean Baptist Church are used in this chapter only.

13. The minutes of Federation meetings were mailed to participants and member congregations as a newsletter called *The Cables*. We were fortunate to have access to an almost complete set of *The Cables* thanks to the Reverend Dr. David Mason, who allowed us access to these documents.

14. Founded by University of Colorado football coach Bill McCartney, the Promise Keepers is a multidenominational group whose stated aim is to reclaim male responsibility and re-establish male leadership. In the autumn of 1977 the organization's rally at the Capitol Mall in Washington drew more than a million men.

Bibliography

Abdennur, A. (1987). *The conflict resolution syndrome: Volunteerism, violence, and beyond*. Ottawa, Canada: University of Ottawa Press.

Ammerman, N. T. (1997). *Congregation and community*. New Brunswick: Rutgers University Press.

Anderson, R. M. (1987). Pentecostal and charismatic Christianity. In: M. Eliade (Ed.) vol. 11. *Encyclopedia of religion* (pp. 229–235). New York: Macmillan.

Apple, D. S. (1999). *Developing the heart of a servant*. Unpublished doctoral dissertation. Eastern Baptist Seminary, Wynnewood, PA.

Ascoli, U., & Cnaan, A. (1997). Volunteering from cross-national perspective: Italy and the United States. *Social Indicators Research, 40*, 299–327.

Barratt, N. S. (1917). *Outline of the history of Old St. Paul Church*. Philadelphia: Colonial Society of Philadelphia.

Bartowski, J. P., & Regis, H. A. (1999). *"Charitable choice" and the feasibility of faith-based welfare reform in Mississippi*. Report submitted to the Joint Center for Poverty Research, Chicago.

Becker, P. E. (2000, August). Religious involvement and volunteering: Implications for civil society. Paper presented at the American Sociological Annual Meeting Anaheim, CA.

Berger, P. L. (1969). *The sacred canopy: Elements of a sociological theory of religion*. Garden City, NY: Doubleday.

Berger, P. L., & Neuhaus, R. J. (1977). *To empower people: The role of mediating structures in public policy*. Washington, DC: American Enterprise Institute for Public Policy Research.

Berrien, J., & Winship, C. (1999). *Should we have faith in the churches? Ten-Point Coalition's effect on Boston's youth violence*. Philadelphia: Public/Private Venture.

Beyers, J. (1999, March). Anchorage: People seeking a "last best chance." *City Voices*, 7.

Billingsley, A. (1992). *Climbing Jacob's ladder: The enduring legacy of African American families*. New York: Simon & Schuster.

———. (1999). *Mighty like a river: The black church and social reform*. New York: Oxford University Press.

Blau, J. R., Land, K. C., & Redding, K. (1992). The expansion of religious affiliation: An explanation of the growth of church participation in the U.S., 1850–1930. *Human Science Research, 21,* 329–352.

Blau, P. M., & Schwartz, J. E. (1984). *Crosscutting social circles: Testing a macrostructural theory of intergroup relations* (2nd ed.). New York: Academic Press.

Bonomi, P. U., & Eisenstadt, P. R. (1982). Church attendance in the eighteenth-century British American colonies. *William and Mary Quarterly, 39,* 245–286.

Brady, H. E., Verba, S., & Schlozman, K. L. (1995). Beyond SES: A resource model of political participation. *American Political Science Review, 89,* 271–294.

Brooks, A. E. (1980). *Profile of the church-related volunteer.* Washington, DC: International Liaison, U.S. Catholic Coordinating Center for Lay Volunteer Ministry.

Brown, E. (1999). Assessing the value of volunteer activity. *Nonprofit and Voluntary Sector Quarterly, 28,* 3–17.

Brown, T. A. (1990). Religious nonprofits and the commercial manner test. *Yale Law Journal, 99,* 1631–1650.

Butler, J. (1997). Protestant success in the new American city, 1870–1920. In: H. S. Stout and D. G. Hart (Eds.), *New directions in American religious history* (pp. 296–333). New York: Oxford University Press.

Byrd, M. (1997). Determining frames of reference for religiously based organizations: A case study of neo-Alinsky efforts to mobilize congregational resources. *Nonprofit and Voluntary Sector Quarterly, 26,* S122–S138.

Carnes, T., Trulear, D. H., & Woo, H. (1998, August). New York City African-American church leaders and their social involvement: A religious, social, and political profile. Paper presented at the ninety-third Annual Meeting of the American Sociological Association, San Francisco.

Chandler, A. (1997). Faith in the nation? The church of England in the 20th century. *History Today, 47* (5), 97–103.

Chang, P. M. Y. (1993). *An institutional analysis of the evolution of the denominational system in American Protestantism, 1790–1980.* Unpublished doctoral dissertation. Stanford University, Palo Alto, CA.

Chaves, M. (1993). Denominations as dual structures: An organizational analysis. *Sociology of Religion, 54,* 147–169.

———. (1999). *Religious organizations and welfare reform: Who will take advantage of "charitable choice"?* Washington, DC: Aspen Institute.

———. (1999b). The congregation's social service activities. Paper presented at the annual meeting of the American Sociological Association. San Francisco, CA.

Chaves, M., & Higgins, L. M. (1992). Comparing the community involvement of black and white congregations. *Journal for the Scientific Study of Religion, 31,* 425–440.

Chong, K. H. (1988). What it means to be Christian: The role of religion in the construction of ethnic identity and boundary among second-generation Korean Americans. *Sociology of Religion, 59,* 259–286.

Clemens, J., & Francis, J. (1998, June 19–26). Estimating the value of volunteering. *Fraser Forum.*

Clydesdale, T. (1999). Toward understanding the role of Bible beliefs and higher education in American attitudes toward eradicating poverty, 1946–1996. *Journal for the Scientific Study of Religion, 38,* 103–118.

Cnaan, R. A. (1997). *Social and community involvement of religious congregations housed in historic religious properties: Findings from a six-city study.* Philadelphia: University of Pennsylvania, Program for the Study of Organized Religion and Social Work.

Cnaan, R. A., with Wineburg, R. J., & Boddie, S. C. (1999). *The newer deal: Social work and religion in partnership.* New York: Columbia University Press.

Cnaan, R. A., Yancey, G., Rodgers, R., & Trulear, D. H. (2002). *Managing local religious congregations in America: Contextual necessities and leadership challenge.* Philadelphia: University of Pennsylvania School of Social Work.

Cnaan, R. A, & Boddie, S. C. (2002). Charitable choice and faith-based welfare: A call for social work. *Social Work* (in press).

Cnaan, R. A., & Cascio, T. (1998). Performance and commitment: Issues in management of volunteers in human service organizations. *Journal of Social Service Research, 24* (3/4), 1–37.

Cnaan, R. A., Kasternakis, A., & Wineburg, R. J. (1993). Religious people, religious congregations, and volunteerism in human services: Is there a link? *Nonprofit and Voluntary Sector Quarterly, 22,* 33–51.

Cohen, J. L., & Arato, A. (1994). *Civil society and political theory.* Cambridge, MA: MIT Press.

Coleman, J. A. (1998). Religion and public life: Some American cases. *Religion, 28,* 155–169.

Coleman, J. S. (1988). Social capital in the creation of human capital. *American Journal of Sociology, 94,* S95–S120.

———. (1990). *Foundations of social theory.* Cambridge, MA: Harvard University Press.

Crary, E. G., Snyder, M., & Ridge, R. (1992). Volunteers' motivations: A functional strategy for the recruitment, placement, and retention of volunteers. *Nonprofit Management and Leadership, 2,* 333–350.

Culhane, D. P., Dejowski, E. F., Ibanez, J., Needham, E., & Macchia, I. (1994). Public shelter admission rates in Philadelphia and New York City: The implications of turnover for sheltered population counts. *Housing Policy Debates, 5,* 107–140.

Cunningham, H. (1995). *God and Caesar at the Rio Grande.* Minneapolis: University of Minnesota Press.

Curtis, J. E., Grabb, E. D., & Baer, D. E. (1992). Voluntary association membership in fifteen counties: A comparative analysis. *American Sociological Review, 57,* 139–152.

Curtis, S. A. (1991). *A consuming faith: The social gospel and American culture.* Baltimore: Johns Hopkins University Press.

Dignan, P. J. (1974; originally published 1933). *A history of the legal incorporation of Catholic Church property in the United States (1784–1932).* Washington, DC: Catholic University of America.

DiIulio, J. J., Jr. (1997, Fall). The Lord's work: The church and the "civil society sector." *Brookings Review,* 27–31.

Douglas, M., & Isherwood, B. (1996). *The world of goods: Towards an anthropology of consumption.* New York: Routledge.

Dorn, J. H. (1993). The social gospel and socialism: A comparison of the thought of Francis Greenwood Peabody, Washington Gladden, and Walter Rauschenbusch. *Church History, 62,* 82–100.

Du Bois, W. E. B. (1996; originally published 1899). *The Philadelphia Negro: A social study.* Philadelphia: University of Pennsylvania Press.

Dudley, C. S., & Johnson, S. A. (1993). *Energizing the congregation: Images that shape your church's ministry.* Louisville, KY: Westminster John Knox Press.

Dudley, C. S., & Roozen, D. A. (2001). *Faith communities today: A report on religion in the United States today.* Hartford, CT: Hartford Seminary.

Dudley, C. S., & Van Eck, T. (1992). Social ideology and community ministries: Implications from church membership surveys. In: K. B. Bedwill & A. M. Jones (Ed.). *Yearbook of Americans and Canadian churches* (pp. 5–11). Nashville: Abingdon Press.

The Economist (1995, July 8). The counter-attack of God. *Economist,* 19–21.

Eiesland, N. L. (1999). *A particular place: Urban restructuring and religious ecology in a Southern exurb.* New Brunswick: Rutgers University Press.

Ellison, C. G. (1995). Rational choice explanations of individual religious behavior: Notes on the problem of social embeddedness. *Journal for the Scientific Study of Religion, 34* (1), 89–98.

Ellison, C. G., & George, L. K. (1994). Religious involvement, social ties and social support in a southeastern community. *Journal for the Scientific Study of Religion, 33,* 46–61.

Ewalt, J. R., & McMann, R. V. (1962). *The churches and mental health: A report to the staff director.* New York: Basic Books (Joint Commission on Mental Illness and Health. Monograph series, no. 8).

Fallding, H. (1978). Mainline Protestantism in Canada and the United States: An overview. *Canadian Journal of Sociology, 3,* 41–60.

Farley, R., & Frey, W. H. (1994). Changes in the segregation of whites from blacks during the 1980s: Small steps toward a more integrated society. *American Sociological Review, 59,* 23–45.

Farnsley, A. (1997, December 21). Considering the 'average' in urban congregations. *Indianapolis Star,* p. B21.

Ferejohn, J. A., & Weingast, B. R. (1997). The new federalism: Can the states be trusted? Stanford: Hoover Institution Press, Stanford University.

Finke, R., & Stark, R. (1992). *The churching of America 1776–1990: Winners and losers in our religious economy*. New Brunswick: Rutgers University Press.

Frankl, V. E. (1963). *Man's search for meaning: An introduction to logotherapy* (rev. ed.). Boston: Beacon Press.

Franklin, R. M. (1997). *Another day's journey: Black churches confronting the American crisis*. Minneapolis: Fortress Press.

Galaskiewicz, J. (1997). An urban grants economy revisited: Corporate charitable contributions in the Twin Cities, 1979–81, 1987–89. *Administrative Science Quarterly, 42*, 445–471.

Gardner, J. W. (1994). *Building community*. Washington, DC: Independent Sector.

Garland, D. R. (1997). Church social work. *Social Work & Christianity, 24* (2), 94–114.

Gaustad, E. S. (1962). *Historic atlas of religion in America*. New York: Harper & Row.

Gelfand, D. E., & Fandetti, D. V. (1986). The emergent nature of ethnicity: Dilemmas in assessment. *Social Casework, 67*, 542–550.

Gelles, R. J., & Straus, M. (1989). *Intimate violence: The causes and consequences of abuse in the American family*. New York: Touchstone.

Gittings, J. (1987, February 2). East Brooklyn churches and the Nehemiah project: Churches in communities: A place to stand. *Christianity and Crisis*, 5–11.

Giving USA (1995). *Giving USA*. New York: American Association of Fund-Raising Counsel Trust for Philanthropy.

Glasser, W. (1965). *Reality therapy: A new approach to psychiatry*. New York: Harper & Row.

Gough, D. M. (1995). *Christ Church, Philadelphia: The nation's church in a changing city*. Philadelphia: University of Pennsylvania Press.

Grath, H. H., & Mills, W. (1958). *From Max Weber: Essays in sociology*. New York: Oxford University Press.

Greeley, A. (1972). *The denominational society*. Glenview, IL: Scott, Foresman.

Grettenberger, S., & Hovmand, P. (1997, December). *The role of churches in human services: United Methodist churches in Michigan*. Paper presented at the twenty-sixth annual meeting of the Association for Research on Nonprofit Organizations and Voluntary Action, Indianapolis.

Hall, D. (1972). *The faithful shepherd*. Chapel Hill: University of North Carolina Press.

Hall, M., & McPherson, L. G. (1997). A provincial portrait of Canada's charities. *Research Bulletin Canadian Centre of Philanthropy, 4* (2/3), 1–12.

Hall, P. D. (1990). The history of religious philanthropy in America. In: R. Wuthnow, V. A. Hodgkinson, & Associates. *Faith and philanthropy in America:*

Exploring the role of religion in America's voluntary sector (pp. 38–62). San Francisco: Jossey-Bass.

Hall, P. D. (1996). *Founded on the rock, built upon shifting sands: Churches, voluntary associations, and nonprofit organizations in public life: 1850–1990.* Unpublished manuscript, Program on Nonprofit Organizations, Yale University, New Haven.

———. (1998, July). Voluntary associations, nonprofit organizations, and religious entities: Associational populations and ecologies in New Haven, Connecticut, 1850–1990. Paper presented at the Program on Nonprofit Organizations, Yale University, New Haven.

Hammack, D. C. (1998). *Making the nonprofit sector in the United States: A reader.* Bloomington: Indiana University Press.

Handlin, O. (1949). *This was America; true accounts of people and places, manners and customs, as recorded by European travelers to the western shore in the eighteenth, nineteenth, and twentieth centuries.* Cambridge: Harvard University Press.

———. (1951). *The uprooted.* Boston: Little, Brown.

Handy, F., & Cnaan, R. A. (1999). Religious nonprofits: Social service provision by congregations in Ontario. In: K. Banting (Ed.). *The nonprofit sector in Canada: Roles and relationships* (pp. 69–106). Montreal: McGill–Queen's University Press.

Handy, F., Cnaan, R. A., Brudney, J., Meijs, L., Ascoli, U., & Ranade, S. (1998, November). Defining who is a volunteer: Cross-cultural comparisons. Paper presented at the annual Association for Research on Nonprofit Organizations and Voluntary Action conference, Seattle.

Harris, M. (1998). *Organizing God's work: Challenges for churches and synagogues.* New York: St. Martin's Press.

Hayghe, H. V. (1991). Volunteers in the U.S.: Who donates time? *Monthly Labor Review, 114* (2), 17–23.

Hill, R. B. (1998). *Report on study of church-based human services.* Baltimore: Associated Black Charities.

Hodgkinson, V. A., & Weitzman, M. S. (1993). *Giving and volunteering in the United States, 1994.* Washington, DC: Independent Sector.

Hodgkinson, V. A., & Weitzman, M. S., with Kirsch, A. D., Noga, S. M., & Gorski, H. A. (1993). *From belief to commitment: The community service activities and finances of religious congregations in the United States, 1993 Edition.* Washington, DC: Independent Sector.

Hodgkinson, V. A., Weitzman, M. S., Noga, S. M., & Knauft, E. B. (1994). *Giving and volunteering in the United States, 1994.* Washington, DC: Independent Sector.

Hoge, D., & Mead, L. B. (1999). Endowed congregations. In: M. Chaves & S. L. Miller (Eds.). *Financing American religion* (pp. 87–94). Walnut Creek, CA: Altamira Press.

Hoge, D. R., Zech, C., McNamara, P., & Donahue, M. J. (1996). *Money matters: Personal giving in American churches.* Louisville, KY: Westminster John Knox Press.

———. (1998). The value of volunteers as resources for congregations. *Journal for the Scientific Study of Religion, 37,* 470–480.

Holifield, E. B. (1994). Toward a history of American congregations. In: J. P. Wind & J. W. Lewis (Eds.). *American congregations: Volume 2—New perspectives in the study of congregations* (pp. 23–53). Chicago: University of Chicago Press.

Hovey, H. A. (1999). Can the states afford devolution? The fiscal implications of shifting federal responsibilities to state and local governments. New York: Century Foundation Press.

Hunter, K. I., & Linn, M. W. (1980–81). Psychological differences between elderly volunteers and non-volunteers. *International Journal of Aging and Human Development, 12,* 205–213.

Iannaccone, L. R. (1994). Why strict churches are strong. *American Journal of Sociology, 99,* 1180–1211.

Iannaccone, L. R., Olson, D. V. A., & Stark, R. (1995, December). Religious resources and growth. *Social Forces, 74* (2), 705–731.

Inglehart, R., et al. (1990). *World value survey, 1981–1983: Computer file and codebook* (2nd ed.). Ann Arbor, MI: Inter-University Consortium for Political and Social Research.

Jackson, E. F., Bachmeier, M. D., Wood, J. R., & Craft, E. A. (1995). Volunteering and charitable giving: Do religious and associational ties promote helping behavior? *Nonprofit and Voluntary Sector Quarterly, 24,* 59–78.

Jackson, M. C., Jr., Schweitzer, J. H., Cato, M. T., & Blake, N., Jr., (1997). *Faith-based institutions' community and economic development programs serving black communities in Michigan.* Kalamazoo: Michigan State University.

Jackuet, C. H., Jr., & Jones, A. M. (1991). *Yearbook of American and Canadian Churches, 1991.* Nashville: Abingdon Press.

Jeavons, T. (1994). *When the bottom line is faithfulness: Management of Christian service organizations.* Bloomington: Indiana University Press.

Jeavons, T., & Cnaan, R. A. (1997). The formation, transformation, and evolution of small religious organizations. *Nonprofit and Voluntary Sector Quarterly, 25,* S62–S84.

Johnson, D. W. *A study of new forms of ministry.* (1991). New York: Department of Research, National Council of Churches of Christ in the U.S.A.

Joseph, M. V. (1987). The religious and spiritual aspects of clinical practice: A neglected dimension of social work. *Social Thought, 13* (1), 12–23.

Jung, S., Boehm, P., Cronin, D., Farley, G., Freudenberger, C. D., Hefferman, J. B., LaBlanc, S., Queen, E. L., II, Ruesink, D. C. (1998). *Rural ministry: The shape and the renewal to come.* Nashville: Abingdon Press.

Kaldor, P., Dixon, R., Powell, R., Bellamy, J., Hughes, B., Moore, S., & Dalziel, J. (1999). *Taking stock: A profile of Australian church attenders.* Adelaide, Australia: Openbook.

Keith-Lucas, A. (1972). *Giving and taking help.* Chapel Hill: University of North Carolina Press.

Kluegel, J. R., & Smith, E. R. (1986). *Beliefs about inequality: Americans' views of what is and what is ought to be.* New York: Aldine de Gruyter.

Ladd, E. C. (1999). *The Ladd report.* New York: Free Press.

Laidlaw, W. (1932). *Population of the city of New York.* New York: Cities Census Committee.

Lammertyn, F., & Hustinx, L. (2000). *Nieuwe stijlen van vrijwilligheid. Een onderzoek bij de hulpdienst vrijwilligers van het Rode Kruis Vlaanderen.* Leuven, Belgium: Katholic University.

Levy, L. W. (1994). *The establishment clause: Religion and the First Amendment.* Chapel Hill: University of North Carolina Press.

Lincoln, C. E., & Mamiya, L. H. (1990). *The black church in the African-American experience.* Durham, NC: Duke University Press.

Lindner, E. W., Mattis, M. C., & Rogers, J. R. (1983). *When churches mind the children: A study of day care in local parishes.* Ypsilanti, MI: High Scope Press.

Lipman, H. (1999, April 22). Parishioners contributed $25 billion to churches in 1997, report says. *Chronicle of Philanthropy,* 16–17.

Lipset, S. M. (1990). *Continental Divide.* New York: Routledge.

Little, D. (1984). *Religion, order, and law: A study in pre-Revolutionary England.* Chicago: University of Chicago Press.

Loconte, J. (1998, November–December). The bully and the pulpit. *Policy Review, 92,* 28–37.

Lodge, M. E. (1964). *The Great Awakening in the middle colonies.* Berkeley: University of California Press.

Loizillon, A., & Hughes, M. A. (1999). *Building revival.* Philadelphia: Public/Private Venture.

Loomis, S. L. (1970; originally published 1887). *Modern cities and their religious problems.* New York: Arno Press.

Lugo, L. (1998). *Equal partners: The welfare responsibility of governments and churches.* Washington, DC: Center for Public Justice.

Lynn, R. W. (1999). Why give. In: M. Chaves & S. L. Miller (Eds.). *Financing American religion* (pp. 55–65). Walnut Creek, CA: Altamira Press.

Maslow, A. H. (1954). *Motivation and personality.* New York: Harper.

Mason, D. (1995). *Leading and managing the expressive dimension: Harnessing the hidden power source of the nonprofit sector.* San Francisco: Jossey-Bass.

Massey, D. S., & Denton, N. A. (1993). *American apartheid: Segregation and the making of the underclass.* Cambridge: Harvard University Press.

Mauss, M. (1990; originally published 1925). *The gift: The form and reason for exchange in archaic societies.* (W. D. Halls, Trans.) New York: W. W. Norton.

Maynard, R., & Jones, B. (1998, August 15). Fighting poverty in Jesus' name. *World,* 12–15.

McAneny, L., & Saad, L. (1993). Strong ties between religious commitment and abortion views. *Gallup Poll Monthly, No. 331*, 35–43.

McDonough, R. (1976). *Working with volunteer leaders in the church*. Nashville, TN: Broadman.

McGavran, D. A., & Winfield, C. A. (1977). *Ten steps for church growth*. New York: Harper & Row.

McLaughlin, A. (1998, September 30). Diet workshops: Churches' many new services. *The Christian Science Monitor*, 1.

McRoberts, K. (1993). *Quebec: Social change and political crisis* (3rd ed.). Toronto: McClelland and Stewart.

Mead, L. M. (1986) *Beyond entitlement: The social obligations of citizenship*. New York: Free Press

Mesch, G. S., & Schwirian, K. P. (1996). The effectiveness of neighborhood collective action. *Social Problems, 43*, 467–483.

Midgley, J., & Livermore, M. (1998). Social capital and local economic development: Implications for community social work practice. *Journal of Community Practice, 5*, 29–40.

Miller, D. E. (1997). *Reinventing American Protestantism: Christianity in the new millennium*. San Francisco: University of California Press.

Miller, D. W. (1999, November 26). Measuring the role of 'the faith factor' in social change: Religion, held at arm's length by sociologists, is attracting more scholarly attention. *Chronicle of Higher Education, 46* (14), A21–A22.

Miller, F. V. (1978). *Bishop by ballot: An eighteenth century ecclesiastical revolution*. New York: Oxford University Press.

Milofsky, C. (1997). Organization from community: A case study of congregational renewal. *Nonprofit and Voluntary Sector Quarterly, 25*, S139–S160.

Miyakawa, T. S. (1969). *Protestants and pioneers*. Chicago: University of Chicago Press.

Moberg, D. (1984). *The church as a social institution* (2nd ed.). Grand Rapids, MI: Baker Book House.

Mock, A. K. (1992). Congregational religion's styles and orientation to society: Exploring our linear assumptions. *Review of Religious Research, 34*, 20–33.

Mollica, R. F., Streets, F. J., Boscarino, J., & Redlich, F. C. (1986). A community study of formal pastoral counseling activities of the clergy. *American Journal of Psychiatry, 143*, 323–328.

Monsma, S. V., & Soper, C. J. (1997). *The challenge of pluralism*. Lanham, MD: Rowman & Littlefield.

Morgan, E. S. (1966). *The Puritan family, religion and domestic relations in seventeenth-century New England*. New York: Harper & Row.

Morris, A. D. (1984). *The origins of the civil right movement: Black communities organizing for change*. New York: Free Press.

Myrom, D. B. (1976). *Why persons volunteer? Theological and sociological factors motivating persons who volunteer to serve in the New England Synod, Lutheran Church in America.* Unpublished doctoral dissertation, Boston University, Boston, MA.

National Council of the Churches of Christ in the U.S.A. (1992). *Church involvement in health: Findings from a national survey.* New York: Columbia University School of Public Health.

National Federation of Community Development Credit Unions (1997). *Faith-based credit unions* (parts 1 and 2). New York: National Federation of Community Development Credit Unions.

Newton, K. (1997). Social capital and democracy. American *Behavioral Scientist, 40,* 575–586.

Olasky, M. N. (1992) *The tragedy of American compassion.* Washington, DC: Regnery Gateway.

Orr, J. B. (1998). *Los Angeles religion: A civic profile.* Los Angeles: University of Southern California, Center for Religion and Civic Culture.

Orr, J. B., Miller, D. E., Roof, W. C., & Melton, J. G. (1994). *Politics of the spirit: Religion and multiethnicity in Los Angeles.* Los Angeles: University of Southern California.

Parker, R. (2000, January). Progressive politics and, uh, . . . God. *American Prospect 11* (5), 32–37.

Pearson, J., & Anhalt, J. (1993). *Community outreach in Denver's black churches.* Denver: Center for Policy Research.

Peck, M. S. (1987). *The different drum: Community making and peace.* New York: Simon & Schuster.

Pew Research Center for the People and the Press. (1996). *The diminishing divide: American churches, American politics.* Washington, DC: Author.

———. (2001). *Faith-based funding backed, but church-state doubts abound.* Http:/www.people-press.org/re101rpt.htm.

Phillips, R. (1999, August). Denominational mandate vs. organizational realities: The case of the missionary work in LDS ward. Paper presented at the sixty-first Annual Meeting of the Association for the Sociology of Religion, Chicago.

Potapchuk, W. R., Crocker, J. P., & Schechter, W. H. (1997). Building community with social capital: Chits and chums or chats with change. *National Civic Review, 86,* 129–140.

Pressley, C. O., & Collier, W. V. (1999). Financing historic black churches. In: M. Chaves & S. L. Miller (Eds.). *Financing American religion* (pp. 21–28). Walnut Creek, CA: Altamira Press.

Printz, T. J. (1998). Faith-based service providers in the nation's capital: Can they do more? Policy Brief No. 2 in *Charting Civil Society.* Washington, DC: Urban Institute, Center on Nonprofits and Philanthropy.

Psacharopoulos, G. (1994). Returns to investment in education: A global update. *World Development, 22,* 1325–1343.

Putnam, R. D. (1995). Bowling alone: America's declining social capital. *Journal of Democracy, 6,* 65–78.

———. (1996, Winter). The strange disappearance of civic America. American Prospect, 34–48.

———. (2000). *Bowling alone: The collapse and revival of American community.* New York: Simon & Schuster.

Putnam, R. D., with Leonardi, R., & Nanetti, R. Y. (1993). *Making democracy work: Civic traditions in modern Italy.* Princeton, NJ: Princeton University Press.

Queen, E. L. (1996). *The religious roots of philanthropy in the West: Judaism, Christianity, and Islam.* Working paper number 96-4. Indianapolis: Indiana University Center on Philanthropy.

Rank, M. K., & Hirschi, T. A. (1999). The likelihood of poverty across the American adult life span. *Social Work, 44,* 202–216.

Rathge, R. W., & Goreham, G. A. (1989). The influence of economic and demographic factors on rural church viability. *Journal for the Scientific Study of Religion, 28,* 59–74.

Regnerus, M. D., & Smith, C. (1998). Selective deprivatization among American religious traditions: The reversal of the great reversed. *Social Forces, 76,* 1347–1372.

Richard, A., Bell, D., & Carlson, J. (2000). Individual religiosity, moral community, and drug user treatment. *Journal for the Scientific Study of Religion, 39,* 240–246.

Roberts, B. B., & Thorsheim, H. I. (1991). Reciprocal ministry: A transforming vision of help and leadership. *Religion and Prevention in Mental Health, 10* (1), 51–67.

Rogers, B. W., & Ronsheim, D. (1998). Interfacing African American churches with agencies and institutions: An expanding continuum of care with partial answers to welfare reform. *Journal of Sociology and Social Welfare, 25* (1), 105–120.

Roof, W. C. (1996). God is in the details: Reflections on religion's public presence in the United States in the mid-1990s. *Sociology of Religion, 57,* 149–162.

Roof, W. C., & McKinney, W. (1987). *American mainline religion.* New Brunswick: Rutgers University Press.

Roozen, D., McKinney, W., & Carroll, J. (1984). *Variations of religious presence: Mission in the public life.* New York: Pilgrim Press.

Ross, A., & Cokorinos, L. (1997). *Promise keepers: The third wave of the American religious right.* New York: Center for Democracy Studies.

Salamon, L. M. (1995) *Partners in public service: Government-nonprofit relations in the modern welfare state.* Baltimore: Johns Hopkins University Press.

Sargeant, K. H. (2000). *Seeker churches: Promoting traditional religion in a nontraditional way.* New Brunswick: Rutgers University Press.

Schneider, J. A. (1999). Trusting that of God in everyone: Three examples of Quaker-based social service in disadvantaged communities. *Nonprofit and Voluntary Sector Quarterly, 28,* 269–295.

Shapiro, J. P., & Wright, A. R. (1996, September 9). Can churches save America? *U.S. News and World Report, 121* (10), 46–53.

Shaw, George Bernard. (1990; originally published 1905). *Man and Superman.* (D. H. Laurence, Ed.) New York: Viking Press.

Silverman, C. (2000). *Faith-based communities and welfare reform: California religious community capacity study.* San Francisco: Institute for Nonprofit Organization Management, University of San Francisco.

Simmel, G., & Wolff, K. (Eds.) (1964). *The sociology of Georg Simmel* (rev. ed.). New York: Free Press.

Smidt, C. E., Green, J. C., Guth, J. L., & Kellstedt, L. A. (1998, October 16–17). Religious involvement, social capital, and political engagement: A comparison of the United States and Canada. Paper presented at the conference on Religion, Social Capital, and Democratic Life, Grand Rapids, MI.

Smith, C. (1998). *American evangelism: Embattled and thriving.* Chicago: University of Chicago Press.

Smith, D. H. (1993). Public benefit and member benefit nonprofit, voluntary groups. *Nonprofit and Voluntary Sector Quarterly, 22,* 53–68.

Smith, S. R., & Lipsky, M. (1993). *Nonprofits for hire: The welfare state in the age of contracting.* Cambridge: Harvard University Press.

Statistics Canada (1998). *Caring Canadians, involved Canadians: Highlights from the 1997 survey of giving, volunteering and participation.* Statistics Canada: Ottawa.

Stehle, V. (1995, July 27). European volunteerism trails U. S. *Chronicle of Philanthropy,* 14–15.

Sullivan, J. L. (1971, October). What organization can do for a church. *Church Administration, 14,* 42–49.

Taylor, R. J., Ellison, C. G., Chatters, L. M., Levin, J. S., & Lincoln, K. D. (2000). Mental health services in faith communities: The role of clergy in black churches. *Social Work, 45,* 73–87.

Thomas, S. B., Quinn, S. C., Billingsley, A., & Caldwell, C. (1994). The characteristics of northern black churches with community health outreach programs. *American Journal of Public Health, 84,* 575–579.

Trost, C. (1988, August 29). Debate over day-care bill spurs odd alliances and raises issue of church-state separation. *Wall Street Journal,* p. 32.

Turner, F. M. (1974). *Between science and religion: The reaction to scientific naturalism in late Victorian England.* New Haven: Yale University Press.

Unruh, H. R. (1999, November 6). Saving souls, saving society: The role of evangelism in church-based social ministries. Paper presented at Religious Research Association Conference, Boston.

United Way of Southeastern Pennsylvania (1999). *Church-based mentoring: A program manual for mentoring ministries.* Philadelphia: United Way of Southeastern Pennsylvania.

Verba, S., Schlozman, K. L., & Brady, H. E. (1995). *Voice and equality: Civic voluntarism in American politics.* Cambridge: Harvard University Press.

Veroff, J., Douvan, E., & Kulka, R. A. (1981). *The inner American: A self-portrait from 1957 to 1976.* New York: Basic Books.

Vineyard, S. (1993). *Megatrends & volunteerism: Mapping the future of volunteer programs.* Downers Grove, IL: Heritage Arts.

Warburton, W., Bp. of Gloucester (1741). *The alliance between church and state: or, The necessity and equity of an established religion and a test-law demonstrated, from the essence and end of civil society, upon the fundamental principles of the law of nature and nations.* (2nd ed. corrected and improved). London: F. Gyles.

Ward, N., Billingsley, A., Simon, A., Burris, J. C. (1994, Summer). Black churches in Atlanta reach out to the community. *National Journal of Sociology, 81,* 49–74.

Warner, W. L., & Lunt, P. S. (1941). *The social life of a modern community.* New Haven: Yale University Press.

Warner, R. S. (1993a). Work in progress toward a new paradigm for the sociological study of religion in the United States. *American Journal of Sociology, 98,* 1044–1093.

———. (1993b). Seeing the world: Congregating. *Christian Century, 110,* 663–665.

———. (1994). The place of the congregation in the contemporary American religious configuration. In: J. P. Wind & J. W. Lewis (Eds.). *American congregations: Volume 2—New perspectives in the study of congregations* (pp. 54–99). Chicago: University of Chicago Press.

Weisbord, B. A. (1988). *The nonprofit economy.* Cambridge: Harvard University Press.

Wilson, J., & Janoski, T. (1995). The contribution of religion to volunteer work. *Sociology of Religion, 56,* 137–152.

Wineburg, R. J. (1988). Welfare reform: What the religious community brings to the partnership. *Journal of Volunteer Administration, 16* (2), 19–26.

Wolfe, J. (1991). *Making things happen: How to be an effective volunteer.* Washington, DC: Island Press.

Wood, R. L. (1994). Faith in action: Religious resources for political success in three congregations. *Sociology of Religion, 55,* 397–417.

———. (1997). Social capital and political culture: God meets politics in the inner city: (Social capital, civil society and contemporary democracy). *American Behavioral Scientist, 40,* 595–605.

Wuthnow, R. (1988). *The reconstructioning of American religion: Society and faith since World War II.* Princeton: Princeton University Press.

———. (1991). *Acts of compassion: Caring for others and helping ourselves.* Princeton: Princeton University Press.

———. (1994a). *God and mammon in America.* New York: Free Press.

Wuthnow, R. (1994b). *Producing the sacred: An essay on public religion.* Urbana: University of Illinois Press.

⸻. (1994c). *Sharing the journey.* New York: Free Press.

⸻. (1997). *The crisis in the churches: Spiritual malaise, fiscal woe.* New York: Oxford University Press.

⸻. (1998). *After heaven: Spirituality in America since the 1950s.* Berkeley, CA: University of California Press.

Wymer, W. W., Jr. (1997). Marketing management in nonprofit organizations: A customer analysis of church volunteers. *Journal of Nonprofit & Public Sector Marketing, 5* (4), 69–90.

Yonish, S. J., & Campbell, D. E. (1998, October 16–17). The grease and the glue: The religious roots of American volunteerism. Paper presented at the conference on Religion, Social Capital, and Democratic Life. Grand Rapids, MI.

Zalnet, K. (1989). *Economic home cookin'.* New York: Community Workshop on Economic Development.

Index

About the Author

Ram Cnaan is associate professor in the School of Social Work and former associate director of the Center for Research on Religion and Urban Civil Society at the University of Pennsylvania, where he is also the founder and director of the Program for the Study of Organized Religion and Social Work. He is the coauthor of *The Newer Deal: Social Work and Religion in Partnership*.

About the Author of the Foreword

John J. DiIulio, Jr., is Frederic Fox Leadership Professor of Politics, Religion, and Civil Society at the University of Pennsylvania. He served as director of the White House Office of Faith-Based and Community Initiatives.